ESL

English as a Second Language

Mathematics
for Standardized Tests

Catherine Price, Ph.D.

Research & Education Association
Visit our website at
www.rea.com

Research & Education Association
61 Ethel Road West
Piscataway, New Jersey 08854
E-mail: info@rea.com

ESL Mathematics for Standardized Tests

Printed in the United States of America

Library of Congress Control Number 2006936339

International Standard Book Number 0-7386-0138-1

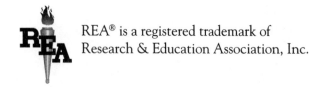

REA® is a registered trademark of
Research & Education Association, Inc.

K06

Your ESL Math Toolbox

REA's *ESL Mathematics for Standardized Tests* answers one of the central questions in ESL education today: How can a student master the special vocabulary and syntax of an academic subject like math while learning the English language itself?

The answer is an approach, used by this book and in classrooms across America, called content-based instruction. This approach allows for the integration of academic content and language learning in a way that recognizes the varied linguistic and ethnic backgrounds of diverse student populations.

REA's *ESL Mathematics for Standardized Tests* presents English language learners with a clear path to learning math with these features:

✓ Easy-to-follow lessons

✓ Step-by-step examples

✓ Problem-solving tips

✓ Review exercises

✓ Exclusive "Focus on English" practice sets

This book can be used both by secondary students and by adult ESL students enrolled in one of the large number of adult ESL programs offered by U.S. community colleges.

In the end, mastering the material in this book will also help you get into the college of your choice. After all, the point of this integrated approach to learning is to aim higher.

Whether for employment, citizenship, high school equivalency, or further education—or *for life itself*—this book serves first as a handy study aid and then as a reliable reference.

Think of this book as a toolbox. Just as a screwdriver is good for some jobs and a hammer is good for others, we give you what you need, when you need it. And we clearly mark off the steps for you to follow to reach your goal of becoming better at math and more fluent in English.

Along the way, you will build your comfort with, and confidence in, the subject matter.

At the same time, you will refine the language skills that will allow you to express yourself clearly in your schoolwork and also as you go about daily living.

Not only will you do better on the all-important standardized tests—which can greatly affect your chances for success for a long time to come—but you will also find that a simple trip to the supermarket will become more pleasant!

If you're an English language learner, this book will put you in command of essential math skills. Where you take it from there is up to you!

Larry B. Kling
Chief Editor

About the Author

Catherine Price (Ph.D., Purdue University) began her academic career at the University of Oklahoma and the University of Wisconsin, Madison. She later moved to Palo Alto College in San Antonio, Texas, and became interested in English as a second language (ESL). She returned to school to pursue a master's in ESL at the University of Texas, San Antonio. Dr. Price is currently adjunct tutor of ESL at Bridgend College, South Wales, United Kingdom.

Author Acknowledgments

I would like to thank Dr. Robert Bayley, Dr. Thomas Ricento, and Dr. Howard Smith of the University of Texas–San Antonio for discussing the need for study guides and textbooks for people who do not necessarily speak standard U.S. English as a first language. I am also grateful to Linda, Martyn, Kathryn, Richard, Sue, Natalie, and Dianne for inspiring me to take up the challenge of writing a mathematics study guide.

About Research & Education Association

Founded in 1959, Research & Education Association (REA) is dedicated to publishing the finest and most effective educational materials—including software, study guides, and test preps—for students in middle school, high school, college, graduate school, and beyond. Today REA's wide-ranging catalog is a leading resource for teachers, students, and professionals.

We invite you to visit us at *www.rea.com* to find out how "REA is making the world smarter."

REA Acknowledgments

In addition to the author, we would like to thank Larry B. Kling, Vice President, Editorial, for supervising development; Pam Weston, Vice President, Publishing, for setting the quality standards for production integrity and managing the publication to completion; Diane Goldschmidt and Anne Winthrop Esposito, Senior Editors, for project management and preflight editorial review and post-production quality assurance; Sandra Rush for copyediting the manuscript; Ellen Gong and Jacqueline Brownstein for proofreading; Christine Saul, Senior Graphic Artist, for cover design; Rachel DiMatteo, Graphic Artist, for her help with page design; and Jeff LoBalbo, Senior Graphic Artist, for annotating design specifications and for post-production file mapping. We also gratefully acknowledge the team at Aquent Publishing Services for designing and typesetting the manuscript.

Contents

Chapter 6—Geometry **203**

Chapter 7—Data Analysis, Logic, and Probability **241**

Chapter 8—Systems of Linear Equations **275**

Chapter 1
Real Numbers

Taking a standardized test in mathematics is an anxiety-provoking experience for many people. The best way to accomplish your goal of passing whatever test you must take is to learn math. Sometimes, this involves learning formulae and rules, but studying mathematics itself will give you the solid foundation that you need to feel confident on the day of your test.

1.0 A Brief Look at Numbers

Let's begin by reviewing several different types of numbers:

- *Whole numbers* include the counting numbers: 0, 1, 2, 3, 4, 5,...

- *Integers* include whole numbers, as well as negative numbers such as -1, -2.

- *Prime numbers* are numbers that can be divided evenly by only themselves and 1. Examples of prime numbers are 2, 3, 5, 7, 11, 13, 17, and 19. The number 2 is the only even prime number. The rest are odd, such as number 7. Zero (0) is not a prime number.

- *Rational numbers* include fractions (but not fractions whose denominator is zero) and their decimal equivalents. Examples are $\frac{2}{3}, \frac{3}{4}$, 1.574, and 7.231. The fraction $\frac{2}{0}$ is not a rational number, because its denominator is zero. The denominator of any whole number is 1, so $3 = \frac{3}{1}$, for example.

- *Irrational numbers* are numbers that cannot be written as fractions. They can be written as decimals that never end and have no pattern, such as 1.743968... (The three dots at the end mean the decimals keep going on forever.)

- *Real numbers* are those that can be placed on a number line, and include both rational and irrational numbers, whole numbers, integers, and prime numbers.

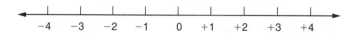

Figure 1.1: A Number Line

1.1 The Number Line

Numbers can be represented on a number line (see fig. 1.1). Notice that the numbers to the right of 0 (zero) are positive ($+$), and those to the left are negative ($-$). Zero itself is neither a positive nor a negative number and is always less than or smaller than any positive number.

For any two unequal numbers, the larger of them will always be located on the number line to the right of the smaller one. For example, is -2 larger than -3, or is -2 less than -3? We can answer this question quickly if we draw a number line like the one shown in figure 1.1. We can see that -2 is to the right of -3, so -2 is larger than -3. We can write this in the following way: $-2 > -3$ ("negative two is greater than negative three"). The symbol $>$ (or $<$) represents "greater than" (or "less than"). The larger number is always at the open end, so $7 > 3$, and $3 < 7$.

Example 1

Fill in the box with one of these three symbols: $>$, $=$, or $<$.

$-8\ \boxed{\phantom{<}}\ -2$

◆ **Step 1**   Draw a number line similar to the one shown in figure 1.1. Your number line should also show the following negative integers placed to the left of zero: $-1, -2, -3, -4, -5, -6, -7, -8\ldots$. Be sure -1 is next to 0, as in figure 1.1.

◆ **Step 2**   Notice that -8 is to the left of -2 on your number line. So -8 must be less than -2.

◆ **Step 3**   Place the less than (or smaller than) symbol in the box:

$-8\ \boxed{<}\ -2$

Ordering Integers in a Sequence

Now that we understand how to construct a number line, we can use this knowledge to position several integers in a sequence.

Example 2

Working from left to right, place the numbers +1, 0, −2, +3, and −3 in a sequence from the largest to the smallest.

◆ **Step 1**   Draw a number line (see fig. 1.2).

◆ **Step 2**   Mark the location of each number on the number line with a dot. Remember that numbers become larger as we move from left to right.

Figure 1.2: Ordering Numbers

◆ **Step 3**   Looking at our number line above, we can see that the largest number is +3, and the next largest is +1. The smallest is −3. Thus, the correct order from the largest to the smallest is:

+3, +1, 0, −2, −3

1.2 Working with Real Numbers

We begin this section by learning about numbers and place value. Each number can be made up of one or more digits. For example, the number 2 can also be written as 2.0 (pronounced "two point zero").

Place Value

Each digit has a place value, depending on its position in the number (see table 1.1).

As we move down the table, we can see that each number is multiplied by 10. Consider the following examples:

1	×	10	=	10
units				tens
100	×	10	=	1,000
hundreds				thousands

Table 1.1: Numbers and Place Values

Number	Place value
1	Units
10	Tens
100	Hundreds
1,000	Thousands
10,000	Ten thousands
100,000	Hundred thousands
1,000,000	Millions

Table 1.2: Digits and Place Value

Thousands	Hundreds	Tens	Units
1	0	2	3

What is the place value of 0 in the number 1,023?

Reading from left to right, enter each digit in a separate box like the one shown in table 1.2.

The digit 0 is in the hundreds box. Thus, the place value of 0 in the number 1,023 is "hundreds."

Example 3

What is the place value of 5 in the number 1,451?

◆ **Step 1**   Draw a box similar to the one shown in table 1.2.

◆ **Step 2**   Note which place value the digit 5 is in.

The answer is "tens."

A number such as 25.321 is called a decimal. Notice that there are digits to the right of the decimal point (.). This rational number is pronounced "twenty-five point three, two, one." The digits 3, 2, and 1 after the decimal point in the number 25.321 also have a place value.

As we move down the table, we can see that each number is divided by 10. Consider the following examples:

$$0.1 \quad \div \quad 10 \quad = \quad 0.01$$
tenths   hundredths

$$0.01 \quad \div \quad 10 \quad = \quad 0.001$$
hundredths   thousandths

Note that we add a "th" to the place value to indicate decimal values. That is, we say "tenths" rather than "tens."

Example 4

How do we read the number 47.005?

◆ **Step 1**   Draw a box showing decimals and place values.

Tenths	Hundredths	Thousandths

◆ **Step 2**   Insert the digits to the right of the decimal point in the box.

Tenths	Hundredths	Thousandths
0	0	5

Thus, we read the number 47.005 as "forty-seven and five thousandths." We can also say "forty-seven point zero, zero, five."

Table 1.3: Decimals and Place Value

Decimals	Place value
0.1	Tenths
0.01	Hundredths
0.001	Thousandths
0.0001	Ten thousandths
0.00001	Hundred thousandths
0.000001	Millionths

Rounding Numbers Up and Down

Rounding a number is a straightforward method of expressing an approximate value for the number. Numbers can be either rounded up to any given place value, or rounded down.

Example 5

Round 38,731 to the nearest thousand (place value).

◆ **Step 1**   Note the given place value (in this example, 8), and then look at the digit immediately to the right (7).

◆ **Step 2**   If the digit to the right of the given place value is equal to or greater than 5, add 1 to the number in the place value position, and replace all the digits to the right of the number with zeros. This is called rounding up. Add 1 to the 8 in the thousands' place value, and replace all the digits to the right with zeros.

The solution is 39,000.

Example 6

Round 27,331 to the nearest thousand (place value).

◆ **Step 1**   Note the given place value (in this example, 7), and then look at the digit immediately to the right (3).

◆ **Step 2**   If the digit to the right of the given place value is less than 5, the number in the given place value remains the same, but all the digits to the right of this number are replaced with zeros. This is called rounding down.

The answer is 27,000.

Changing Decimals to Fractions

Example 7 shows us how to change a decimal number to a fraction.

Example 7

How do we change 19.54 to fractional notation?

◆ **Step 1** How many numbers are to the right of the decimal point? Two—the digits 5 and 4.

19.54

◆ **Step 2** Move the decimal point two places to the right. Begin writing a fraction with 1954 as the numerator (the number on the top of a fraction).

19.54
→

Remember that the denominator of any number is 1.

$\dfrac{1954}{?}$

Since the decimal point in the numerator was moved two places, the decimal point in the denominator (the number on the bottom) is also moved two places. So it is 1 followed by two zeros.

The answer is $\dfrac{1954}{100}$.

Example 8

Express 0.753 in fractional notation.

◆ **Step 1** How many numbers are to the right of the decimal point? Three—the numbers 7, 5, and 3.

◆ **Step 2** Move the decimal point three places to the right.

0.753
→

◆ **Step 3** Write a fraction with 753 as the numerator.

◆ **Step 4**   Since the decimal point in the numerator was moved three places, the denominator is 1 followed by three zeros.

$$\frac{753}{?}$$

The result: $\frac{753}{1000}$

Changing Fractions to Decimals

To change a fraction to a decimal, we divide the fraction's numerator by its denominator.

Example 9

Change $\frac{4}{5}$ to decimal notation.

◆ **Step 1**   Divide the numerator 4 by the denominator 5.

$$5\overline{)4}$$

Remember that 4 is the same as 4.0.

Divide until the remainder is 0 (zero) or, as we will see in the next example, the division may repeat itself. (Often an exercise will tell you how many places to go, such as "Change $\frac{4}{7}$ to decimal notation to two places.")

$$\begin{array}{r} 0.8 \\ 5\overline{)4.0} \\ \underline{40} \\ 0 \end{array}$$

The answer is 0.8.

Since the remainder equals zero, the result is called a *terminating decimal*.

Example 10

Change $\frac{2}{3}$ to decimal notation.

◆ **Step 1**   Divide the numerator 2 by the denominator 3.

$$3\overline{)2}$$

The remainder is 2, and this pattern keeps repeating itself.

$$
\begin{array}{r}
0.666 \\
3\overline{)2.000} \\
\underline{18} \\
20 \\
\underline{18} \\
20 \\
\underline{18} \\
2
\end{array}
$$

The solution is $\frac{2}{3} = 0.66\overline{6}$.

Since the remainder repeats itself, the decimal is called a *repeating decimal*. The bar sign over the last 6 indicates that the decimal is a repeating one.

Ordering Real Numbers in a Sequence

To order real numbers in a sequence, we build upon the knowledge we learned about number lines, place value, fractions, and decimals. All real numbers can be positioned on a number line. These include, but are not limited to, integers, fractions, and decimals (see fig. 1.3).

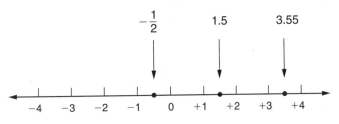

Figure 1.3: Ordering Real Numbers

Example 11

Place the following numbers from smallest to largest on a number line: 0, 3.5, −1.5, 2.75, 1

◆ **Step 1**   Draw a number line similar to the one shown in figure 1.3.

◆ **Step 2**   Mark the numbers on the line.

◆ **Step 3**   Write down the numbers in order from smallest to largest.

> The answer: $-1.5, 0, 1, 2.75, 3.5$

Notice that for positive numbers, we do not have to place the plus sign $(+)$ in front of the number. For example, $+3.5$ is usually written as 3.5.

Example 12

> Jack is working in his parents' hardware store during the summer vacation. If Jack is asked to stock packets of nails on the shelf from the left to the right, from the smallest size in inches (in.) to the largest, in which order would he arrange the nails whose sizes are $\frac{5}{8}$ in., $\frac{3}{16}$ in., $\frac{3}{4}$ in., and $\frac{9}{32}$ in.?

◆ **Step 1**   Express each fraction as a decimal:

$$
\begin{array}{r}
.625 \\
8\overline{)5.000} \\
48 \\
\hline
20 \\
16 \\
\hline
40 \\
40 \\
\hline
0
\end{array}
\qquad
\begin{array}{r}
.1875 \\
16\overline{)3.0000} \\
16 \\
\hline
140 \\
128 \\
\hline
120 \\
112 \\
\hline
80 \\
80 \\
\hline
0
\end{array}
\qquad
\begin{array}{r}
.75 \\
4\overline{)3.00} \\
28 \\
\hline
20 \\
20 \\
\hline
0
\end{array}
\qquad
\begin{array}{r}
.28125 \\
32\overline{)9.00000} \\
64 \\
\hline
260 \\
256 \\
\hline
40 \\
32 \\
\hline
80 \\
64 \\
\hline
160 \\
160 \\
\hline
0
\end{array}
$$

◆ **Step 2**   Compare the decimals for each fraction. The smallest fraction is the one with the smallest decimal. Thus, we order the fractions from left to right, from smallest to largest as follows:

.1875, .28125, .625, .75, or

$$\frac{3}{16}, \frac{9}{32}, \frac{5}{8}, \frac{3}{4}$$

Stocking the shelf from left to right, Jack begins with the $\frac{3}{16}$ in. nails, then continues with the $\frac{9}{32}$ in., the $\frac{5}{8}$ in., and ends with the largest nails, $\frac{3}{4}$ in.

Comparing Fractions

You can compare fractions by converting to their decimals, as shown in example 12. Or, for a quicker answer, you can use a method called cross multiplication to find out which of two fractions is the larger or the smaller.

Example 13

Is $\frac{7}{8}$ larger than $\frac{3}{4}$?

◆ **Step 1**   Begin at the bottom (the denominator position of the fraction) and multiply diagonally (follow the arrows shown in fig. 1.4). The result obtained from multiplication is called the product.

$$4 \times 7 = 28 \qquad 8 \times 3 = 24$$

$$\frac{7}{8} \diagup\!\!\!\!\diagdown \frac{3}{4}$$

Figure 1.4: Cross Multiplying

◆ **Step 2**   Write down the products next to each of the two fractions.

◆ **Step 3**   Write down which of the two products is the larger. The larger is 28.

◆ **Step 4**   The fraction located next to the larger product is the larger fraction of the two.

Thus, $\frac{7}{8}$ is larger than $\frac{3}{4}$.

Example 14

Is $\frac{3}{5}$ larger than $\frac{9}{10}$?

◆ **Step 1**   Use the cross multiplication method shown in figure 1.4.

◆ **Step 2**   Write down the product next to each one of the two fractions.

$10 \times 3 = 30$ $5 \times 9 = 45$

$$\frac{3}{5} \times \frac{9}{10}$$

◆ **Step 3**   The two products are 30 and 45. Notice that 30 is less than 45.

Thus, $\frac{3}{5}$ is smaller than $\frac{9}{10}$.

1.3 Properties of Real Numbers

In this section, we study several properties of real numbers that help us to understand mathematics better.

The Associative Property of Addition

The associative property of addition means that it doesn't matter in which order we group numbers; we always obtain the same result. Thus, for any real numbers a, b, and c:

$$a + (b + c) = (a + b) + c$$

Let's test this property by assigning values to the letters a, b, and c.

Example 15

Let $a = 2$, $b = 1$, and $c = 3$.
$a + (b + c) =$
$2 + (1 + 3) =$
$2 + (4)\ \ \ \ =$
$2 + 4\ \ \ \ \ \ = 6$
and
$(a + b) + c =$
$(2 + 1) + 3 =$
$(3) + 3\ \ \ \ =$

$$3 + 3 \quad = 6$$

Notice we obtained the same answer—the number 6.

The Commutative Property of Addition

For any real numbers a and b,

$$a + b = b + a$$

The commutative property of addition means that the order in which we add numbers is not significant, because $a + b$ will give us the same result as $b + a$.

Example 16

Let $a = 5$ and $b = 4$.
$a + b =$
$5 + 4 = 9$
and
$b + a =$

$4 + 5 = 9$

The Additive Identity Property

When any real number a is added to zero (which is called the additive identity), the result is the original number a. Thus,

$$a + 0 = a$$

Example 17

If $a = 7$, then
$a + 0 =$

$7 + 0 = 7$

MATH TIPS

Multiplication & Division Symbols

Several ways are used to indicate that two or more numbers are to be multiplied or divided.

The following symbols all denote multiplication as shown by the examples:

$3 \cdot 3$

3×3

$3(3)$

$(3)(3)$

Here are two symbols used in examples that denote division:

$3 \div 3$

$\dfrac{3}{3}$

The Associative Property of Multiplication

For any real numbers a, b, and c:

$$a(bc) = (ab)c$$

The associative property of multiplication states that the way in which we group numbers when we multiply them is not significant, because we obtain the same product regardless of how a, b, and c are grouped.

Example 18

Let $a = 1$, $b = 2$, and $c = 3$.
$a(bc)$ =
$1(2 \times 3)$ =
$1(6)$ = 6

and
$(ab)c \quad =$
$(1 \times 2)3 =$

$(2)3 \quad = 6$

The Commutative Property of Multiplication

For any real numbers a and b,

$$ab = ba$$

The commutative property of multiplication states that no matter how we order a and b, we obtain the same product.

Example 19

If $a = 4$ and $b = 1$, then
$ab \ = 4 \times 1 \quad = 4$ and

$ba \ = 1 \times 4 \quad = 4$

The Multiplicative Identity Property

When any real number a is multiplied by 1 (called the multiplicative identity), the result is the original number a. Thus,

$$a \times 1 = a$$

Example 20

Let $a \ = 5.$
$a \times 1 \ =$

$5 \times 1 \ = 5$

MATH TIPS

Subtract

Subtract means *to take away*. For example, when we are required to subtract 5 from 9, we write this mathematically as $9 - 5$.

The Distributive Property

Unlike other properties, the distributive property involves multiplication and either addition or subtraction. This property states that for any real numbers a, b, and c:

$$a(b + c) = ab + ac$$
$$\text{or}$$
$$a(b - c) = ab - ac$$

Example 21

Let $a = 1$, $b = 2$, and $c = 3$.

$a(b + c) \quad =$

$1(2 + 3) \quad =$

$1(5) \qquad = 5$

and

$ab + ac \quad =$

$1(2) + 1(3) \quad =$

$2 + 3 \qquad = 5$

Thus, $a(b + c) = ab + ac$.

Example 22

Let $a = 1$, $b = 3$, and $c = 2$.

$a(b - c) \ =$

$1(3 - 2) \ =$

$1(1) \qquad = 1$

and

$$ab - ac \quad =$$
$$1(3) - 1(2) =$$
$$3 - 2 \quad = 1$$

Thus, $a(b - c) = ab - ac$.

1.4 Absolute Value

This section on absolute value serves as the foundation for further work on the addition, subtraction, multiplication, and division of real numbers. We can define absolute value as the distance of a number from zero (its point of origin) on a number line. The symbol $|x|$ is used to indicate the absolute value of a number x. Figure 1.5 shows that the number 3 is three units from zero on the number line. Thus, we say that the absolute value of 3 is 3. However, -3 is also three units from zero, so the absolute value of -3 is also 3. We can say, then, that the absolute value of a number, with the exception of 0 (zero), is always positive.

Figure 1.5: Absolute Value

Example 23

What is the absolute value of 4?
There are 4 units between 0 and 4 on the number line, so the absolute value of 4 is 4.

$$|4| = 4$$

Example 24

Find: $|-3|$
There are 3 units between zero and -3, so the absolute value of -3 is 3, which is the numerical part of the number.

$$|-3| = 3$$

Example 25

Evaluate: $|-8| + 6$

◆ **Step 1**   Evaluate $|-8|$, and then add 6.

$$(8) + 6 = 14$$

Example 26

Evaluate: $8 + |-8| -2$

◆ **Step 1**   Evaluate $|-8|$.

$$8 + (8) - 2$$

◆ **Step 2**   Add and subtract.

$$8 + (8) - 2 =$$

$$16 - 2 \quad\quad = 14$$

1.5 Addition with Negatives

Adding Negative Numbers

Figure 1.6 illustrates the addition of negative numbers. For example, when we add -2 and -1, we can begin by locating 0 on a number line. We count two units to the left of zero (for -2), and then one more unit, also to the left of zero

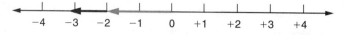

Figure 1.6: Adding Two Negative Numbers

(for -1). We can see that when we count two units to the left, we reach -2 on the number line, and moving to the left one more unit brings us to the -3 position.

Thus, to add two or more negative numbers, add the absolute values of the numbers and put a negative sign in front of the result.

Example 27

Add: -3 and -9

◆ **Step 1**   Add the absolute values of the two numbers.

$3 + 9 = 12$

◆ **Step 2**   Write a negative sign in front of the sum.

$-3 + (-9) = -12$

Adding Numbers with Different Signs

The number line illustrated in figure 1.7 shows how to add the negative integer -1 and the positive integer $+2$. Beginning at zero on the number line, count one unit to the left of zero (for -1), and then, from the -1 position, count two units to the right (for $+2$).

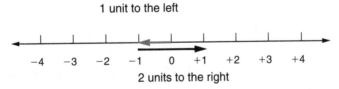

Figure 1.7: Adding Numbers with Different Signs

Looking at figure 1.7, we can see that we arrive at the number $+1$. Thus, when we add numbers with different signs, we actually subtract the absolute values of the numbers and we write in front of the result the sign that is the same as the number with the largest absolute value.

Example 28

Add: -8 and $+3$

◆ **Step 1** Write down the absolute value of both numbers.

$|-8| = 8$ and

$|+3| = 3$

◆ **Step 2** Subtract the smaller absolute value from the larger:

$8 - 3 = 5$

◆ **Step 3** Decide which sign to use. Remember that we use the sign of the number that has the larger absolute value. Since the absolute value of -8 (negative 8) is larger than the absolute value of $+3$ (positive 3), we write down a negative sign in front of our result.

$-8 + 3 = -5$

1.6 Subtraction with Negatives

Subtracting Negative Numbers

If we subtract two negative numbers, such as -2 from -1, we can write this as follows: $-1 - (-2)$. Subtracting a number is the same as adding its opposite.

Example 29

Subtract: $-1 - (-2)$

◆ **Step 1** Find the opposite of -2, the number that we are subtracting from -1. The opposite of -2 is $+2$.

◆ **Step 2** Add $+2$ to -1.

$-1 + 2 = 1$

Example 30

What is $-18 - (-11)$?

◆ **Step 1** Find the opposite of -11. The result is $+11$.

◆ **Step 2** Add $+11$ to -18.

$$-18 + 11 = -7$$

Subtracting Numbers with Different Signs

In examples 31 and 32, we subtract numbers that have different signs.

Example 31

Subtract: $+21 - (-5)$

◆ **Step 1** Find the opposite of -5. The answer is $+5$.

◆ **Step 2** Add $+5$ to $+21$.

$$21 + 5 = 26$$

Example 32

Subtract: $-6 - (+4)$

◆ **Step 1** Find the opposite of $+4$. The answer is -4.

◆ **Step 2** Add -4 to -6.

$$-6 + (-4) =$$

$$-6 - 4 \quad = -10$$

1.7 Multiplication with Negatives

When we multiply two numbers, the result is called the product. It is very important to learn several rules governing the multiplication of negative numbers and the multiplication of numbers with different signs.

- A negative number multiplied by a negative number yields a product with a positive sign. For example, $-3\,(-2) = +6$.

- A positive number multiplied by a negative number yields a product with a negative sign. For example, $4\,(-3) = -12$.

- A negative number multiplied by a positive number yields a product with a negative sign. For example, $-3\,(+9) = -27$.

- A positive number multiplied by a positive number yields a product with a positive sign. For example, $5\,(3) = 15$.

If you find it hard to remember these rules, try the following summary:

- If two numbers have different signs, their product is a negative number.

- If two numbers have the same sign, their product is a positive number.

Example 33

Multiply: $(-3) \times (-5)$

♦ **Step 1**   Apply the rule for multiplying two negative numbers. Both numbers are negative, so their product is a positive number.

$(-3) \times (-5) = +15$

1.8 Division with Negatives

When we divide one number by another, the result is called the quotient. Listed below are the basic rules for dividing negative numbers or dividing numbers with different signs.

- A negative number divided by a negative number gives us a quotient with a positive sign. For example, $\frac{-8}{-4} = +2$.

- A positive number divided by a negative number yields a quotient with a negative sign. For example, $\frac{10}{-5} = -2$.

- A negative number divided by a positive number yields a quotient with a negative sign. For example, $\frac{-12}{2} = -6$.

- A positive number divided by a positive number yields a quotient with a positive sign. For example, $\frac{14}{7} = +2$.

Again, we can simplify these rules by remembering the following:

- If two numbers have different signs, their quotient is a negative number.

- If two numbers have the same sign, their quotient is a positive number.

Example 34

Divide: $\frac{-24}{3}$

◆ **Step 1**   Apply the rule for dividing two numbers with different signs. One is a negative number (-24), and the other is a positive number ($+3$). Thus, the quotient is a negative number.

$$\frac{-24}{3} = -8$$

1.9 Positive Exponents

Exponential notation is a useful way of indicating that a number is to be multiplied by itself a designated number of times. Consider the expression a^n. The letter a can represent a number and is called the base, whereas the superscript letter n is referred to as the exponent, or power. For example, 2^4 (pronounced "two to the power of four" or "two to the fourth power") equals 2 multiplied four times, or $2 \times 2 \times 2 \times 2 = 16$.

Example 35

Evaluate: 3^3

◆ **Step 1** 3^3 is equal to $3 \times 3 \times 3$.

◆ **Step 2**   Multiply.

$3 \times 3 \times 3 =$

$(9) \times 3 \quad =$

$9 \times 3 \quad = 27$

    Two specific types of powers, called squares and cubes, are frequently used in many branches of mathematics, including algebra, arithmetic, and geometry. Briefly, squaring a number means raising it to the second power, so $5^2 = 5 \times 5 = 25$. The number 5^2 is pronounced "five squared." To cube a number requires us to raise it to the third power. For example, 2^3 equals $2 \times 2 \times 2 = 8$. The number 2^3 is pronounced "two cubed." We must be careful, however, to note the difference between expressions such as $(-2)^4$ and -2^4. At first glance, they look very similar, but they must be evaluated differently (see example 36).

Example 36

Evaluate: $(-2)^4$

$(-2)^4 = (-2)(-2)(-2)(-2)$

◆ **Step 1**   Multiply, working from left to right and remembering the rules for multiplying negative and positive numbers.

$(-2)(-2)(-2)(-2) =$

$(4)(-2)(-2) \qquad =$

$(-8)(-2) \qquad\qquad = +16$ (positive number)

but

$-2^4 \qquad\qquad\qquad =$

$$-(2)(2)(2)(2) \; = $$

$$(-4)(2)(2) \quad = $$

$$(-8)(2) \qquad = -16 \; \text{(negative number)}$$

1.10 Negative Exponents

The expression 2^{-2} has a negative exponent. How do we work with this type of exponent? A negative exponent simply means the reciprocal of the number with a positive exponent. *Reciprocal* means switching the numerator and denominator of a fraction, so the reciprocal of 3 is $\frac{1}{3}$, since 3 is the same as $\frac{3}{1}$.

Example 37

Change 2^{-2} to a positive number.

◆ **Step 1**   Change the negative exponent by building a fraction with the number 1 in the numerator position, and 2^2 in the denominator position.

◆ **Step 2**   Simplify as follows:

$$2^{-2} \quad =$$

$$\frac{1}{2^2} \quad =$$

$$\frac{1}{(2)(2)} = \frac{1}{4}$$

Example 38

Evaluate: $(-2)^{-3}$

◆ **Step 1**   Change the negative exponent by building a fraction with the number 1 in the numerator position and -2^3 in the denominator position.

◆ **Step 2**   Simplify as follows:

$$\frac{1}{(-2)^3} =$$

$$\frac{1}{(-2)(-2)(-2)} =$$

$$\frac{1}{(4)(-2)} =$$

$$\frac{1}{-8} = -\frac{1}{8}$$

Example 39

Evaluate: $\left(\frac{1}{2}\right)^{-2}$

◆ **Step 1** Remove the negative sign in the exponent by switching the numerator and the denominator (writing the reciprocal).

$$\left(\frac{1}{2}\right)^{-2} =$$

$$\left(\frac{2}{1}\right)^{2} =$$

◆ **Step 2** Evaluate the result.

$$2^2 = 4$$

1.11 More About Exponents

Several rules regarding exponents must be learned in order to work successfully with exponential expressions:

- The exponent 0: For any real number (except zero), $a^0 = 1$.

- The exponent 1: For any real number, a, $a^1 = a$.

- The product rule for exponents states that $a^x a^y = a^{x+y}$.

- The power rule for exponents states that $a^x b^x = (ab)^x$.

- The quotient rule for exponents states that $\frac{a^x}{a^y} = a^{x-y}$.

- The power rule for quotients states that $\frac{a^x}{b^x} = \left(\frac{a}{b}\right)^x$.

- To raise a number with an exponent to a higher power, we follow this rule:
  $(a^x)^y = a^{xy}$

- To change from a negative to a positive exponent, we follow this rule:
  $\frac{a^{-m}}{b^{-n}} = \frac{b^n}{a^m}$

The product rule for exponents and the power rule for exponents are sometimes confused. Table 1.4 shows how they differ.

Table 1.4: The Product and Power Rules for Exponents

Product rule for exponents	Power rule for exponents
The bases are the *same*. Do *not* multiply the bases.	The bases are *not* the same. *Multiply* the bases.
Add the exponents.	Do *not* add the exponents.
Example: $6^2 \times 6^3 = 6^5$	Example: $2^3 \times 4^3 = 8^3$

Example 40

Multiply: $2^3 \times 2^4$

◆ **Step 1**   To multiply, we use the product rule for exponents, $a^x a^y = a^{x+y}$, since the base (the number 2) is the same.

◆ **Step 2**   Add the exponents.

$2^3 \times 2^4 =$

$2^{3+4} \quad = 2^7$

Example 41

Multiply: 3×3^2

◆ **Step 1** To multiply, we again use the product rule for exponents, $a^x a^y = a^{x+y}$, because the base (the number 3) is the same. Remember that $3 = 3^1$ (the exponent 1 rule).

◆ **Step 2** Add the exponents.

$3 \times 3^2 =$

$3^1 \times 3^2 =$

$3^1 \times 3^2 = 3^3$

Example 42

Multiply: $2^3 \times 4^3$

◆ **Step 1** The bases are different, but the exponents are the same, so we need to use the power rule for exponents, $a^x b^x = (ab)^x$, to multiply.

$2^3 \times 4^3 =$

$(2 \times 4)^3 =$

$(8)^3 =$

Table 1.5: The Quotient Rule for Exponents and the Power Rule for Quotients

Quotient rule for exponents	Power rule for quotients
The bases are the *same*. Do *not* divide the bases.	The bases are *not* the same. Use *division* when working with the bases.
Subtract the exponents.	Raise the quotient to the *common power*. Do *not* subtract the exponents.
Example: $\dfrac{6^4}{6^2} = 6^{4-2} = 6^2$	Example: $\dfrac{8^2}{4^2} = 2^2$

$$8^3 \quad =$$

$$8 \times 8 \times 8 = 512$$

The quotient rule for exponents and the power rule for quotients also are sometimes confused. Table 1.5 shows how they differ.

Example 43

Divide: $\dfrac{6^4}{6^2}$

◆ **Step 1**   To divide, we use the quotient rule for exponents, $\dfrac{a^x}{a^y} = a^{x-y}$, since the base (the number 6) is the same.

$$\frac{6^4}{6^2} \quad =$$

$$6^{4-2} \quad =$$

$$6^2 \quad = 36$$

Example 44

Divide: $\dfrac{8^2}{4^2}$

◆ **Step 1**   To divide, we use the power rule for quotients, $\dfrac{a^x}{b^x} = \left(\dfrac{a}{b}\right)^x$, since the exponent (the number 2) is the same.

$$\frac{8^2}{4^2} \quad =$$

$$\left(\frac{8}{4}\right)^2 \quad =$$

$$(2)^2 \quad =$$

$$2^2 \quad = 4$$

Example 45

Simplify: $(3^2)^4$

◆ **Step 1** This simplification requires us to follow the rule for raising a number with an exponent to a higher power, represented by $(a^x)^y = a^{xy}$.

◆ **Step 2** Multiply the exponents.

$(3^2)^4 =$

$(3)^8 =$

3^8

Note that when you are asked to simplify an expression, you just have to write it in a simpler form. You don't have to do the actual multiplication, which in this case would be 3 multiplied by itself eight times—a very large number.

Here is an example that involves a negative exponent.

Example 46

Simplify: $(2^{-2})^3$

◆ **Step 1** Multiply the exponents, remembering the rule for multiplying numbers with different signs.

$\left(2^{-2}\right)^3 =$

$(2)^{-6} =$

$2^{-6} =$

$\dfrac{1}{2^6}$

Example 47

Simplify: $\dfrac{3^{-2}}{4^{-4}}$

◆ **Step 1** To work with this expression, we need to follow the rule for changing from a negative to a positive exponent, $\dfrac{a^{-m}}{b^{-n}} = \dfrac{b^n}{a^m}$.

$$\frac{3^{-2}}{4^{-4}} =$$

$$\frac{4^4}{3^2}$$

This is simplified as far as it can go, because neither the bases nor the exponents are the same.

1.12 Square Roots and Cube Roots

Since $3^2 = 3 \times 3 = 9$, we say that 9 is the square of 3, or the number 3 is the square root $\left(\sqrt{} \right)$ of 9. In order to find the positive square root of any number a, it is necessary to find a number b that, when multiplied by itself, equals a, or $b \times b = a$. What is the positive square root of 25? It is 5, because 5 multiplied by 5 equals 25. Be careful not to misread expressions containing square roots. For example, $\sqrt{16+9}$ is not equal to $\sqrt{16} + \sqrt{9}$. To simplify $\sqrt{16+9}$, first add the two numbers under the square root symbol, and then find the square root of the sum of the two numbers: $\sqrt{16+9} = \sqrt{25} = 5$. (Adding $\sqrt{16}$ and $\sqrt{9}$ would give us a different answer: $\sqrt{16} = 4$ and $\sqrt{9} = 3$; therefore, $\sqrt{16} + \sqrt{9} = 4 + 3 = 7$).

Example 48

What is the square root of 36?

◆ **Step 1**   Find a number that, when multiplied by itself, equals 36.

$$\sqrt{36} = 6$$

The symbol for cube root $\left(\sqrt[3]{} \right)$ is similar to the square root sign, but it includes a small superscript number 3 immediately to the left of the root symbol. In order to find the positive cube root of any number a, it is necessary to find a number b that, when multiplied three times, equals a, or $b \times b \times b = a$.

Example 49

What is the cube root of 27?

◆ **Step 1**   Express the cube root of 27 by finding a number that, when multiplied three times, equals 27. The answer is 3.

$$(3)(3)(3) =$$

$$(9)(3)\quad =$$

$$(27)\quad =$$

27

Thus, $\sqrt[3]{27} = 3$.

Many square roots, such as $\sqrt{2}$ and $\sqrt{3}$, cannot be expressed as integers. They can be written as decimals, but they are irrational numbers. Most standardized tests require students to know only the most commonly used *perfect* square roots, as shown in table 1.6. From these perfect squares, as they are known, you can estimate other square roots. For example, since $\sqrt{16} = 4$ and $\sqrt{25} = 5$, you know that $\sqrt{21}$ is some number between 4 and 5, and it is probably an irrational number. (In fact, $\sqrt{21} = 4.583\ldots$)

There are also two rules that we need to know when working with square roots:

- If two numbers a and b are either positive or 0, then $\sqrt{ab} = \sqrt{a}\sqrt{b}$.

- If two numbers a and b are positive (and b is not equal to zero), then $\sqrt{\dfrac{a}{b}} = \dfrac{\sqrt{a}}{\sqrt{b}}$.

Table 1.6: Common Square Roots

$\sqrt{0} = 0$	$\sqrt{36} = 6$
$\sqrt{1} = 1$	$\sqrt{49} = 7$
$\sqrt{4} = 2$	$\sqrt{64} = 8$
$\sqrt{9} = 3$	$\sqrt{81} = 9$
$\sqrt{16} = 4$	$\sqrt{100} = 10$
$\sqrt{25} = 5$	$\sqrt{144} = 12$

Example 50

Simplify: $\sqrt{18}$

◆ **Step 1** Write down the number 18 as a product of its factors (we will be working more with factors in chapter 4).

$1 \times 18 = 18$

$2 \times 9 = 18$

$3 \times 6 = 18$

◆ **Step 2** If possible, choose the factor that contains a perfect square. Notice that the factor 9 is the perfect square of 3, so $\sqrt{9} = 3$.

◆ **Step 3** Follow the rule $\sqrt{ab} = \sqrt{a}\sqrt{b}$. Rewrite $\sqrt{18}$ as $\sqrt{9}\sqrt{2}$.

◆ **Step 4** Simplify.

$\sqrt{18} =$

$\sqrt{9}\sqrt{2} =$

$(3)\sqrt{2} =$

$3\sqrt{2}$

Example 51

Simplify: $\sqrt{\dfrac{16}{25}}$

◆ **Step 1** Follow the rule $\sqrt{\dfrac{a}{b}} = \dfrac{\sqrt{a}}{\sqrt{b}}$. Rewrite $\sqrt{\dfrac{16}{25}}$ as $\dfrac{\sqrt{16}}{\sqrt{25}}$.

$$\sqrt{\frac{16}{25}} =$$

$$\frac{\sqrt{16}}{\sqrt{25}} =$$

◆ **Step 2**   Simplify. (The square root of 16 is 4, and the square root of 25 is 5.)

$$\frac{4}{5}$$

1.13 Scientific Notation

Scientific notation is a mathematical shorthand for expressing very large or very small numbers. A number expressed in scientific notation is written as a product of two factors. The first factor is an integer equal to or greater than 1 but less than 10, and the second is the number 10 raised to some power, either a positive integer, a negative integer, or zero.

Example 52

Change 3,200,000 (standard form) to scientific notation.

◆ **Step 1**   Write the number in standard form: 3,200,000

Remember that the number can be written as a decimal by putting a decimal point at the end of the zeros:

3,200,000. ⟵

◆ **Step 2**   Create the first factor by moving the decimal point to the left until we create the decimal 3.2 (a real number that is greater than 1 and less than 10). How many places to the left did we move the decimal point to create the first factor? We moved the decimal point six places.

3200000.

3.200000 ⟵

◆ **Step 3**   The second factor is 10 raised to the power of 6, since we moved the decimal point six places to the left. The exponent 6 is a positive integer, because the standard form number was greater than 1.

◆ **Step 4**   Write down the two factors:

3.2×10^6

Example 53

How do we write 0.0000005 in scientific notation?

◆ **Step 1**   Create the first factor by moving the decimal point seven places to the right.

0.0000005   The first factor is 5.

◆ **Step 2**   Since the number in standard form is less than 1, the second factor is 10 raised to the power of a negative integer, in this case -7.

5×10^{-7}

Example 54

Change 6.24×10^4 to standard form.

◆ **Step 1**   Notice that the exponent is positive, so the decimal point will move to the right.

◆ **Step 2**   Move the decimal point four places to the right to obtain the standard form number.

6.2400

The standard form number is 62,400.

Note that we had to put zeros in as placeholders when we moved the decimal point to the right.

Example 55

Change 3.21×10^{-2} to standard form.

◆ **Step 1**   Notice that the exponent is negative, so the decimal point will move to the left.

◆ **Step 2**   Move the decimal point two places to the left to obtain the standard form number.

03.21
↵

The standard form number is .0321, which we can also write as 0.0321.

Note that we had to put a zero in as a placeholder when we moved the decimal point to the left.

Multiplying in Scientific Notation

In order to multiply in scientific notation, we need to use the product rule for exponents discussed in section 1.11, as well as the associative property of multiplication discussed in section 1.3.

Example 56

Multiply: $(2 \times 10^3)(4 \times 10^5)$

◆ **Step 1**   Rewrite as $(2 \times 4)(10^3 \times 10^5)$

$$(2 \times 4)(10^3 \times 10^5) =$$

◆ **Step 2**   Multiply.

$$8(10^3 \times 10^5) =$$

◆ **Step 3**   Since the base 10 is the same, add the exponents.

$8(10^{3+5}) =$

$8(10^8)$

The solution is 8×10^8.

Example 57

Multiply: $(4 \times 10^3)(7 \times 10^5)$

◆ **Step 1**   Rewrite as $(4 \times 7)(10^3 \times 10^5)$

◆ **Step 2**   Multiply.

$(4 \times 7)(10^3 \times 10^5) =$

$28(10^3 \times 10^5) \quad =$

◆ **Step 3**   Since the base 10 is the same, add the exponents.

$28(10^{3+5}) \quad =$

28×10^8

◆ **Step 4** 28×10^8 is not yet in scientific notation, because 28 is greater than 10. Express 28 as a decimal: 28.0. Move the decimal point one digit to the left: 2.8.

◆ **Step 5**   Since we moved the decimal point one place to the left, we must *add* 1 to the exponent of 10. Thus, 10^8 becomes 10^9.

The solution: 2.8×10^9

Dividing in Scientific Notation

In order to divide in scientific notation, we need to use the quotient rule for exponents,

$$\frac{a^x}{a^y} = a^{x-y}, \text{ where } a = \text{ the base 10 in scientific notation.}$$

Example 58

Divide: $\frac{(4 \times 10^5)}{(2 \times 10^3)}$

◆ **Step 1** Rewrite as $\left(\frac{4}{2}\right)\left(\frac{10^5}{10^3}\right)$.

◆ **Step 2** Divide and use the quotient rule for exponents.

$$\frac{4}{2} \times \frac{10^5}{10^3} \; = $$

$$2 \times 10^{5-3} \; = $$

$$2 \times 10^2$$

The solution is 2×10^2.

Example 59

Divide: $\frac{1.5 \times 10^5}{3.0 \times 10^2}$

◆ **Step 1** Rewrite as $\left(\frac{1.5}{3.0}\right)\left(\frac{10^5}{10^2}\right)$ and divide.

$$\left(\frac{1.5}{3.0}\right)\left(\frac{10^5}{10^2}\right) = $$

$$0.5 \times \frac{10^5}{10^2} \; = $$

$$0.5 \times 10^{5-2} \; = $$

$$0.5 \times 10^3$$

◆ **Step 2** 0.5×10^3 is not yet in scientific notation, because 0.5 is less than 1. To change 0.5×10^3 to scientific notation, move the decimal point in 0.5 one place to the right and *subtract* 1 from the exponent of 10.

$0.5 \times 10^3 \quad =$

$5.0 \times 10^{3-1} =$

5×10^2

The solution is 5×10^2.

1.14 The Metric System

The metric system was first proposed by French officials and was adopted in 1795 by the French Revolutionary Assembly. There was a lot of resistance to the system at first, but its use was made compulsory in France in 1837. Between 1850 and 1900, the metric system was adopted throughout continental Europe, in Latin America, and in many countries elsewhere. The Treaty of the Meter (1875) established the International Bureau of Weights and Measures, which presides over what is called the International System of Units (the metric system, or SI). The 22nd General Conference met in October 2003. The United States and Great Britain have resisted the metric system over the years, but Great Britain has now started to use it. The United States, however, still uses the older Imperial System of weights and measures. Today many European Union (EU) countries do not allow products in their countries unless they are manufactured to metric system standards, increasing pressure on the United States to adopt the metric system, now the world's common language of measurement.

From Imperial to Metric

Example 60

Tim has a soda that is 10 fluid ounces in volume. Convert this volume to the metric system.

◆ **Step 1**   Check table 1.7 for converting fluid ounces to milliliters. The table says to multiply fluid ounces by 30.

$10 \times 30 = 300$ mL

Table 1.7: Converting from the Imperial System to the Metric System

Imperial symbol	When you know	Multiply by	Metric system	Symbol
Length				
in	inches	2.5	centimeters	cm
ft	feet	30.0	centimeters	cm
yd	yards	0.9	meters	m
mi	miles	1.6	kilometers	km
Mass				
oz	ounces	28.0	grams	g
lb	pounds	0.45	kilograms	kg
Volume				
fl oz	fluid ounces	30.0	milliliters	mL
pt	pints	0.47	liters	L
qt	quarts	0.95	liters	L
gal	gallons	3.8	liters	L
ft^3	cubic feet	0.003	cubic meters	m^3
yd^3	cubic yards	0.76	cubic meters	m^3
Temperature				
°F	degrees Fahrenheit	Subtract 32 and multiply by $\frac{5}{9}$	degrees Celsius	°C

From Metric to Imperial

Example 61

If the temperature in San Francisco is 25° Celsius, what is this temperature in degrees Fahrenheit?

◆ **Step 1** Check table 1.8 to find out how to convert degrees Celsius to degrees Fahrenheit. We have to multiply by $\frac{9}{5}$ and add 32.

$$25 \times \frac{9}{5} = 45$$

◆ **Step 2** Add 32.

$$45 + 32 = 77° \text{ Fahrenheit}$$

Table 1.8: Converting from the Metric System to the Imperial System

Metric system	When you know	Multiply by	Imperial system	Symbol
Length				
mm	millimeters	0.04	inches	in
cm	centimeters	0.4	inches	in
m	meters	3.3	feet	ft
m	meters	1.1	yards	yd
km	kilometers	0.6	miles	mi
Mass				
G	grams	0.035	ounces	oz
kg	kilograms	2.2	pounds	lb
Volume				
mL	milliliters	0.03	fluid ounces	fl oz
L	liters	2.1	pints	pt
L	liters	1.06	quarts	qt
L	liters	0.26	gallons	gal
m^3	cubic meters	35.0	cubic feet	ft^3
m^3	cubic meters	1.3	cubic yards	yd^3
Temperature				
°C	degrees Celsius	Multiply by $\frac{9}{5}$ and add 32	degrees Fahrenheit	°F

1.15 The Order of Operations

We are now familiar with the operations of addition, subtraction, multiplication, and division. Often we have to use more than one operation when solving problems, so it is extremely important that we know in which order to perform the operations. Here is the order of operations that we must learn:

1. Working from left to right, first evaluate the expressions in the grouping symbols, such as parentheses ( ), braces { }, brackets [ ], or absolute value | |. If there are numbers in parentheses embedded within braces—for example, {8 + (4 · 1)}—work first from the inside (the parentheses), and then to the outside { }.

2. Simplify expressions with exponents or roots (for example, 8^2 or $\sqrt{16}$).

3. Working from left to right, multiply and/or divide.

4. Working from left to right, add and/or subtract.

Many instructors use a well-known saying to help students remember the order of operations:

Please	*Excuse*	*My*	*Dear*	*Aunt*	*Sally*
parentheses	exponents	multiply	divide	add	subtract

Example 62

Simplify: $9 + 8 - 3$

◆ **Step 1** Working from left to right, add and then subtract.

$9 + 8 - 3 =$

$17 - 3 \quad = 14$

Example 63

Simplify: $(6 + 2)^2 - 5$

◆ **Step 1** Work inside the parentheses first, and then evaluate the exponent.

$(6 + 2)^2 - 5 =$

$(8)^2 - 5 \quad =$

$(8)(8) - 5 \quad =$

$64 - 5 \quad =$

◆ **Step 2** Subtract.

$64 - 5 = 59$

Example 64

Simplify: $12 - 8 \div 2$

◆ **Step 1**   Divide first.

$$12 - 8 \div 2 =$$

$$12 - 4 \quad =$$

◆ **Step 2**   Subtract.

$$12 - 4 = 8$$

Note that if you subtracted first and then divided, you would get a different (and incorrect) answer.

Example 65

Simplify: $6 - 2\left[2 - 4(2 - 4)\right] + 2^{-2} + \dfrac{3}{4}$

◆ **Step 1**   Work inside the parentheses ( ) first.

$$6 - 2\left[2 - 4(-2)\right] + 2^{-2} + \frac{3}{4} =$$

◆ **Step 2**   Work inside the brackets [ ].

$$6 - 2\left[2 + 8\right] + 2^{-2} + \frac{3}{4} =$$

$$6 - 2\left[10\right] + 2^{-2} + \frac{3}{4} =$$

◆ **Step 3**   Work with the exponent, expressing it as a positive exponent.

$$6 - 2\left[10\right] + \frac{1}{2^2} + \frac{3}{4} =$$

$$6 - 2[10] + \frac{1}{(2)(2)} + \frac{3}{4} =$$

$$6 - 2[10] + \frac{1}{4} + \frac{3}{4}$$

◆ **Step 4** Multiply.

$$6 - 20 + \frac{1}{4} + \frac{3}{4}$$

◆ **Step 5** Working from left to right, subtract and add.

$$-14 + \frac{1}{4} + \frac{3}{4} =$$

$$-14 + 1 \quad = -13$$

Problems

1. Simplify: $-10 + 20 \div (-5)$

2. Simplify: $6 - 3[2 - 4(2 - 4)]$

3. Simplify: $(2 + 1)^3 + 5$

4. Evaluate: $-(-5)^4$

5. Evaluate: 7^{-2}

6. Divide: $\dfrac{4^4}{4^2}$

7. Multiply: $4^3 \cdot 3^3$

8. Simplify: $\sqrt[3]{125}$

9. Simplify: $3\sqrt{49} + 6\sqrt{81}$

10. What is the place value of 1 in the number 1,384?

11. Change from standard form to scientific notation: 0.00674219

12. The star Sirius, also known as the Dog Star, is 8.1833325×10^{13} kilometers from Earth. Express this distance in standard notation.

13. Change from scientific notation to standard form: 4.80305×10^{-2}

14. Multiply: $(1.1 \times 10^{-7})(3 \times 10^{-3})$

15. Arranging from right to left, Mrs. Patel placed her buttons from smallest to largest in size. If the buttons are the following sizes in inches, $\frac{3}{8}, \frac{7}{8}, \frac{2}{8}, \frac{3}{16}$, and $\frac{3}{4}$, in what order did she arrange them?

Focus on English

Grammar

Its

Its is a possessive pronoun like *his* or *her*. Many people make the mistake of spelling *its* as *it's*. *It's* is not a possessive pronoun but is the contracted form of *it is*.

Example: "I like this pattern. *Its* colors are very bright."

Other possessive pronouns are as follows:

Mine: That book is mine.

Yours: It's not Elizabeth's; it's yours!

His: His work is very good.

Hers: That jacket is hers.

Ours: No, you can't have that computer; it's ours!

Theirs: The car is theirs.

Larger, Smaller

Adjectives are words that describe nouns. For example, Mr. Smith is an honest man. *Honest* is the adjective, and *man* is the noun. *Smaller* and *larger* are called comparatives of the adjective, while *smallest* and *largest* are the superlative forms. We use *smaller* or *larger* when we are comparing, for example, two boxes: *The red box is smaller than the green box.* If we have more than two boxes, we use the superlative to describe them. For example, *The blue box is the largest.* Fill in the blanks below, and practice writing sentences using the comparative and the superlative forms of adjectives.

Example: (short) Mrs. Sanchez is short**er** than Mrs. Garza. (comparative)

Example: (tall) Mr. Tang is the tall**est** man in the room. (superlative)

Example: (large) Which is the larg**est** box? It is the blue one. (superlative)

1. (thick) The expensive tires are _____ than the cheap ones. (comparative)

2. (safe) Flying is _____ than driving. (comparative)

3. (hot) August is the _____ month of the year in San Antonio. (superlative)

4. (high) Carl's scores were _____ than he expected. (comparative)

5. (kind) Mrs. Smith is the _____ woman in the store. (superlative)

Parents'

We often make errors when we write the general possessive form of regular plural nouns that end with the letter *s*. For example, *parent* is a singular noun, and the plural form is *parents*. If we write about a child of one parent, we can say "the *parent's child*." But if we are discussing a child of two parents, we put the apostrophe mark (') after the *s* in *parents* so that it becomes "the *parents' child*." Practice writing sentences using the possessive form of regular plural nouns that end with the letter *s*.

Example: Mrs. Samuel placed her **cats'** toys in their basket.

Improving Mathematical Vocabulary

1. In the fraction $\frac{3}{4}$, which number is the denominator, and which number is the numerator?

2. Write down the symbol for positive and the symbol for negative.

3. How do we say these three symbols in English?

    >

    <

    =

4. What does cross multiplication mean?

5. What is the difference between a square root and a cube root?

6. How do you define absolute value?

7. What is scientific notation? For what reason do mathematicians use scientific notation?

8. Why is it so important to learn the order of operations?

 Dictionary Work

Define the following words:

Decimal

Product

Exponent

Numerator

Denominator

Quotient

Chapter 2
Linear Equations

We begin this chapter by studying some of the basic concepts of algebra, such as variables, terms, numerical coefficients, like terms, and unlike terms.

2.0 Introduction to Algebra

Variables

The following linear equation contains the variable x:

$$x + 21 = 40$$

A variable (which can be any letter, such as x or y) represents a number whose value we do not yet know but are seeking to discover. In the above equation, the value of x is 19, since $19 + 21 = 40$.

Terms

A term can include any one of the following:

- A variable, such as x

- The product of a number and a variable—for example, $7y$

- The quotient of a number and a variable: $\frac{10}{x}$

- A constant, which is a number, such as 15, whose value never changes

- The product of a number and a variable raised to a power—for example, $4a^2$

Numerical Coefficients

The numerical coefficient is the numerical part of a term. For example, the numerical coefficient of $8x^2$ is 8, whereas the coefficient of $-9x$ is -9. Does the variable y have a numerical coefficient? Yes, since y is the same as $1y$, the coefficient is 1. Similarly, the coefficient of $-x$ is -1. The numerical coefficient of $\frac{11}{z}$ is 11; and that of $\frac{a}{3}$ is $\frac{1}{3}$, since the coefficient of a is 1.

Like Terms

Like terms are terms that have the same variables raised to the same power:

$4x$ and $7x$	same variable
$8yz$ and $2zy$	same variables: yz and zy are equivalent by the commutative property of multiplication
$-9a^2$ and $3a^2$	same variable raised to the same power

We combine like terms that contain a common variable by using the distributive property (introduced in chapter 1), which can be written as

$$ax + bx = (a + b)x$$
$$ax - bx = (a - b)x$$

Example 1

Add: $5x + 8x$

◆ **Step 1**   Use the distributive property to group the coefficients.

$5x + 8x =$

$(5 + 8)x =$

◆ **Step 2**   Add the coefficients.

$(13)x =$

$13x$

Example 2

Simplify: $18z - 6z$

$$18z - 6z \;=\;$$

$$(18 - 6)z \;=\;$$

$$(12)z \quad =$$

$$12z$$

Example 3

Combine like terms: $4x + 8x + 2x$

◆ **Step 1**   Use the distributive property to group the coefficients.

$$4x + 8x + 2x =$$

$$(4 + 8 + 2)x \;=\;$$

◆ **Step 2**   Add the coefficients.

$$(14)x =$$

$$14x$$

Unlike Terms

Unlike terms are terms with different variables, or the same variable raised to different powers.

$6a$ and $9b$	different variables, a and b
$4yz$ and $7zya$	different variables, yz and zya
$9x^2$ and $5y^5$	different variables and exponents
$8x^2$ and $7x^3$	same variables but different exponents

It is very important to remember that we cannot combine unlike terms. If your automobile engine needs 5 quarts of oil to function properly, imagine what would happen to your car's engine if you tried to combine 3 quarts of oil with

2 quarts of water. We can express this mathematically as $3o + 2w$, where o represents quarts of oil, and w represents quarts of water. Thus, when working with terms, check very carefully whether the terms are like or unlike.

Simplifying More Complex Algebraic Expressions

Example 4 illustrates how to work with more complex algebraic expressions.

Example 4

Use the distributive property to simplify $12x + 2(6 + 3x)$.

◆ **Step 1**   Rearrange the terms.

$12x + 2(6 + 3x)$ =

$12x + 2(6) + 2(3x)$ =

$12x + 12 + 6x$ =

◆ **Step 2**   Combine like terms.

$12x + 6x + 12 =$

$18x + 12$

This expression cannot be simplified further, because $18x$ and 12 are unlike terms.

Example 5

Simplify: $5(2t - 3) - 2(4t - 9) + 4c$

◆ **Step 1**   Use the distributive property.

$5(2t - 3) - 2(4t - 9) + 4c$ =

$5(2t) + 5(-3) - 2(4t) - 2(-9) + 4c =$

◆ **Step 2**   Rearrange the terms.

$10t - 15 - 8t + 18 + 4c =$

◆ **Step 3**   Combine like terms.

$10t - 8t + 4c - 15 + 18 =$

$2t + 4c + 3$

Example 6

If $x = 1$ and $y = 2$, evaluate $13x(2 - 3) - 2(y + 8) + 14$.

◆ **Step 1**   Insert the known values for x and y.

$13(1)(2 - 3) - 2(2 + 8) + 14 =$

◆ **Step 2**   Work inside the parentheses first.

$13(1)(-1) - 2(10) + 14 =$

◆ **Step 3**   Multiply; then add and subtract.

$13(-1) - 2(10) + 14 =$

$-13 - 20 + 14 \qquad =$

$-33 + 14 \qquad\quad =$

-19

Understanding Linear Equations

An equation is a mathematical statement indicating the equality of expressions such as $4y = 12$, $5c - 2c + 2 = 11$, and $2 + x = 4$.

Such equations are called linear equations, because the variables are raised to the power of 1 (that is, $x = x^1$). In order to solve a linear equation, we must determine the value of the variable in an equation so that both sides of the equal sign ($=$) are equal in value. For example, when we solve for x in the linear equation $x + 3 = 5$, we find the value of x so that when it is added to the number 3, the sum is equal to 5. In other words, which number, when added to 3, gives us 5? The solution is 2. Thus, we say that $x = 2$ in the equation $x + 3 = 5$.

2.1 Solving by Addition or Subtraction

Solving by Addition

When solving linear equations by addition, we use the addition property of equality, which states that if $a = b$, then for any real number c, the following is true:

$$a + c = b + c$$

This means that whatever we add to one side of the equation, we must also add to the other side. This property enables us to solve for the variable by isolating it on one side of the equation. The word "isolate" in math has the same meaning as it does in everyday language—"to set apart."

Example 7

Solve for x: $x - 5 = 10$

◆ **Step 1**   Add 5 to both sides of the equation to isolate x.

$$x - 5 + 5 = 10 + 5$$

$$x + 0 \quad = 10 + 5$$

◆ **Step 2**   Solve for x.

$$x = 10 + 5$$

$$x = 15$$

Example 8

Solve for b: $9 = -5(2b - 1) - (-11b + 6)$

◆ **Step 1** Use the distributive property.

$$9 = -5(2b - 1) - (-11b + 6)$$

$$9 = -10b + 5 + 11b - 6$$

◆ **Step 2** Rearrange the terms.

$$9 = -10b + 11b + 5 - 6$$

◆ **Step 3** Combine like terms.

$$9 = 1b + 5 - 6$$

$$9 = 1b - 1$$

$$9 = b - 1$$

◆ **Step 4** Isolate the variable by adding 1 to both sides, and solve for b.

$$9 + 1 = b - 1 + 1$$

$$10 \quad = b$$

$$b \quad = 10$$

Solving by Subtraction

We can also solve linear equations by using the subtraction property of equality, which states that if $a = b$, then for any real number c, the following is true:

$$a - c = b - c$$

Thus, whatever we subtract from one side of the equation, we must also subtract from the other side.

Example 9

Solve for x: $x + 3 = 12$

◆ **Step 1**   Subtract 3 from both sides of the equation to isolate x.

$x + 3 - 3 = 12 - 3$

◆ **Step 2**   Solve for x.

$x = 12 - 3$

$x = 9$

Example 10

Solve for a: $2a + 3a - 5 + 9 = 10a + 3 - 6a - 5$

◆ **Step 1**   Combine like terms.

$2a + 3a - 5 + 9 = 10a + 3 - 6a - 5$

$5a - 5 + 9 \quad = 4a + 3 - 5$

$5a + 4 \quad\quad = 4a - 2$

◆ **Step 2**   Subtract 4 from both sides of the equation.

$5a + 4 - 4 = 4a - 2 - 4$

$5a \quad\quad = 4a - 6$

◆ **Step 3**   Subtract $4a$ from both sides.

$5a - 4a = 4a - 6 - 4a$

$$1a = -6$$

$$a = -6$$

2.2 Solving by Multiplication or Division

Solving by Multiplication

Solving linear equations by adding or subtracting is straightforward, but there are times when these methods are inadequate and we have to use two other properties—the multiplication property of equality and the division property of equality. The multiplication property of equality states that if $a = b$, then for any real number c, the following is true:

$$ac = bc$$

This means that whatever we multiply one side of the equation by, we must also multiply the other side by.

Example 11

Solve for x: $\frac{1}{2}x = 4$

◆ **Step 1**   Isolate the variable x, by multiplying both sides of the equation by 2 or $\frac{2}{1}$, the reciprocal of $\frac{1}{2}$.

$$\frac{2}{1} \cdot \frac{1}{2}x = 4 \cdot \frac{2}{1}$$

◆ **Step 2**   Solve for x.

$$\frac{\cancel{2}}{\cancel{2}}x = \frac{8}{1}$$

$$x = 8$$

Example 12

Solve for x: $3x + 5 = 20$

◆ **Step 1**   Isolate the term $3x$ by subtracting 5 from both sides of the equation.

$$3x + 5 - 5 = 20 - 5$$

$$3x \qquad = 15$$

◆ **Step 2**   Multiply both sides by the reciprocal $\frac{1}{3}$.

$$3x \cdot \frac{1}{3} = 15 \cdot \frac{1}{3}$$

$$\frac{\cancel{3}}{\cancel{3}} x = \frac{15}{3}$$

◆ **Step 3**   Solve for x.

$$x = 5$$

Example 13

Solve for x: $\frac{1}{7}x = 3$

◆ **Step 1**   Multiply both sides of the equation by the reciprocal $\frac{7}{1}$.

$$\frac{1}{7}x \cdot \frac{7}{1} = 3 \cdot \frac{7}{1}$$

$$\frac{\cancel{7}}{\cancel{7}} x = \frac{21}{1}$$

◆ **Step 2**   Solve for x.

$$x = 21$$

Solving by Division

The division property of equality can also be used to solve linear equations. This property states that if $a = b$, then for any real number c (except for zero), the following is true:

$$\frac{a}{c} = \frac{b}{c}$$

This means that whatever we divide one side of the equation by, we must also divide the other side by.

Example 14

Solve for x: $4x = 24$

◆ **Step 1**

Isolate the variable x by dividing both sides of the equation by 4 (this is the same as multiplying by its reciprocal $\frac{1}{4}$).

$$\frac{1}{4} \cdot \frac{4}{1} x = 24 \cdot \frac{1}{4}$$

$$\frac{\cancel{4}}{\cancel{4}} x = \frac{24}{4}$$

◆ **Step 2**   Solve for x.

$x = 6$

Example 15

Solve for c: $4c + 3 - 7 + 1 = 3 + 7c - 9$

◆ **Step 1**   Combine like terms.

$$4c + 3 + 1 - 7 = 7c + 3 - 9$$

$$4c + 4 - 7 = 7c - 6$$

$$4c - 3 = 7c - 6$$

◆ **Step 2** Subtract $7c$ from both sides.

$$4c - 3 - 7c = 7c - 6 - 7c$$

$$-3c - 3 = -6$$

◆ **Step 3** Add $+3$ to both sides of the equation.

$$-3c - 3 + 3 = -6 + 3$$

$$-3c = -3$$

◆ **Step 4** Divide both sides by -3 (or multiply by $-\frac{1}{3}$).

$$\frac{\cancel{-3}c}{\cancel{-3}} = \frac{-3}{-3}$$

$$c = 1$$

We can discover if we have the correct solution for an equation by replacing the variable with its value to see if the equation is true. For example, in example 15,

let $c = 1$ in the original equation $4c + 3 - 7 + 1 = 3 + 7c - 9$.

$$4(1) + 3 - 7 + 1 = 3 + 7(1) - 9$$

$$4 + 3 - 7 + 1 = 3 + 7 - 9$$

$$7 - 7 + 1 = 10 - 9$$

$$0 + 1 = 1$$

$$1 = 1$$

The equation is true; thus, we know that $c = 1$ in example 15.

Solving Linear Equations Containing Fractions

In order to solve linear equations containing fractions, we begin by finding the lowest common denominator, or LCD. The following equation has three denominators (6, 3, and 2):

$$\frac{s}{6} + \frac{2}{3} = \frac{1}{2}$$

We determine the LCD of these three denominators by finding the least common multiple (LCM) of 6, 3, and 2. That is, we find which number is the smallest common multiple of 6, 3, and 2. The answer is 6, because 2, 3, and 6 are all factors of 6:

$$2 \times 3 = 6$$

$$3 \times 2 = 6$$

$$6 \times 1 = 6$$

Note that 12 is also a common multiple, but it is easier to work with the *least* (lowest) common multiple.

Because 6 is the LCD of the three denominators in the equation $\frac{s}{6} + \frac{2}{3} = \frac{1}{2}$, we multiply by 6 throughout the equation to clear the fractions. We then solve for s.

Example 16

Solve for s: $\frac{s}{6} + \frac{2}{3} = \frac{1}{2}$

◆ **Step 1**   Multiply each side of the equation by the LCD 6 to clear the fractions.

$$6\left(\frac{s}{6} + \frac{2}{3}\right) = 6\left(\frac{1}{2}\right)$$

◆ **Step 2**   Use the distributive property and simplify the terms.

$$6\left(\frac{s}{6}\right) + 6\left(\frac{2}{3}\right) = 6\left(\frac{1}{2}\right)$$

$$\left(\frac{\cancel{6}s}{\cancel{6}}\right) + \left(\frac{12}{3}\right) = \left(\frac{6}{2}\right)$$

$$s + 4 = 3$$

◆ **Step 3**   To isolate the variable s, subtract 4 from both sides of the
             equation.

$$s + 4 - 4 = 3 - 4$$

$$s \qquad = -1$$

Example 17

Solve for x: $\dfrac{x+3}{8} + \dfrac{1}{2} = 5$

◆ **Step 1**   Determine the LCD of 8 and 2. It is 8, since $8 \times 1 = 8$ and $2 \times 4 = 8$. Multiply each side of the equation by 8.

$$8\left(\frac{x+3}{8} + \frac{1}{2}\right) = 8(5)$$

◆ **Step 2**   Use the distributive property.

$$8\left(\frac{x+3}{8}\right) + 8\left(\frac{1}{2}\right) = 8(5)$$
$$(x+3) \quad + \frac{8}{2} \quad = 40$$
$$x + 3 \quad + 4 \quad = 40$$
$$x + 7 \qquad\qquad = 40$$

◆ **Step 3**   Subtract 7 from both sides to isolate the variable x.

$$x + 7 - 7 = 40 - 7$$

$$x \qquad = 33$$

Solving Linear Equations Containing Decimals

Solving linear equations containing decimals is straightforward if we remember the basic concept that whatever operation we perform on one side of the equation, we must also perform on the other side.

Example 18

If $3.7x - 2.7 = 15.8$, what is the value of x?

◆ **Step 1**   Isolate the term with the variable by adding 2.7 to both sides of the equation.

$$3.7x - 2.7 + 2.7 = 15.8 + 2.7$$

$$3.7x \qquad\qquad = 18.5$$

◆ **Step 2**   Divide by 3.7 on both sides of the equation.

$$\frac{\cancel{3.7}x}{\cancel{3.7}} = \frac{18.5}{3.7}$$

$$x = 5$$

We can check our solution by inserting the value 5 for x in the original equation.

$$3.7(5) - 2.7 = 15.8$$

$$18.5 - 2.7 = 15.8$$

$$15.8 = 15.8$$

We can also solve equations containing decimals by first multiplying by 10 (or a power of 10) across the equation to clear the decimals.

Example 19

Solve for x: $3.7x - 2.7 = 15.8$

◆ **Step 1**   Multiply by 10 on both sides of the equation and simplify.

$$10(3.7x - 2.7) \qquad = 10(15.8)$$

$$(10)3.7x - (10)2.7 = (10)15.8$$

$$37x - 27 \qquad\qquad = 158$$

◆ **Step 2**   Add 27 to both sides of the equation to isolate the term with the variable.

$$37x - 27 + 27 = 158 + 27$$

$$37x = 185$$

◆ **Step 3**   Divide by 37 on both sides of the equation to isolate the variable x.

$$\frac{37x}{37} = \frac{185}{37}$$

$$x = 5$$

Example 20

Solve for x: $2x + 0.6 = 23.4$

◆ **Step 1**   Multiply by 10 across the equation to clear the decimals.

$$10(2x) + 10(0.6) = 10(23.4)$$

$$20x + 6 = 234$$

◆ **Step 2**   Subtract 6 from both sides of the equation.

$$20x + 6 - 6 = 234 - 6$$

$$20x = 228$$

◆ **Step 3**   Divide by 20 to isolate the variable.

$$\frac{20x}{20} = \frac{228}{20}$$

$$x = 11.4$$

2.3 Solving Linear Equations Containing Parentheses

In chapter 1, we learned the order of operations for solving mathematical problems. When we work with linear equations containing parentheses, the order of operations continues to apply. This means that we must work inside the parentheses first before performing other operations.

Example 21

Solve for x: $2(x - 3) + (3 \times 2) - (4 \div 2) = 2(4 + 3) - 4$

◆ **Step 1** Work inside the parentheses first.

$2(x - 3) + (3 \times 2) - (4 \div 2) = 2(4 + 3) - 4$

$2x + 2(-3) + (6) - (2) = 2(7) - 4$

$2x - 6 + 6 - 2 = 14 - 4$

$2x - 2 = 10$

◆ **Step 2** Add 2 to both sides of the equation to isolate the x term.

$2x - 2 + 2 = 10 + 2$

$2x = 12$

◆ **Step 3** Divide by 2.

$$\frac{2x}{2} = \frac{12}{2}$$

$x = 6$

Example 22

Solve for y: $3 + (2 - 3) - 4(y - 2) = (3 - 4)2$

◆ **Step 1**   Work with the parentheses first.

$$3 + (2 - 3) - 4(y - 2) = (3 - 4)2$$

$$3 + (-1) - (4y) + (8) = (-1)2$$

$$3 - 1 - 4y + 8 \qquad = -2$$

◆ **Step 2**   Combine like terms.

$$10 - 4y = -2$$

◆ **Step 3**   Subtract 10 from both sides of the equation.

$$10 - 4y - 10 = -2 - 10$$

$$-4y \qquad = -12$$

◆ **Step 4**   Divide both sides by -4.

$$\frac{\cancel{-4}y}{\cancel{-4}} = \frac{-12}{-4}$$

$$y \qquad = 3$$

2.4 Solving Linear Equations Containing Percentages

Understanding Percentages

A percentage is a fraction whose denominator is always 100. In fact, the symbol % comes from 1, 0, 0, or 100. For example, we can write 25% as $\frac{25}{100}$.

Example 23

How do we write the following as a percentage? Ninety-seven out of every 100 households in the United States have at least one television:

$$\frac{97}{100} = 97\%$$

Example 24

How do we express the following as a fraction? The school computer club raised 145% of the amount of money it raised the previous year.

$$145\% = \frac{145}{100}$$

We can also write a percentage as a decimal and a decimal as a percentage.

To express a percentage as a decimal, eliminate the percentage sign (%), and move the decimal point two places to the left, which is what you do when you divide by 100. To write a decimal as a percentage, do just the opposite: Move the decimal point two places to the right, and write a percentage symbol at the end of the number.

Example 25

How do we write 25% as a decimal?

◆ **Step 1**   Remove or eliminate the percentage sign.

25%

25

◆ **Step 2**   Move the decimal point two places to the left.

25.

0.25

Example 26

How do we write 3.195 as a percentage?

◆ **Step 1**   Move the decimal point two places to the right.

3.195

319.5

◆ **Step 2**   Write down the percentage symbol.

319.5%

Example 27

Write the fraction $\frac{2}{5}$ as a percentage.

◆ **Step 1**   Change the fraction to a decimal by dividing 2 by 5.

$$5\overline{)2.0} \quad \begin{array}{r} 0.4 \\ \hline \end{array}$$
$$\underline{20}$$
$$0$$

$$\frac{2}{5} = 0.4$$

◆ **Step 2**   Change the decimal 0.4 (which we can also write as 0.40) to a percentage by moving the decimal point two places to the right and adding a percentage sign.

0.40
→

40%

Linear Equations and Percentages

We solve problems involving percentages by translating them into English statements that we can express mathematically.

Example 28

What is 26% of 50?

◆ **Step 1**   Write this mathematically. In general, "of" means multiply and "is" means equals.

What is 26% of 50?

$$n = 26\% \times 50$$

$$n = \frac{26}{100} \times 50$$

$$= 0.26 \times 50$$

$$= 13$$

13 is 26% of 50.

Example 29

Maureen bought a new stereo system for $575. If she made a down payment of 20% to put the stereo in layaway until the end of the month, what was her down payment?

◆ **Step 1**   Write down the problem in English.

How much is 20% of $575?

◆ **Step 2**   Express this sentence mathematically.

$x = 0.20 \times 575$, where x equals the amount of the down payment.

$$= 115$$

◆ **Step 3**   State the solution in English.

Maureen's down payment for her stereo was $115.

Percent Increase and Percent Decrease

Some problems deal with determining percent increase or percent decrease. We solve these problems by using the formula:

$$\frac{change}{starting\ point} = percent\ change$$

Example 30

Mrs. Lin has lived in the same house for 4 years. During this period of time, her rent has increased from $800 per month to $1,200 per month. By what percent has her rent increased?

◆ **Step 1**   Let x equal the percent increase in the rent.

◆ **Step 2**   Calculate the change in the rent. Subtract $800 from $1,200. The result is $400.

◆ **Step 3**   Use the formula $\frac{change}{starting\ point} = percent\ change$ to find the percent increase in the rent, where change is $400, starting point is $800, and x is the percent increase in the rent.

$$\frac{400}{800} = x$$
$$\frac{1}{2} = x$$

◆ **Step 4**   Change $\frac{1}{2}$ to a decimal by dividing the numerator 1 by the denominator 2.

$$2\overline{)1.0} = x$$
$$0.5$$
$$\underline{10}$$
$$\ \ 0$$

◆ **Step 5**   Change the decimal 0.5 to a percentage by moving the decimal point two places to the right and adding a percentage sign.

Mrs. Lin's rent has increased by 50% over a period of 4 years.

Example 31

What is the percent decrease of a $300 coat on sale for $225?

◆ **Step 1**   Let x = percent decrease in the price of the coat.

◆ **Step 2**   Find the change in the price by subtracting 225 from 300. The result is 75.

◆ **Step 3**   Use the formula $\dfrac{\text{change}}{\text{starting point}}$ = percent change to find the percent decrease (or discount) in the price of the coat.

$$\frac{75}{300} = x$$

$$\frac{1}{4} = x$$

◆ **Step 4**   Change or convert the fraction to a decimal, and then express the result as a percentage.

$$
\begin{array}{r}
0.25 \\
4\overline{)1.00} \\
\underline{8} \\
20 \\
\underline{20} \\
0
\end{array}
$$

0.25 = 25%
The percent decrease in the price of the coat is 25%.

Ratio and Proportion

When we write ratios, we indicate a mathematical relationship between two or more numbers. For example, the ratio of a number represented by x to another number represented by y may be expressed in three ways:

$$\frac{x}{y} \qquad x \text{ to } y \qquad x : y$$

Example 32

How do we write the ratio of 2 parts of sesame oil to 6 parts of vinegar?

$\dfrac{2}{6}$, or 2 to 6, or 2 : 6

When two ratios are equal, they are in proportion to each other. This means they represent the same percentage (or fractional) value. For example, $\frac{1}{4} = \frac{2}{8}$ is a proportion, because the ratios are equal:

$$\frac{1}{4} = \frac{\cancel{2}^{1}}{\cancel{8}_{4}} = \frac{1}{4}$$

In order to determine whether two ratios are in proportion, we use the cross-multiplication method that we learned in chapter 1 to compare the values of two fractions. If the ratios are in proportion, cross multiplication will yield the same numbers.

Example 33

Are the ratios $\frac{1}{3}$ and $\frac{2}{6}$ in proportion?

◆ **Step 1** Cross multiply.

$3 \times 2 = 6$ and $6 \times 1 = 6$

Cross multiplying 3 and 2 yielded a product of 6, and cross multiplying 6 and 1 also gave us a product of 6, so we can say that the two ratios are in proportion. We can use this method to solve a variety of proportion and percentage problems.

Example 34

Twenty-four is what percent of 120?

◆ **Step 1** Use the cross-multiplication method to solve this problem. Set up the proportion in the following way, where x is the unknown percentage. Remember that percentage means "divided by 100."

$$\frac{24}{120} = \frac{x}{100}$$

◆ **Step 2** Cross multiply.

$120x = 100(24)$

$120x = 2{,}400$

◆ **Step 3**   Divide both sides of the equation by 120.

$$\frac{\cancel{120}\,x}{\cancel{120}} = \frac{2{,}400}{120}$$

$$x = \frac{20}{1}$$

$$x = 20$$

> Twenty-four is 20% of 120.

Another method to solve the problem in example 34 is to convert the English sentence to math language.

$$24 \quad \text{is what percent of 120}$$

$$24 \quad = \quad \frac{x}{100} \quad \cdot \; 120$$

$$2{,}400 = \quad 120x$$

> 20   = x, so 24 is 20% of 120.

Example 35

> After grading the first test, Mr. Suganami found that 24 out of the 32 students in his class had earned an A grade. What percentage of his students made an A on their first examination?

◆ **Step 1**   Set up the proportion in this way where x is the unknown percentage:

$$\frac{24}{32} = \frac{x}{100}$$

◆ **Step 2**   Cross multiply.

$$\frac{24}{32} = \frac{x}{100}$$

$$32x = 100(24)$$

$$32x = 2{,}400$$

◆ **Step 3**   Divide both sides of the equation by 32 to isolate the variable x.

$$\frac{32x}{32} = \frac{2,400}{32}$$
$$x = 75$$

◆ **Step 4**   Add the percent sign.

$$x = 75\%$$

> Seventy-five percent of Mr. Suganami's students earned an A grade.

Example 36

> If a baker sells 500 loaves of bread every 10 days, how many would she sell in 25 days?

◆ **Step 1**   Write down the proportion in this way:

$\frac{500}{10} = \frac{x}{25}$, where x = the number of loaves sold in 25 days, and the proportion represents $\frac{\text{loaves}}{\text{days}}$.

◆ **Step 2**   Cross multiply.

$$10x = 25(500)$$

$$10x = 12,500$$

◆ **Step 3**   Divide both sides of the equation by 10.

$$\frac{10x}{10} = \frac{12,500}{10}$$
$$x = 1,250$$

> The baker would sell 1,250 loaves of bread in 25 days.

Example 37

The ratio of mathematics books to history books sold at the college bookstore is 9 to 6. If the bookstore sold 960 history books, how many math books did it sell?

◆ **Step 1** Let m equal the number of mathematics books sold.

◆ **Step 2** Set up the proportion of $\dfrac{\text{math books}}{\text{history books}}$.

$$\frac{9}{6} = \frac{m}{960}$$

◆ **Step 3** Cross multiply.

$$6m = 960(9)$$
$$6m = 8,640$$
$$m = \frac{8,640}{6}$$
$$m = 1,440$$

The bookstore sold 1,440 mathematics books.

2.5 Linear Equations with No Solutions

So far in this chapter, we have found that all the linear equations we worked on had a single solution. There are times, however, when linear equations either cannot be solved or have so many possible solutions that we must conclude that the equation has no single solution.

Example 38

Solve for x: $x + 4 = x + 6$

◆ **Step 1** Let's try to obtain a single solution for x. Subtract x from both sides of the equation.

$$x + 4 = x + 6$$

$$x - x + 4 = x - x + 6$$

> 4 = 6
>
> This is false. Since $4 \neq 6$, there is no solution for this equation. We write this as either {} or $\varnothing$. Actually, $x + 4 = x + 6$ should not be called an equation, because the two sides can never be equal.

Example 39

> Solve for x: $4x - 12 = 4(x - 3)$

◆ **Step 1**   Work with the terms inside the parentheses first.

$$4x - 12 = 4(x - 3)$$

$$4x - 12 = 4x - 12$$

◆ **Step 2**   Add 12 to both sides of the equation.

$$4x - 12 + 12 = 4x - 12 + 12$$

◆ **Step 3**   Subtract $4x$ from both sides.

$$4x \qquad = 4x$$

$$4x - 4x = 4x - 4x$$

> $$0 \qquad = 0$$

Notice that the variable has disappeared. When this occurs, we can say that the equation is true for all x, since x can be any real number. Thus, we say that the equation $4x - 12 = 4(x - 3)$ has an infinite number of solutions.

2.6 More About Word Problems

We use algebra to solve word problems, including those we can apply in our daily life. Table 2.1 lists some key words and phrases that often appear in word problems. Use the blank spaces in the table to add any other words and phrases that

Table 2.1: Words and Phrases Often Found in Word Problems

Words and phrases that mean addition	Words and phrases that mean subtraction	Words and phrases that mean multiplication	Words and phrases that mean division
plus	minus	product	ratio
more than	less than	times	quotient
sum	difference	of	divided by
greater than	fewer than	twice	half of
increase	decrease	multiplied by	quarter of
larger than	smaller than		third of
rise	drop		
enlarge	diminish		
grow	reduced by		
bigger than	lower		
together			

you have also found in word problems. Using the table as a guide, practice translating phrases into algebraic expressions such as the ones in the examples below.

Example 40

How do we express "the product of a number and 5"?

◆ **Step 1**   Let the variable n represent the number.

◆ **Step 2**   "Product" signals multiplication, so the "product of a number and 5" is:

$5n$

Example 41

How do we express "four times a number, decreased by one-half of another number"?

◆ **Step 1**   Let the first number be x, and the second number be y.

◆ **Step 2**   Since "times" signals multiplication, we express "four times a number x" as

$4x$

◆ **Step 3**   "Decreased" signals subtraction, so we write

$4x -$

◆ **Step 4**   One-half of the other number y is

$\frac{1}{2}y$

◆ **Step 5**   Write down mathematically "four times a number, decreased by one-half of another number" as

$$4x - \frac{1}{2}y$$

Now that we've practiced translating words and phrases into algebraic expressions, let's try working with several complete word problems.

Example 42

For his last big party, Gordon ordered a 20-inch submarine sandwich from the local deli. When it arrived, he found that it had broken into two pieces in such a way that the longer piece was four times as long as the shorter piece. Find the length of both pieces.

◆ **Step 1**   Let x represent the shorter piece of the sandwich. Thus, the longer piece, which is four times (multiplication) as long as the shorter piece, is $4x$.

◆ **Step 2**   Both pieces together make up one submarine sandwich whose total length is 20 inches. So x (the shorter piece) together with (which signals addition) $4x$ (the longer piece) make up (equal) a sandwich of 20 inches in length. We write this as

$x + 4x = 20$

◆ **Step 3** Solve for x.

$$x + 4x = 20$$
$$5x = 20$$
$$\frac{5x}{5} = \frac{20}{5}$$
$$x = 4$$

We know that the shorter piece x is 4 inches long. What is the length of the longer piece?

$$20 - 4 = 16$$

Thus, the shorter piece of the sandwich is 4 inches long, and the longer piece (which is four times as long as the shorter one) is 16 inches long.

2.7 Literal Equations

Literal equations (equations with letters) are similar to the equations we have already studied, except they can contain several variables. Treat them the same way.

Example 43

Solve for R: $RT - W = Z$

◆ **Step 1** Add W to both sides of the equation to isolate R.

$$RT - W + W = Z + W$$

$$RT = Z + W$$

◆ **Step 2** Divide both sides of the equation by T.

$$\frac{RT}{T} = \frac{Z + W}{T}$$
$$R = \frac{Z + W}{T}$$

Example 44

Solve for Z: $\dfrac{Z}{V} = XY + A$

◆ **Step 1**   Multiply both sides of the equation by V.

$$\cancel{V}\left(\dfrac{Z}{\cancel{V}}\right) = V(XY + A)$$

$$Z \qquad = VXY + VA$$

2.8 Working with Rectangles and Squares

This section introduces us to two geometric shapes—rectangles and squares. We will work with more complex geometric figures in a later chapter. Some standardized tests give students the various formulas (or formulae) on the examination sheet itself. However, it is a good idea to memorize a few basic formulas in case the information is not provided to you when you take your test.

Area and Perimeter

The area of a two-dimensional figure, such as a rectangle, is the entire surface area of the figure. The perimeter of a two-dimensional figure is the total distance around the edges of the figure.

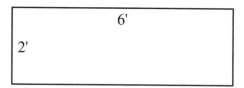

Figure 2.1: Rectangle 1

Figure 2.1 shows a rectangle whose length is 6 feet and width is 2 feet. In order to calculate the area (A) of a rectangle, we multiply the length (l) by the width (w).

Thus,

$$A = lw$$

Example 45

Figure 2.1 shows a rectangle with a width of 2 feet and length of 6 feet. Calculate the area of the rectangle.

◆ **Step 1** Use the formula $A = lw$ to calculate the area of the rectangle.

◆ **Step 2** Let A = unknown area, l = 6 feet, and w = 2 feet.

◆ **Step 3** Write down the equation, and solve for A.

$A = lw$

$A = 6(2)$

$A = 12$ square feet, or 12 ft^2

Example 46

Find the width in inches of a rectangle with length = 6 inches and area = 24 square inches, or 24 in.^{2}

◆ **Step 1** Use the formula $A = lw$.

◆ **Step 2** Insert the known values into the formula $A = lw$.

$24 = 6(w)$

◆ **Step 3** Divide both sides of the equation by 6 to isolate the variable w.

$$\frac{24}{6} = \frac{\cancel{6}w}{\cancel{6}}$$
$$4 = w$$

The width of the rectangle is 4 inches.

To calculate the perimeter (P) of a rectangle, multiply the length (l) by 2, multiply the width (w) by 2, and add the products of both. Thus, the perimeter of a rectangle can be expressed mathematically as follows:

$$P = 2(l) + 2(w)$$

Example 47

Figure 2.2 shows a rectangle with width = 1 foot and length = 4 feet. Calculate the perimeter of this rectangle.

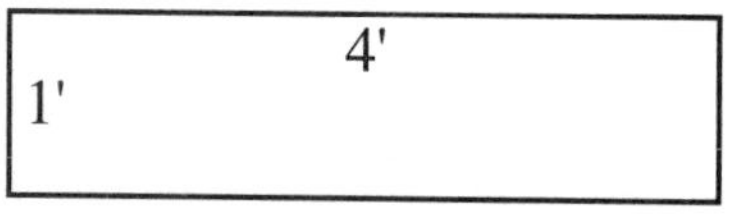

Figure 2.2: Rectangle 2

◆ **Step 1**   Use the formula $P = 2(l) + 2(w)$.

◆ **Step 2**   Insert the known values into the formula, and solve for P.

$P = 2(4) + 2(1)$

$P = 8 + 2$

$P = 10$

The perimeter of the rectangle shown in figure 2.2 is 10 feet.

Area and Perimeter of Squares

A square is a two-dimensional geometric figure with four equal sides. To find the area (A) of a square with side (s), use the following formula:

$$A = s^2$$

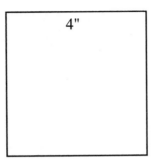

4"

Figure 2.3: A Square

Example 48

Figure 2.3 shows a square with side (s) = 4 inches. What is the area (A) of the square?

◆ **Step 1**   Use the formula $A = s^2$, where s = 4 inches.

$A = 4(4)$

$A = 16$ in.^{2}

Example 49

If the area of a square is 64 in.^{2}, what is the length of each side?

◆ **Step 1**   Use the formula $A = s^2$, where A is 64 in.^{2}

$64 = s^2$

◆ **Step 2**   To calculate the value of s, find the square root on both sides of the equation.

$\sqrt{64} = \sqrt{s^2}$
$8 \quad = s$

Each side of the square measures 8 inches.

It is easy to calculate the perimeter of a square. Simply multiply one side (s) by 4, since four sides of equal length make up a square. The formula:

$$P = 4s$$

Example 50

If the perimeter of a square is 48 inches, what is the length of each side?

◆ **Step 1**   Use the formula $P = 4s$, where $P = 48$ and s is one side of a square.

$$48 = 4s$$

◆ **Step 2**   Divide both sides of the equation by 4 to isolate the variable s.

$$\frac{48}{4} = \frac{\cancel{4}s}{\cancel{4}}$$
$$12 = s$$

The length of each side of the square is 12 inches.

2.9 Linear Equations: Simple Interest and Money

Linear Equations and Simple Interest Problems

The following examples involve calculating simple interest by using the formula

$$I = PRT$$

where I = simple interest, P = principal (the total amount of money invested), R = the annual interest rate (for example, 8%) expressed as a decimal, and T = time in years.

Example 51

When LaDonna Johnson's grandmother passed away, she left LaDonna an inheritance of $15,000. If LaDonna decides to invest it at 7%, how much simple interest will her investment earn in one year?

◆ **Step 1**   Use the formula $I = PRT$, and insert the known values.

$I = 15,000 \times 7\% \times 1$

◆ **Step 2**   Convert 7% to a decimal.

0.07

◆ **Step 3**   Solve for I.

$I = 15,000 \times 0.07 \times 1$

$I = 1,050$

LaDonna's investment will earn $1,050 in one year.

Example 52

Peter Lau borrowed money from a relative who charged him only simple interest at an annual rate of 10%. If Peter paid $900 in simple interest during the first year, how much did he borrow?

◆ **Step 1**   Use the formula $I = PRT$, where $I = 900$, $R = 10\%$ (or 0.10), $T = 1$, and $P =$ the amount of money Peter borrowed.

◆ **Step 2**   Solve for P.

$900 = P(0.10) \times 1$

$900 = P(0.10)$

◆ **Step 3**   Multiply by 100 across the equation to clear the decimal.

$900(100) = P(0.10)(100)$

$90,000 = P(10)$

$$\frac{90,000}{10} = \frac{P(\cancel{10})}{\cancel{10}}$$

$9,000 = P$

Peter borrowed $9,000 in one year.

Linear Equations and Money Problems

Money problems often look very complicated, but they are easy to solve if we organize the data accurately.

Example 53

When fourth grader James counted his savings, he discovered that he had 15 more dimes than nickels. If the total of his savings is $15, how many of each type of coin does he have?

◆ **Step 1**   Let x = the number of nickels and $x + 15$ = the number of dimes.

◆ **Step 2**   Since the money is not expressed in the same denomination, we must determine the common monetary value of the coins before solving the problem.

The value of a nickel is 5 cents (or 5 pennies).

The value of a dime is 10 cents (or 10 pennies).

Thus, the value of the nickels is $5x$, and the value of the dimes is $10(x + 15)$.

Together, they total $15, or 1,500 pennies.

◆ **Step 3**   Set up the equation and solve for x.

$$5x + 10(x + 15) = 1,500$$

$$5x + 10x + 150 = 1,500$$

$$15x + 150 \quad = 1,500$$

◆ **Step 4**   Subtract 150 from both sides of the equation to isolate x.

$$15x + 150 - 150 = 1,500 - 150$$
$$15x \qquad\quad = 1,350$$

◆ **Step 5**   Divide each side of the equation by 15.

$$\frac{\cancel{15}x}{\cancel{15}} = \frac{1,350}{15}$$
$$x \quad = 90$$

◆ **Step 6**   Determine how many of each coin James has.

$$x \quad = \text{the number of nickels}$$

$$x + 15 = \text{the number of dimes}$$

Thus, James has 90 nickels and $90 + 15 = 105$ dimes.

2.10 Linear Equations and Variation

Direct and Inverse Variation

Variation deals with specific relationships between two variables. If two numbers, represented by x and y, are in a relationship in which the ratio is constant, this is direct variation. Thus, if Ralph can read 25 pages in 1 hour, 50 pages in 2 hours, and 75 pages in 3 hours, then the ratio of pages read to time is $\frac{25}{1}$. In other words, the number of pages Ralph reads varies directly as the time elapses or passes.

Two numbers can also be in a relationship called inverse variation. For example, imagine that Christine is visiting a neighboring town 25 miles from her home. If weather conditions are hazardous and she can travel the distance at only 25 miles per hour, then it will take her 1 hour to complete the trip. If she travels at 50 miles per hour, she can reach her destination in 30 minutes $\left(\frac{1}{2}\text{hour}\right)$; but if she speeds at 75 miles per hour, it will take her only 20 minutes $\left(\frac{1}{3}\text{hour}\right)$ to complete the distance. The time t that it takes Christine to travel 25 miles at a rate of speed r may be expressed as $t = \frac{25}{r}$, where t varies inversely as r. In an inverse relationship, as one variable increases, the other variable decreases.

Example 54

The librarian estimated that for every 1 book on tropical fish that was kept in the reference section in the library, there were 200 books on the same subject located on the general shelves. If the librarian found 5 books on tropical fish in the reference area of the library, how many were kept on the general shelves?

◆ **Step 1**   Let f = the number of books on tropical fish kept in the reference section of the library, and let s = the number of books on the same topic kept on the general shelves.

◆ **Step 2**   We know that f varies directly as s, and the constant $k = 200$. Write down the equation and solve for s.

$s = kf$

$s = 200(5)$

$s = 1,000$

There are 1,000 books on tropical fish kept on the general shelves.

Example 55

A village's annual turtle race covers a distance of 6 feet. It usually takes Bert's pet turtle (traveling at 2 inches per minute) 36 minutes to complete the course. If his turtle had a good year and completed the course in only 30 minutes, how fast was the turtle traveling down the course?

◆ **Step 1**   Let t = time (30 minutes) it takes for the turtle to cover the course, let r = rate of speed, and let d = distance (72 inches, or 6 feet).

◆ **Step 2**   Write down the equation and solve for r.

$$r = \frac{d}{t}$$
$$r = \frac{72}{30}$$
$$r = 2.4$$

Bert's turtle was traveling at a rate of 2.4 inches per minute.

Problems

1. Simplify: $6(2b - 3) - 2(4b + 4) + 5b$

2. If $x = 4$ and $y = 6$, evaluate:

    $(-6)^0 - |3x - 6y| - 4^2 + xy$

3. Solve for x: $7(x + 3) = 3x + 25$

4. Solve for x: $\frac{x}{8} + 1 = 3$

5. Solve for x: $-4(3x - 1) = 5(x - 5) + 114$

6. Solve for x: $\frac{x+1}{6} + \frac{x-1}{7} = 0$

7. Mike eats a total of 90,000 calories per month from saturated fat, enriched flour, and refined sugar. Mike gets half of his monthly calorie total from refined sugar alone, and the number of sugar calories he takes in is five times what he gets from saturated fat. How many calories does Mike eat per month in saturated fat and enriched flour?

8. Solve for W: $WT - V = Z$

9. Solve for T: $XZ + Y = \frac{T}{S}$

10. Find the width in inches of a rectangle with length = 4 in. and area = 36 sq. in.

11. The perimeter of a rectangle with sides A, B, C, and D is 24 feet, and the sum of sides A and C is one-third of the perimeter. What is the length of side B?

12. Solve the proportion for x: $\frac{25}{2x+1} = \frac{26}{2x+2}$

13. What is the percentage decrease of a $450 overcoat on sale for $360?

14. Catalina, a mixed-media artist, made a mosaic using pieces of red glass, white glass, and yellow glass. If the mosaic contains 440 pieces of red glass, 340 pieces of white glass, and 55 pieces of yellow glass, what is the ratio of red glass to yellow glass in the mosaic?

15. Market analysis found that the local car salesman sold 5 trucks for every 3 compact cars. If the salesman sold a total of 640 vehicles, which proportion could be used to find t, the number of trucks sold?

Focus on English

Grammar

Wh Questions

A *wh* question is one that begins with the letters *w* and *h*. *Wh* questions are *what*, *when*, *where*, *who*, *why*, and *which*.

Read the following e-mail and match Laura's information with the following *wh* questions.

From: Laura [lauralopez@zenmail.com]

To: Steven [stevemills@zenmail.com]

Hi, Steven!

My name's Laura. I was born in Cuba, but I now live in Miami in the United States. I'm a receptionist at a hotel, and I take classes in English in the evenings. My first language is Spanish. I want to learn English for my job and to watch English-language TV. I have a big family. I have three sisters and a brother. They are all at school. I'm 20, my three sisters are 18, 16, and 14, and my brother is 12. I like music, especially Gloria Estefan. I also like to watch sports. Please write soon.

Laura

1. Which languages does Laura speak?

2. What does she do?

3. Where is she from?

4. Why does she want to learn English?

Do

To do is an auxiliary, or "helper," verb that is difficult for second-language speakers of English to master. Notice the following differences in questions:

Example: He knows Mr. Smith?

Example: Does he know Mr. Smith?

Example: I passed the course?

Example: Did I pass the course?

Practice by asking questions in the present and simple past tenses.

Present Tense

Do I?

Do you? (singular)

Does he?

Does she?

Does it?

Do we?

Do you? (plural)

Do they?

Past

Did I?

Did you? (singular)

Did he?

Did she?

Did it?

Did we?

Did you? (plural)

Did they?

QUASI

QUASI stands for question word, auxiliary (or "helper") verb, subject (for example, *I*), and the infinitive form of the verb (such as *to go*). *I go*, *you go*, and *he goes* are examples of the verb *to go* conjugated in the present tense. An infinitive verb is one that has *not* been conjugated.

QU	A	S	I
Where	does	she	go?
Why	did	he	leave?
When	did	they	arrive?
Why	didn't	they	come?

Practice asking questions using the QUASI rule.

Improving Mathematical Vocabulary

x

Mathematicians often use the letters *a*, *b*, *c*, *x*, *y*, and *z* when doing algebra problems. The English language has 5 vowels (a, e, i, o, and u) and 21 consonants, such as *x*, *y*, and *z*. Here is the English alphabet:

a, b, c, d, e, f, g, h, i, j, k, l, m, n, o, p, q, r, s, t, u, v, w, x, y, z (lowercase or small letters)

A, B, C, D, E, F, G, H, I, J, K, L, M, N, O, P, Q, R, S, T, U, V, W, X, Y, Z (uppercase or capital letters)

Ask your teacher or instructor how to pronounce each letter of the English alphabet if you are not certain how to do so.

Area and Perimeter

The area of a two-dimensional figure, such as a rectangle, is the entire surface area of the figure. The perimeter of a two-dimensional figure, such as a rectangle, is the total distance around the four edges of the figure. Practice asking questions in class: Ask your teacher or instructor to draw a rectangle and show you the difference between the area of a rectangle and the perimeter of a rectangle.

Mathematical Words and Phrases

How do you define the following words and phrases that are commonly used in mathematics? Write down two examples after each word or phrase.

1. variable

2. numerical coefficient

3. like terms

4. unlike terms

5. constant

6. lowest common denominator

7. least common multiple

Dictionary Work

Define the following words:

denomination

principal

principle

term

Chapter 3
Linear Inequalities

3.0 The Concept of Inequality

In the previous chapter, we dealt with the concept of equality, discovering that what was on the left side of an equation was equal to what was on the right side. In this chapter, we explore the concept of linear inequality. In linear inequalities, the variables usually represent many real numbers. The important thing is that whatever mathematical statement is declared must be true for all values of the variable in the solution. If we were to declare, for example, that $x < 4$, then x must be any real number less than 4, including zero and negative numbers.

How do we determine what constitutes linear inequalities? Whereas an equation has an equal ($=$) sign, as in the equation $5x + 2 = 12$, a linear inequality can have any one of four possibilities, $<$, $\leq$, $>$, and $\geq$. For example,

$x + 4 < 10$ (x plus four is less than ten)

$x + 4 \leq 10$ (x plus four is less than or equal to ten)

$x + 4 > 10$ (x plus four is greater than ten)

$x + 4 \geq 10$ (x plus four is greater than or equal to ten)

If we look at the first example, $x + 4 < 10$, we know that x cannot be 6, because the inequality tells us that the sum of x and 4 must be less than 10. Thus, the solution for x in the inequality $x + 4 < 10$ must include every real number (including roots, fractions, decimals, negative numbers, and so on) that, when added to 4, is less than 10.

Let's look at the second example, $x + 4 \leq 10$. Is 6 a possible solution for x? Yes, because the condition of the inequality states that the sum of x and 4 can either be equal to 10 or less than 10. Thus, the solution for x in this example includes all real numbers that are less than or equal to 6.

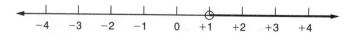

Figure 3.1: Graphing $x > 1$ on a Number Line

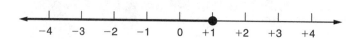

Figure 3.2: Graphing $x \leq 1$ on a Number Line

In the third example, $x + 4 > 10$, the value of x cannot be 6, because the condition of the inequality here states that the sum of x and 4 must be greater than 10. So, the value of x must be greater than 6. But in our last example, $x + 4 \geq 10$, x can be equal to 6 or any real number that is greater than 6.

3.1 Graphing Inequalities in One Variable

The solutions of problems involving inequalities can be illustrated, or graphed, on a number line. For example, a graph of all the real numbers that are solutions of the inequality $x > 1$ is shown in figure 3.1. The open circle indicates that 1 is not included in all the possible solutions for x. The line pointing to the right indicates that the value of x can be any real number that is greater than 1. If we want to graph the inequality $x \geq 1$, we would have shown that 1 is a possible solution by placing a closed circle at the $+1$ location on the number line.

Figure 3.2 shows how to graph the inequality $x \leq 1$. Notice that we use a closed circle to indicate that 1 is a possible solution for x (x is equal to or less than 1), and an arrow that points to the left, illustrating that the value of x can also be any real number that is less than 1.

3.2 Solving by Addition

Solving linear inequalities is somewhat similar to solving linear equations. To solve a linear inequality by addition, we must remember that whatever we add to one side of the inequality sign, we must also add to the other side.

Example 1

Solve: $x - 5 > 2$

◆ **Step 1** Add 5 to both of sides of the inequality symbol $>$.

$x - 5 + 5 > 2 + 5$

$x \qquad > 7$

We can check the solution by assigning a possible value to x such that $x > 7$. Let's say that x is 8. Is $8 - 5 > 2$? Yes. In example 1, $x > 7$ indicates that its solution is the set of all real numbers greater than 7. One way that mathematicians show the solution set $x > 7$ is to use a special symbol called set-builder notation. The solution set for $x > 7$, for example, can be written as $\{x \mid x > 7\}$. We read this as follows: "The set of all x such that x is greater than 7." We can also graph the solution set on a number line (see fig. 3.3).

Example 2

Solve: $x - 5 \geq 1$

◆ **Step 1** Add 5 to both sides of the inequality sign.

$x - 5 + 5 \geq 1 + 5$

$x \qquad \geq 6$

$\{x \mid x \geq 6\}$, or "the set of all x such that x is greater than or equal to 6."

Example 3

Solve: $-x - 3 < -2x - 2$

◆ **Step 1** Add 3 to both sides of the inequality sign.

Figure 3.3: Graphing $x > 7$ on a Number Line

$$-x - 3 + 3 < -2x - 2 + 3$$

$$-x < -2x + 1$$

◆ **Step 2**   Move the term with the variable that is located on the right side to the left side of the inequality sign by adding 2x to both sides.

$$-x + 2x < -2x + 1 + 2x$$

$$x < +1$$

$$x < 1$$

$$\{x \,|\, x < 1\}$$

3.3 Solving by Subtraction

To solve a linear inequality by subtraction, we must remember that whatever we subtract from one side of the inequality sign, we must also subtract from the other side.

Example 4

Solve: $x + 3 > 4 - 2$

◆ **Step 1**   Subtract 3 from both sides of the inequality sign.

$$x + 3 > 2$$

$$x + 3 - 3 > 2 - 3$$

$$x > -1$$

$$\{x \,|\, x > -1\}$$

Example 5

Solve: $4x + 5 \leq 3x + 2$

◆ **Step 1**   Subtract 5 from both sides of the inequality sign.

$$4x + 5 - 5 \leq 3x + 2 - 5$$

$$4x \qquad \leq 3x - 3$$

◆ **Step 2**   Subtract $3x$ from both sides of the inequality sign.

$$4x - 3x \leq 3x - 3 - 3x$$

$$x \qquad \leq -3$$

$$\{x \mid x \leq -3\}$$

3.4 Solving by Multiplication or Division

Solving linear inequalities by using the addition and subtraction methods is very similar to solving linear equations. However, when we solve inequalities by multiplication or division, a very important distinction can be seen, and it is this difference that we must note and remember. When we multiply or divide both sides of an inequality by a *negative* number, we must *reverse the sign* of the inequality.

Example 6

Solve: $-\dfrac{1}{2}x < 3$

◆ **Step 1**   Multiply both sides by -2, remembering to reverse the sign of the inequality because we are multiplying by a negative number.

$$-2 \cdot \left(-\frac{1}{2}x\right) > 3 \cdot (-2)$$

$$-\frac{2}{1}\left(-\frac{1}{2}x\right) > 3 \cdot (-2)$$

◆ **Step 2**   Simplify.

$$-\frac{\cancel{2}}{1}\left(-\frac{1}{\cancel{2}}x\right) > 3\cdot(-2)$$
$$x \qquad\qquad > -6$$

> The solution is $x > -6$, or $\{x \mid x > -6\}$.

Example 7

> Solve: $-\frac{1}{4}x \geq 1$

◆ **Step 1**   Multiply both sides of the inequality sign by $-\frac{4}{1}$ to remove the fraction and reverse the inequality sign.

$$-\frac{\cancel{4}}{1}\cdot\left(-\frac{1}{\cancel{4}}x\right) \leq 1\cdot\left(-\frac{4}{1}\right)$$

◆ **Step 2**   Simplify.

$$x \leq -4$$

> The solution is $x \leq -4$, or $\{x \mid x \leq -4\}$.

Example 8

> Solve: $2x \leq 4$

◆ **Step 1**   Divide by 2 on both sides of the inequality sign to isolate the variable.

$$\frac{2x}{2} \leq \frac{4}{2}$$
$$x \;\; \leq 2$$

> The solution is $x \leq 2$.

We do not need to reverse the inequality sign, because we are dividing by a positive number. We reverse the inequality sign only if we are multiplying or dividing by a negative number.

Example 9

Solve: $-4y > 12$

◆ **Step 1**   Divide both sides by -4 and reverse the inequality sign.

$$\frac{-4y}{-4} < \frac{12}{-4}$$

◆ **Step 2**   Simplify.

$$y < -3$$

3.5 Solving by Using Multiple Operations

In sections 3.2 to 3.4, we solved linear inequalities by using the properties of addition, subtraction, multiplication, and division. In this section, we use more than one property to solve more complicated linear inequalities.

Example 10

Solve: $4y + 2 > 2y - 4$

◆ **Step 1**   Subtract 2 from both sides of the inequality sign.

$$4y + 2 - 2 > 2y - 4 - 2$$

$$4y \qquad > 2y - 6$$

◆ **Step 2**   Subtract $2y$ from both sides.

$$4y - 2y > 2y - 6 - 2y$$

$$2y \qquad > -6$$

◆ **Step 3**   Divide both sides by 2.

$$\frac{2y}{2} > \frac{-6}{2}$$

$$y > -3$$

We should bear in mind two points when we are solving linear inequalities containing parentheses:

* The order of operations that we studied in chapter 1 requires us to first work inside parentheses, brackets, braces, and absolute value symbols.

* The multiplication and division rules governing inequalities that we studied in this chapter continue to apply. That is, when we multiply or divide by a negative number, we must reverse the direction of the inequality symbol.

Example 11

Solve: $4(a - 2 + 4) - 6a \geq 4(a - 3) + 8$

◆ **Step 1**   Work inside the parentheses first.

$$4(a + 2) - 6a \geq 4a - 12 + 8$$

$$4a + 8 - 6a \geq 4a - 12 + 8$$

◆ **Step 2**   Subtract 8 from both sides.

$$4a + 8 - 8 - 6a \geq 4a - 12 + 8 - 8$$

$$4a - 6a \qquad \geq 4a - 12$$

◆ **Step 3**   Subtract 4a from both sides of the inequality sign to isolate the variable on the left side.

$$4a - 4a - 6a \geq 4a - 4a - 12$$

$$-6a \qquad \geq -12$$

◆ **Step 4**   Divide both sides by -6 and reverse the inequality sign.

$$\frac{-6a}{-6} \leq \frac{-12}{-6}$$

$a \leq 2$, or
$\{a \,|\, a \leq 2\}$

Example 12

Solve: $3(2z - 4) + 2^3 - 2 > 4[4 - 2(4 + 1)]$

◆ **Step 1**   Work inside the parentheses first, and then the brackets.

$6z - 12 + 2^3 - 2 > 4[4 - 2(5)]$

$6z - 12 + 2^3 - 2 > 4[4 - 10]$

$6z - 12 + 2^3 - 2 > 4[-6]$

$6z - 12 + 2^3 - 2 > -24$

◆ **Step 2**   Evaluate the exponent.

$6z - 12 + (2)(2)(2) - 2 > -24$

$6z - 12 + (4)(2) - 2 \;\; > -24$

$6z - 12 + 8 - 2 \qquad > -24$

$6z - 6 \qquad\qquad > -24$

◆ **Step 3**   Add 6 to both sides.

$6z - 6 + 6 > -24 + 6$

$6z \qquad\quad > -18$

◆ **Step 4**   Divide both sides by 6.

$$\frac{6z}{6} > \frac{-18}{6}$$

$$z > -3, \text{ or } \{z \mid z > -3\}$$

3.6 Solving Linear Inequalities Containing Fractions

Solving linear inequalities containing fractions is not difficult as long as we remember to remove the fractions first by multiplying throughout the inequality by the lowest common denominator (LCD). Again, we must reverse the inequality symbol when multiplying or dividing by a negative number.

Example 13

Solve: $\dfrac{a+5}{2} + \dfrac{1}{2} < 2a - \dfrac{a-2}{8}$

◆ **Step 1**   Determine the lowest common denominator of 2 and 8.

The answer is 8, since 2 is a factor of 8.

◆ **Step 2**   Remove the fractions by multiplying by 8 throughout the inequality.

$$8\left(\frac{a+5}{2} + \frac{1}{2}\right) < 8\left(2a - \frac{a-2}{8}\right)$$

$$8\left(\frac{a+5}{2}\right) + 8\left(\frac{1}{2}\right) < 8(2a) - 8\left(\frac{a-2}{8}\right)$$

$$\overset{4}{\cancel{8}}\left(\frac{a+5}{\underset{1}{\cancel{2}}}\right) + \overset{4}{\cancel{8}}\left(\frac{1}{\underset{1}{\cancel{2}}}\right) < 8(2a) - \cancel{8}\left(\frac{a-2}{\cancel{8}}\right)$$

◆ **Step 3**   Work with the parentheses and combine like terms.

$$4(a) + 4(5) + 4(1) < 8(2a) - a - (-2)$$

$$4a + 20 + 4 < 16a - a + 2$$

$$4a + 24 < 15a + 2$$

◆ **Step 4**   Subtract 24 from both sides.

$$4a + 24 - 24 < 15a + 2 - 24$$

$$4a \qquad < 15a - 22$$

◆ **Step 5**   Subtract 15a from both sides of the inequality.

$$4a - 15a < 15a - 15a - 22$$

$$-11a \quad < -22$$

◆ **Step 6**   Divide by −11 and reverse the inequality sign (because we are dividing by a negative number).

$$\frac{-11a}{-11} > \frac{-22}{-11}$$

$$a \quad > 2$$

Example 14

Solve: $3y + \left(\dfrac{2+y}{3}\right) \le 5 - \left(\dfrac{y+5}{6}\right)$

◆ **Step 1**   Remove the fractions by multiplying by 6 (the LCD) throughout the inequality. Combine like terms.

$$6(3y) + {}^{2}6\left(\frac{2+y}{3_1}\right) \le 6(5) - {}^{1}6\left(\frac{y+5}{6_1}\right)$$

$$18y + 2(2) + 2y \quad \le 30 - y - 5$$

$$18y + 4 + 2y \qquad \le 30 - y - 5$$

$$20y + 4 \qquad\qquad \le 25 - y$$

◆ **Step 2**   Subtract 4 from both sides of the inequality.

$$20y + 4 - 4 \le 25 - 4 - y$$

$$20y \qquad\quad \le 21 - y$$

◆ **Step 3**   Add y to both sides of the inequality.

$20y + y \leq 21 - y + y$

$21y \qquad \leq 21$

◆ **Step 4**   Divide by 21 on both sides of the inequality.

$$\frac{21y}{21} \leq \frac{21}{21}$$

$y \quad \leq 1$

3.7 Solving Three-Part Linear Inequalities

A three-part, or compound, inequality is one that states that a number is within the range of two other numbers. For example, $-2 < x \leq 4$ is a compound inequality that we read as "negative two is less than x, and x is less than or equal to four," or "x is greater than negative two and less than or equal to four." Figure 3.4 illustrates this compound inequality on a number line.

Figure 3.4: Graphing $-2 < x \leq 4$ on a Number Line

Example 15

Solve: $5 \leq 4x - 3 < 9$

◆ **Step 1**   Isolate $4x$ (the term with the variable) by adding 3 to each part of the compound inequality.

$5 + 3 \leq 4x - 3 + 3 < 9 + 3$

$8 \quad \leq 4x \qquad < 12$

◆ **Step 2**   Divide each part by 4 to isolate the variable x.

$$\frac{8}{4} \le \frac{\cancel{4}x}{\cancel{4}} < \frac{12}{4}$$

$$2 \le x \quad < 3$$

$2 \le x < 3$

Two is less than or equal to x, and x is less than three, or x is greater than or equal to two and less than three.

Example 16

Solve: $-2 < \frac{1}{2}y - 3 < 1$

◆ **Step 1**　Multiply each part by 2 to remove the fraction.

$$2(-2) < 2\left(\frac{1}{2}y - 3\right) < 2(1)$$

$$-4 \quad < y - 6 \quad\quad < 2$$

◆ **Step 2**　Add 6 to each part.

$$-4 + 6 < y - 6 + 6 < 2 + 6$$

$$2 \quad\quad < y \quad\quad\quad < 8$$

$2 < y < 8$

3.8　Solving Absolute Value Inequalities

We learned in chapter 1 that the absolute value of a number is the distance of that number from zero, its point of origin, on a number line. We know, for example, that the real number -4 is four units from zero, so we say that the absolute value of -4 is 4. The solution set of an absolute value inequality of the form $|x| < 4$ includes all numbers whose distance from zero is less than 4 units. We write this in set-builder notation as $\{x \mid -4 < x < 4\}$. When we solve an absolute value inequality of the form $|x| < a$, we can state that if a is positive, then the following is true:

$$|x| < a \text{ is the same as } -a < x < a$$
$$\text{and}$$
$$|x| \leq a \text{ is the same as } -a \leq x \leq a$$

Example 17

Solve for y, $|y - 3| < 2$

◆ **Step 1** Using the rule that $|x| < a$ is the same as $-a < x < a$, let $a = 2$ and let $x = y - 3$. Thus, in this example, $-a < x < a$ is expressed as $-2 < y - 3 < 2$.

◆ **Step 2** Add 3 to all parts of the compound inequality.

$$-2 + 3 < y - 3 + 3 < 2 + 3$$

$$1 \qquad < y \qquad < 5$$

$$1 < y < 5$$

Example 18

Solve for b and graph the solution: $|2b + 4| + 1 \leq 3$

◆ **Step 1** Before applying the absolute value inequality rule for the form $|x| < a$, isolate the absolute value expression by subtracting 1 from both sides of the inequality sign.

$$|2b + 4| + 1 - 1 \leq 3 - 1$$

$$|2b + 4| \qquad \leq 2$$

◆ **Step 2** Apply the absolute value rule $|x| < a$, with $a = 2$ and $x = 2b + 4$.

$$-2 \leq 2b + 4 \leq 2$$

◆ **Step 3** Subtract 4 from each part to isolate the term with the variable.

$$-2 - 4 \le 2b + 4 - 4 \le 2 - 4$$

$$-6 \quad \le 2b \quad \le -2$$

◆ **Step 4**   Divide each part by 2.

$$\frac{-6}{2} \le \frac{2b}{2} \le \frac{-2}{2}$$

$$-3 \le b \le -1$$

◆ **Step 5**   Graph the solution $-3 \le b \le 1$ on a number line.

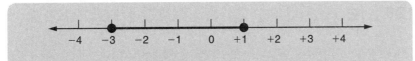

Figure 3.5: Graphing $-3 \le b \le 1$ on a Number Line

So, an absolute value inequality of the form $|x| < a$ has a solution between two values. However, when we solve an absolute value inequality of the form $|x| > a$, we state that if a is a positive number, the solution is outside of two values. Therefore, the following is true:

> $|x| > a$ is the same as $x < -a$ or $x > a$
> and
> $|x| \ge a$ is the same as $x \le -a$ or $x \ge a$

Note that the solutions use the word "or," because both choices cannot be true at the same time.

So, how do we graph the solution set $|x| \ge 1$? Because the solution set of the form $|x| \ge a$ can be expressed as $x \le -a$ or $x \ge a$, the solution set for our example $|x| \ge 1$ contains 1 and all numbers greater than 1, and -1 and all numbers less than -1 (see fig. 3.6).

Example 19

Solve for y, $|y - 3| > 2$

Figure 3.6: Graphing the Solution Set $\{x | x \le -1 \text{ or } x \ge 1\}$

◆ **Step 1**   Using the rule $|x| > a$ is the same as $x < -a$ or $x > a$, let $a = 2$ and $x = y - 3$.

$y - 3 < -2$ or $y - 3 > 2$

◆ **Step 2**   Add 3 to each part.

$$
\begin{array}{ccc}
y - 3 + 3 < -2 + 3 & & y - 3 + 3 > 2 + 3 \\
y \qquad\quad < 1 & \text{or} & y \qquad\quad > 5
\end{array}
$$

$y < 1$ or $y > 5$

3.9 Linear Inequalities and Word Problems

In the previous chapter, we used linear equations to solve word problems. However, sometimes word problems contain phrases, such as "must be more than" or "is at least," that cannot be solved by using linear equations. Instead, we must translate word problems into linear inequalities to arrive at solution sets. Using table 3.1 as a guide, we begin this section by learning to translate word problems into inequalities. Use the blank areas in the table to add any words or phrases that signal to you that a word problem involves a linear inequality.

Table 3.1:   Phrases Used in Word Problems Involving Inequalities

Phrases that require $<$	Phrases that require $\leq$	Phrases that require $>$	Phrases that require $\geq$	Phrases that require $< x <$
is less than	is at most must not be more than is less than or equal to cannot exceed up to	is more than is greater than must exceed	is at least is greater than or equal to cannot be less than	is between

Example 20

Translate the following into an inequality: Scientists estimate that the water wrung out from a typical household sponge used to wipe down the kitchen sink and countertops contains at least 10 million bacteria.

◆ **Step 1**   Let b represent the bacteria in the sponge water. "At least" means "equal to or more than," or $\geq$, so "at least 10 million bacteria" can be expressed mathematically as

$b \geq 10,000,000$

Example 21

Steven has no more than $382 in his chess club fund. He decides to treat members of the club to an end-of-the-semester dinner, but first he has to decide whether to invite the club members to a pizza café or to a steak restaurant. The pizza café charges $30 to rent a room and $11 a person for pizza, salad, breadsticks, and a beverage. The steak restaurant charges $11 per dinner, plus a 15% tip (calculated on the cost of the dinner only) and a $0.35 service charge per person. If Steven wants to invite as many people as he can afford, which restaurant should he choose if he wants to have the greatest number of people he can invite, including himself?

◆ **Step 1**   Let x represent the number of people Steven hopes to invite to the pizza café. He has $382 total to spend on dinner and services. Translate and solve the inequality.

30              $+ 11(x)$ ≤ 382
(room rental) (cost of food per person)   (must be less than or equal to $382)

$30 + 11(x) \leq 382$

◆ **Step 2**   Subtract 30 from both sides of the inequality.

$30 - 30 + 11x \leq 382 - 30$

$11x \qquad\quad \leq 382 - 30$

$11x \qquad\quad \leq 352$

◆ **Step 3**   Divide each side by 11.

$\dfrac{11x}{11} \leq \dfrac{352}{11}$
$x \quad \leq 32$

Thus, the largest number of people that Steven can invite to the pizza café (including himself) is 32.

◆ **Step 4**   Now let's consider the steak restaurant. Let y represent the number of people Steven is considering inviting to the steak restaurant. Before proceeding, calculate the total cost of the dinner, gratuity, and service charge per person.

11	+ 15% of 11	+ 0.35	=
(dinner)	(gratuity)	(service charge)	

| 11 | + (0.15)(11) | + 0.35 | = |

| 11 | + 1.65 | + 0.35 | = 13 |

The total cost per person to eat at the steak restaurant is $13. So the steak restaurant inequality is $13y \le 382$.

◆ **Step 5**   Divide each side by 13.

$$\frac{13y}{13} \le \frac{382}{13}$$
$$y \quad \le 29+$$

Thus, Steven can invite more guests to the pizza café than he can to the steak restaurant.

Problems

1. Translate the following to an inequality: nine less than one-half of a number n is greater than or equal to 30.

2. Translate the following to an inequality: Z is less than the product of the square of the sum of x and y and the quotient of x and $4y$.

3. Graph the inequality $x \geq -1$ on a number line.

4. Graph the inequality $-3 \leq y < 4$ on a number line.

5. Write an inequality involving the variable z that describes the set of numbers graphed on the number line in figure 3a below.

6. Figure 3b below shows a graph of which solution set (use set-builder notation and the variable x)?

7. Solve the inequality $-0.03x \leq -0.06$.

8. Solve the inequality $5x + 1 \geq 3x - 9$.

9. Solve the inequality $\frac{2}{3}(a+3) < -\frac{2}{3}(a-5)$.

10. Solve the inequality and express the solutions in set-builder notation:
$$\frac{x+1}{6} + \frac{x-5}{12} \geq 3$$

11. Solve the inequality and express the solutions in set-builder notation:
$2z - (4z + 3) < 6z + 3(z + 4) + 7$

12. Solve the inequality $-5 \leq 2x - 3 \leq 5$.

Figure 3a

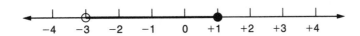

Figure 3b

13. Solve the absolute value inequality $|a + 2| + 1 \leq 3$.

14. Three consecutive odd integers are arranged in ascending order (from smallest to largest). Twice the middle integer is at least 9 more than the largest integer. What is the minimum sum of the three integers?

15. Sarah keeps a jar on her desk for spare nickels and dimes. If she knows that she has three times as many dimes as nickels and that the total value of the coins is no more than $21, what is the maximum number of nickels there can be in the jar?

Focus on English

Grammar

Of, On, To, With

Of, on, to, and *with* are called prepositions. For example, "I'm going *with* David *to* the concert." Complete the sentences with *of, on, to,* or *with.*

1. They have their radio _____ very loud.

2. She's arguing _____ her husband.

3. The couch is in front _____ the closet.

4. She lives _____ the second floor.

5. The chair is next _____ the couch.

Prepositions of Time: In, On, At

Here are some examples of how we use prepositions of time:

In	On	At
the morning	Friday morning	3 o'clock
the afternoon	the Fourth of July	midnight
the evening	my birthday	lunchtime
September		night
the winter		the weekend
2006		New Year

Complete the following sentences with one of the three prepositions (*in, on, at*) of time:

1. I'll be home _____ midnight.

2. He celebrates his birthday _____ February 13.

3. _____ the winter, it always snows in Wisconsin.

4. Many people give presents _____ Christmas.

5. In the United States, people usually start work _____ nine o'clock.

6. In the United Kingdom, many shops are closed _____ Sundays.

7. In Spain it's usually very hot _____ the summer.

Spelling

Here are some basic rules for spelling plural nouns.

Singular	Plural	Spelling
A book	books	add -s
A pen	pens	
A watch	watches	add -es after *ch, sh, s, x*
A box	boxes	
A country	countries	consonant + *y* > *ies*
An inequality	inequalities	
A possibility	possibilities	

And, Or, But, Because

And, or, but, and *because* are called connectors. For example, "I have coffee, juice, *and* a muffin for breakfast." Complete the following sentences with one of those four connectors.

1. I like coffee _____ I don't like tea.

2. I like Sundays _____ I don't have to work.

3. I don't like baseball _____ football.

4. In the evening I go dancing with my friends _____ I watch TV at home.

5. I wake up at 7:00 _____ I don't get up until 8:00.

6. I have three brothers _____ a sister.

 ## Improving Mathematical Vocabulary

Graph

What does "to graph" mean? Draw an example of a graph.

Set-Builder Notation

What is set-builder notation? Write down three examples of set-builder notation.

 ## Dictionary Work

Define the following words:

Constitute

Condition

Wring (present tense of *wrung*)

Chapter 4

Polynomials and Factoring

Before we begin working with polynomials, let's review from chapter 2 some of the words and phrases that are central to our understanding of algebra. Remember that a term includes numbers, variables, the product or quotient of numbers and variables, or numbers and variables raised to powers. Thus, -2, y, $16a$, $\frac{3}{x}$, and $6a^2$ are all terms.

Moreover, the numerical coefficient is the number that is written or implied in all terms. For example, the numerical coefficient of $\frac{3}{x}$ is 3, and that of y is 1.

Terms that have the same variables or that have the same variables raised to the same power (for example, $3x^2$ and $7x^2$) are called like terms, whereas unlike terms are those that contain different variables or variables raised to different powers (such as $3x^2$, $4x^3$, and $3b^2$). Now we're ready for some new vocabulary and definitions.

4.0 Understanding Polynomials

Degree of a Term

The degree of a term that contains variables is the sum of the exponents of the variables. For example, the term $4y^2$ has degree 2, and the term $4a^3b^2$ has degree 5 (the sum of the exponents 3 and 2). Furthermore $4bc^2$ has degree 3 (the sum of the exponents 1 and 2). Terms that consist of only a number, such as 3, are called constant terms, or constants. Zero itself has no degree.

Monomials and Polynomials

Monomial, *polynomial*, *binomial*, and *trinomial* are all words that refer to specific types of algebraic expressions. If we look carefully at the first part of each word, we can figure out what each one means. *Mono* is a prefix, or a beginning part of a word, that means *one* or *single*. We see this prefix in words such as *mono*logue, a speech made by one person, or *mono*rail, a train on one track. So, a monomial is a mathematical expression consisting of only one term. For example, $4x$, 5, -11, and $4ab^2$ are all monomials.

Poly is a prefix that derives from the Greek language and means *many*, or *more than one*. It is used as a prefix in many technical terms and some other words, such as *polyglot* (a person who can speak several languages). A polynomial, then, is an algebraic expression containing more than one term. As you might guess by now, *nomial* refers to *term*. So, $-3x^3 + 5x - x + 4$ is a polynomial consisting of four terms: $-3x^3$, $5x$, $-x$, and 4. This example is a polynomial in one variable (x), but polynomials can also contain several variables, such as $5x^5 + 2y^2 + z + 3$. It is important to remember that the variables in a polynomial expression are raised to positive integer powers. So, $3x^4 - 3yz$ is a polynomial, because x, y, and z are raised to positive numbers. In contrast, $3x^{-4} - 3yz$ is not a polynomial, because the variable x is raised to a negative integer power. Moreover, because a negative exponent means the variable is a reciprocal, a polynomial cannot contain variables in the denominator position of a fraction. For example, $5a^3 + 3b + \dfrac{2}{x^3}$ is not a polynomial, because the variable x raised to the third power is in the denominator of the fractional expression $\dfrac{2}{x^3}$. Note that this term is the same as $2x^{-3}$.

Binomials and Trinomials

Binomials and trinomials are specific types of polynomials. The prefix *bi* comes from the Latin language and means *two*. Human beings, for instance, are *bipeds*, because we have two feet, or a *bicycle* has two wheels. We can quickly determine, then, that a binomial is a mathematical expression made up of only two terms. For example, $2y - 3x$ is a binomial, as is $4x + 5$.

Tri refers to three, as in *tricycle*, a cycle with three wheels, or *triangle*, a three-angled (or three-sided) figure. Thus, a trinomial is a polynomial that contains three terms, such as $4x^3 - 4x^2 + 9$.

Degree of a Polynomial

The degree of a polynomial is the largest degree of all its member terms. For example, the degree of the trinomial $2x^5 + yz^3 - 4$ is five, because the term $2x^5$ is the member term with the largest degree. As for the binomial $4x^3 + 3x^2$, the exponent 3 is larger than the exponent 2, so the degree of this binomial is 3. Mathematicians often write polynomials in one variable in what is called descending order. This means that the terms are arranged in such a way that the exponents decrease as we proceed from left to right. Notice, for example, in the polynomial $14x^5 + 14x^4 - 6x^2 + 3$ that the exponents are written down in descending order (5, 4, 2, followed by the constant term 3).

To summarize, the degree of a polynomial is the largest degree of all of its terms, and the degree of a term is the sum of all the exponents of the variables in the term. So the degree of the polynomial $7a^2b^2 + 3a^2b + 4ab + 6$ is 4 (the degrees of each term, in order, are 4, 3, 2).

4.1 Evaluating Polynomials

We evaluate a polynomial by first replacing each variable in the polynomial with a given number and then following the order of operations that we discussed in chapter 1.

Example 1

Evaluate the trinomial $x^3 + x + 21$ when $x = 2$.

◆ **Step 1** Replace the variable x with the number 2 (the given value for x).

$x^3 + x + 21 \quad =$

$(2)^3 + (2) + 21 =$

◆ **Step 2** Evaluate the exponent and then multiply.

$(2)(2)(2) + 2 + 21 =$

$(4)(2) + 2 + 21 \quad =$

◆ **Step 3** Add.

$(8) + 2 + 21 =$

$10 + 21 \quad = 31$

Example 2

Evaluate the polynomial $3a^2b - ac + 12$ when $a = 2$, $b = 4$, and $c = 5$.

◆ **Step 1**   Replace the variables a, b, and c with their respective values 2, 4, and 5.

$3a^2b - ac + 12 \qquad =$

$3(2)^2(4) - (2)(5) + 12 =$

◆ **Step 2**   Evaluate the exponent.

$3(2)(2)(4) - (2)(5) + 12 =$

$3(4)(4) - (2)(5) + 12 \qquad =$

◆ **Step 3**   Multiply.

$12(4) - (10) + 12 =$

$48 - 10 + 12 \qquad =$

◆ **Step 4**   Subtract and add.

$38 + 12 = 50$

4.2 Adding and Subtracting Polynomials

In chapter 2, we learned that algebraic expressions could be simplified by combining like terms. For example, $5x + 3x = 8x$. Note, however, that we cannot combine $3x + 2y$, because they are unlike terms. The concept of like terms is very important—it is central to our understanding of how polynomials are added and subtracted.

Adding by Using the Horizontal Method

There are two methods for adding polynomials. Practice both of them to determine which one works better for you. Example 3 shows us how to add polynomials by using the horizontal method.

Example 3

Add: $4x^3 - 2x^2 + 3$ and $-2x^3 + 4x^2 - 2$

◆ **Step 1**   Place all the like terms next to each other, using a plus sign between them.

$$4x^3 + (-2x^3) + (-2x^2) + 4x^2 + 3 - 2 =$$

◆ **Step 2**   Regroup, remembering the rule for adding numbers with different signs.

$$4x^3 - 2x^3 - 2x^2 + 4x^2 + 3 - 2 =$$

◆ **Step 3**   Add and subtract like terms.

$$2x^3 + 2x^2 + 1$$

Adding by Using the Vertical Method

Example 4 demonstrates how to add polynomials by using the vertical method.

Example 4

Add the trinomials: $4x^3 - 2x^2 - 3$ and $-2x^3 + 4x^2 - 2$

◆ **Step 1**   Place all like terms in separate columns.

$$4x^3 \qquad -2x^2 \qquad -3$$

$$-2x^3 \qquad +4x^2 \qquad -2$$

◆ **Step 2**   Add each column vertically.

$$
\begin{array}{ccc}
4x^3 & -2x^2 & -3 \\
-2x^3 & +4x^2 & -2 \\
\hline
2x^3 & 2x^2 & -5
\end{array}
$$

◆ **Step 3**   Write down the sum of each column:

$$2x^3 + 2x^2 + (-5) = 2x^3 + 2x^2 - 5$$

Subtracting Polynomials

Subtracting polynomials requires more concentration than adding them, because we have to remember, when subtracting one polynomial from another, to change the sign in front of each term of the polynomial that is being subtracted and then add like terms. We can add by using either the horizontal or vertical method discussed above.

Example 5

Subtract $6y^3 + 4y^2 + 3$ from $10y^3 + 6y^2 - 4$.

◆ **Step 1**   Determine which polynomial is to be subtracted. Here it is:

$6y^3 + 4y^2 + 3$

◆ **Step 2**   Change the sign in front of each term of that polynomial to indicate subtraction (equivalent to adding a negative).

$$6y^3 \quad +4y^2 \quad +3$$
$$\downarrow \qquad \searrow \qquad \searrow$$
$$-6y^3 \quad -4y^2 \quad -3$$

◆ **Step 3**   Add the two polynomials $10y^3 + 6y^2 - 4$ and $-6y^3 - 4y^2 - 3$. In this example, we use the vertical method.

$$
\begin{array}{rrr}
10y^3 & +6y^2 & -4 \\
-6y^3 & -4y^2 & -3 \\
\hline
4y^3 & 2y^2 & -7
\end{array}
$$

The solution:

$4y^3 + 2y^2 - 7$

4.3 Multiplying Polynomials

In this section, we learn how to do four things—to multiply monomials, to multiply a monomial and a polynomial, to multiply two binomials, and finally to multiply a variety of polynomials.

Multiplying Monomials

We can multiply monomials by grouping like bases and then applying the product rule for exponents, which states that when we multiply exponential expressions whose bases are the same, we add the exponents.

Example 6

Multiply: $(3x^3)(5x^4)$

◆ **Step 1** Group like bases.

$(3 \cdot 5)(x^3 \cdot x^4) =$

◆ **Step 2** Multiply the constants, and add the exponents because the base, x, is the same.

$(3 \cdot 5)(x^{3+4}) =$

$15x^7$

Example 7

Multiply: $(4x^3y^2z^2)(3x^5y^4z)$

◆ **Step 1** Group like bases.

$(4 \cdot 3)(x^3 \cdot x^5)(y^2 \cdot y^4)(z^2 \cdot z^1) =$

◆ **Step 2** Multiply the constants, and add the exponents for each base.

$(12)(x^8)(y^6)(z^3) =$

$12x^8y^6z^3$

Multiplying Monomials and Polynomials

We find the product of a monomial and a polynomial by using the distributive property and the product rule for exponents.

Example 8

Find the product of the monomial $4x$ and the polynomial $4x^2 - 3x + 5$.

◆ **Step 1**   Multiply each term of the polynomial by the monomial $4x$.

$$4x(4x^2) + 4x(-3x) + 4x(5) =$$

◆ **Step 2**   Group like bases for each term.

$$(4 \cdot 4)(x \cdot x^2) + (4 \cdot -3)(x \cdot x) + (4 \cdot 5)(x) =$$

◆ **Step 3**   Multiply.

$$(16)(x^3) + (-12)(x^2) + 20(x) =$$

$$16x^3 - 12x^2 + 20x$$

Multiplying Two Binomials

Two binomials can be multiplied in two basic ways. Choose the one you prefer. Example 9 shows one method of multiplying two binomials.

Example 9

Multiply the binomials $x + 6$ and $x + 3$.

◆ **Step 1**   Multiply the binomial $x + 6$ by each term of the binomial $x + 3$.

$$(x + 3)(x + 6) \qquad =$$

$$x(x + 6) + 3(x + 6) =$$
$$x^2 + 6x + 3x + 18 \quad =$$

◆ **Step 2**   Combine like terms.

$$x^2 + 9x + 18$$

Example 10 illustrates another method of multiplying binomials. It is called the FOIL method and, with practice, is a relatively fast method of finding the product of two binomials.

Example 10

Use the FOIL method to find the product of $(x + 3)$ and $(x + 5)$.

◆ **Step 1** $(x + 3)(x + 5)$ **F**   Multiply the first terms:

$(x)(x) = x^2$ (*first*)

◆ **Step 2** $(x + 3)(x + 5)$ **O**   Multiply the outside terms:

$(x)(5) = 5x$ (*outside*)

◆ **Step 3** $(x + 3)(x + 5)$ **I**   Multiply the inside terms:

$(3)(x) = 3x$ (*inside*)

◆ **Step 4** $(x + 3)(x + 5)$ **L**   Multiply the last terms:

$(3)(5) = 15$ (*last*)

◆ **Step 5**   Combine the like terms $5x$ and $3x = 8x$.

◆ **Step 6**   Write down the sum of the FOIL steps after combining like terms. The solution:

$x^2 + 8x + 15$

Multiplying a Binomial and a Trinomial

When multiplying a trinomial by a binomial, multiply each term of the trinomial by both terms of the binomial.

Example 11

Multiply $(x + 3)$ and $(x^2 + 3x + 4)$.

◆ **Step 1**   Multiply each term in the trinomial by each term in the binomial.

$(x)(x^2 + 3x + 4) + (3)(x^2 + 3x + 4) =$

$x^3 + 3x^2 + 4x + 3x^2 + 9x + 12 \quad =$

◆ **Step 2**   Group and combine like terms.

$$x^3 + 3x^2 + 3x^2 + 4x + 9x + 12 =$$

$$x^3 + 6x^2 + 13x + 12$$

The product of trinomials and binomials can also be found by using the long multiplication method, as the next example shows.

Example 12

Multiply: $y^2 + 5y$ and $3y^3 - 2y^2 + 4y$

◆ **Step 1**   Arrange the polynomials in the following way:

$$3y^3 - 2y^2 + 4y$$

$$y^2 + 5y$$

◆ **Step 2**   Multiply each term in the top row by $5y$, and then multiply each term in the top row by y^2.

$$
\begin{array}{r}
3y^3 - 2y^2 + 4y \\
y^2 + 5y \\
\hline
15y^4 - 10y^3 + 20y^2 \\
3y^5 - 2y^4 + 4y^3
\end{array}
$$

◆ **Step 3**   Add like terms vertically. The solution:

$$3y^5 + 13y^4 - 6y^3 + 20y^2$$

Multiplying a Binomial and a Polynomial

The product of polynomials and binomials can be found by using a method similar to either example 11 or example 12.

Example 13

Multiply: $(2y + 1)(y^3 - 4y^2 + 3y - 2)$

◆ **Step 1** Multiply each term in the trinomial with both terms of the binomial. Be careful when working with positive and negative signs.

$$2y(y^3 - 4y^2 + 3y - 2) + 1(y^3 - 4y^2 + 3y - 2) =$$

$$2y^4 - 8y^3 + 6y^2 - 4y + y^3 - 4y^2 + 3y - 2 \quad =$$

◆ **Step 2** Group and combine like terms.

$$2y^4 - 8y^3 + y^3 + 6y^2 - 4y^2 - 4y + 3y - 2 =$$

$$2y^4 - 7y^3 + 2y^2 - y - 2$$

4.4 Special Products

Many standardized tests in mathematics include problems that test the student's knowledge of two groups of special products relating to binomials. The first group deals with the square of a binomial, and the second group is known as a difference of squares. Both groups of special products reveal patterns that help us to both recognize them quickly and solve them quickly.

The Square of a Binomial

The square of the binomial $(x + 2)^2$ may be written as two binomials: $(x + 2)(x + 2)$. Similarly, the square of the binomial $(x - 3)^2$ can be expressed as $(x - 3)(x - 3)$. If we were asked to find the product of two binomials $(x + 2)(x + 2)$, we might decide to use the FOIL method. Let's use the FOIL method in an example, and perhaps we will see a pattern emerging that will help us to find the product even faster.

Example 14

Multiply: $(x + 2)^2$

◆ **Step 1** Use the FOIL method to find the product.

$(x + 2)(x + 2)$ **F** Multiply the first terms:

$(x)(x) = x^2$

$(x + 2)(x + 2)$ **O** Multiply the outside terms:

$(x)(2) = 2x$

$(x + 2)(x + 2)$ **I**   Multiply the inside terms:

$(2)(x) = 2x$

$(x + 2)(x + 2)$ **L**   Multiply the last terms:

$(2)(2) = 4$

◆ **Step 2**   Combine the terms.

The solution:

$$x^2 + 2x + 2x + 4 =$$
$$x^2 + 4x + 4$$

Example 15

Multiply: $(x - 3)^2$

◆ **Step 1**   Use the FOIL method to find the product.

$(x - 3)(x - 3)$ **F**   Multiply the first terms:

$(x)(x) = x^2$

$(x - 3)(x - 3)$ **O**   Multiply the outside terms:

$(x)(-3) = -3x$

$(x - 3)(x - 3)$ **I**   Multiply the inside terms:

$(-3)(x) = -3x$

$(x - 3)(x - 3)$ **L**   Multiply the last terms:

$(-3)(-3) = 9$

◆ **Step 2**   Combine the terms.

The solution:

$$x^2 - 3x - 3x + 9 = $$
$$x^2 - 6x + 9$$

Look carefully at examples 14 and 15. Notice that in both, the outside and the inside products are the same. This pattern holds true for all squares of binomials, giving us this rule:

> The square of a binomial $(a + b)^2$ or $(a - b)^2$ is the square of the first term a^2, plus twice the product of the two terms that make up the binomial, $(2ab)$, plus the square of the last term b^2.
> Thus:
>
> $$(a + b)^2 = (a^2 + 2ab + b^2)$$
> $$(a - b)^2 = (a^2 - 2ab + b^2)$$

A Difference of Squares

We may be required to find the product of two binomials, such as $(x + 3)$ and $(x - 3)$. They look similar except that the first binomial is the sum of the two terms $(x + 3)$ and the second binomial is the difference of the two terms $(x - 3)$. Let's use the FOIL method on another example.

Example 16

Multiply: $(x + 3)(x - 3)$

◆ **Step 1**   Use the FOIL method to find the product.

$(x + 3)(x - 3)$ **F**   Multiply the first terms:

$(x)(x) = x^2$

$(x + 3)(x - 3)$ **O**   Multiply the outside terms:

$(x)(-3) = -3x$

$(x + 3)(x - 3)$ **I**   Multiply the inside terms:

$(3)(x) = 3x$

$(x + 3)(x - 3)$ **L**   Multiply the last terms:

$(3)(-3) = -9$

◆ **Step 2**   Combine the terms.

$x^2 - 3x + 3x - 9 =$

$$x^2 - 9$$

Notice that when we multiplied the binomials in example 16, the inside and outside products cancelled each other out. We have identified the difference of squares rule, which states:

> The product of the sum and difference of two terms $(a + b)(a - b)$ is the difference of their squares. Thus, $(a + b)(a - b) = a^2 - b^2$.

4.5 Polynomials and Division

Dividing a Polynomial by a Monomial

When we divide a polynomial by a monomial to obtain a quotient, we must divide each term in the polynomial by the term in the monomial.

Example 17

Divide $9x^6 + 15x^4$ by $3x^2$.

◆ **Step 1**   Divide each term of $9x^6 + 15x^4$ by $3x^2$.

$$\frac{9x^6 + 15x^4}{3x^2} =$$

$$\frac{9x^6}{3x^2} + \frac{15x^4}{3x^2} =$$

◆ **Step 2**   Reduce the coefficients of the variables.

$$\frac{3x^6}{1x^2} + \frac{5x^4}{1x^2} =$$

◆ **Step 3**   Subtract the exponents according to the quotient rule for dividing when the base is the same (for example, $\frac{3x^6}{1x^2} = 3x^{6-2}$). The solution:

$$3x^4 + 5x^2$$

Example 18

Find the quotient: $\dfrac{3a^4b^2 + 15a^3b + 6a}{6a^2b^3}$

◆ **Step 1**   Divide each term by $6a^2b^3$.

$$\frac{3a^4b^2 + 15a^3b + 6a}{6a^2b^3} =$$

$$\frac{3a^4b^2}{6a^2b^3} + \frac{15a^3b}{6a^2b^3} + \frac{6a}{6a^2b^3} =$$

◆ **Step 2**   Reduce the coefficients of the variables.

$$\frac{^1\cancel{3}a^4b^2}{_2\cancel{6}a^2b^3} + \frac{^5\cancel{15}a^3b}{_2\cancel{6}a^2b^3} + \frac{^1\cancel{6}a}{_1\cancel{6}a^2b^3} =$$

$$\frac{1a^4b^2}{2a^2b^3} + \frac{5a^3b}{2a^2b^3} + \frac{1a}{1a^2b^3} =$$

$$\frac{a^4b^2}{2a^2b^3} + \frac{5a^3b}{2a^2b^3} + \frac{a}{a^2b^3} =$$

◆ **Step 3**   Subtract the exponents according to the quotient rule for dividing when the base is the same. The solution:

$$\frac{a^2}{2b} + \frac{5a}{2b^2} + \frac{1}{ab^3}$$

Note that the variables in each term are in the numerator or denominator of each fraction, according to where the variable with the larger exponent was.

Polynomials and Long Division

When we divide a number, such as 8, by another number, such as 4, the number 8 is called the dividend and the number 4 is called the divisor. When the divisor and the dividend are both polynomials, we can use a method called long division to find the quotient. Two points must be remembered:

- We must make sure that both the dividend and the divisor are written in descending order of exponents. Thus, we can proceed to divide $x^3 + x^2 + 4$ by $x^2 + x - 1$, but not $x^3 + x^2 + 4$ by $1 + x + x^2$.

- Both the dividend and the divisor must follow the same sequence of exponents. If any of the exponents in the sequence are "missing," we fill in with $0x$ raised to the missing power.

For example, let's say that we want to divide $2x^4 + 2x^3 + 4x - 2$ by $x^2 + x - 1$. We can see that the divisor has the variable x raised to the second power (x^2) in its sequence, but the dividend does not. In this case, we rewrite the dividend as $2x^4 + 2x^3 + 0x^2 + 4x - 2$.

Example 19

> Divide $y^2 + 3y + 3$ by $y + 2$.

◆ **Step 1**   Check the dividend and divisor to make sure they are written in descending order of exponents. In this case, they are.

◆ **Step 2**   Look to see if there are any terms missing in the sequence of either the dividend or the divisor. In this case, there are no missing terms.

◆ **Step 3**   Use long division. Remember when subtracting to change the signs and add the terms.

$$
\begin{array}{r}
y + 1 \\
y + 2 \overline{)\, y^2 + 3y + 3} \\
+y^2 + 2y \\
\hline
-y^2 - 2y \\
\hline
0 \;\; + y \; + 3 \\
+y \;\; + 2 \\
\hline
-y \;\; - 2 \\
\hline
0 \; + 1
\end{array}
$$

The quotient, located on the top line, is $y + 1$, and the remainder is 1. We therefore write the solution:

$$y + 1 + \dfrac{1}{y + 2}$$

This is similar to dividing 7 by 2: $2\overline{)7}$ with quotient 3, $\frac{6}{1}$, where we put the remainder over the divisor and get $3\dfrac{1}{2}$.

Example 20

Divide: $4a^2 - 9$ by $2a - 3$

◆ **Step 1**   Check the dividend and divisor to make sure they are written in descending order of exponents. In this case, they are.

◆ **Step 2**   Look to see if there are any terms missing in the sequence of either the dividend or the divisor. The dividend is missing a term with degree 1, so insert $0a$ to give us the polynomial $4a^2 + 0a - 9$.

◆ **Step 3**   Use long division.

$$
\begin{array}{r}
2a + 3 \\
2a - 3 \overline{)4a^2 + 0a - 9} \\
+4a^2 - 6a \\
-4a^2 + 6a \\
\hline
0 \;\; + 6a - 9 \\
+6a - 9 \\
-6a + 9 \\
\hline
0
\end{array}
$$

The quotient is $2a + 3$, and there is no remainder.

4.6 Polynomials and Word Problems

Polynomials have a role to play in solving everyday problems. For example, scientists testing new medications can use polynomials to test the concentration of a trial drug in a volunteer's bloodstream after a specific period of time. Furthermore, when we work with the area or the volume of geometric figures—such as circles, squares, and cubes—we may need to use polynomials. The following examples illustrate how polynomials are applied to word problems.

Example 21

Imagine that scientists testing a new treatment for anxiety disorder have determined that the polynomial $-0.04h^2 + 2h + 3$ represents in parts per million the concentration of the drug in a test volunteer's blood after h hours. What is the concentration after 4 hours?

◆ **Step 1**   Let h represent hours elapsed.

◆ **Step 2**   Insert the value for h (which is 4), and evaluate the polynomial.

$-0.04h^2 + 2h + 3 \quad =$

$-0.04(4)^2 + 2(4) + 3 =$

$-0.04(16) + 2(4) + 3 =$

$-0.04(16) + 8 + 3 \quad =$

$-0.64 + 11 \qquad = 10.36$

The concentration is 10.36 parts per million after 4 hours.

Example 22

Letreece is furnishing her new condominium. So far, her living room contains a couch whose base measures 3 feet by 6 feet. In front of the couch is a rectangular coffee table, 2 feet wide and x feet long, and by the side of the couch is a decorative tree in a container whose base has an area of 3 square feet. If Letreece's living room is a square with each side ($x + 10$ feet), and she intends to install wall-to-wall carpeting throughout the room, construct a polynomial to represent the area of the carpet that is still visible after the couch, coffee table, and potted tree have been moved in.

◆ **Step 1**   Draw a diagram to represent Letreece's living room.

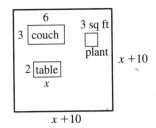

◆ **Step 2**   The area of the carpet that is visible is the total area of the wall-to-wall carpeting minus the total area of the bases of the couch, decorative container base, and the coffee table. Find the area in square feet of the wall-to-wall carpet. Notice that this is a binomial squared, so we should be able to write the product right away by using the rule $(a + b)^2 = a^2 + 2ab + b^2$.

$(x + 10)(x + 10) = x^2 + 20x + 100$

◆ **Step 3**   What is the area in square feet of the coffee table?

$2 \times x = 2x$ sq ft

What is the area in square feet of the container?

3 sq ft

What is the area in square feet of the couch?

$6 \times 3 = 18$ sq ft

Add the total in square feet of the three items:

$2x + 3 + 18$

◆ **Step 4**   Subtract the total in square feet of the three items from the area in square feet of the wall-to-wall carpeting to determine how much of the carpet will not be covered.

$(x^2 + 20x + 100) - (2x + 3 + 18) =$

$(x^2 + 20x + 100) - (2x + 21)\quad =$

$x^2 + 20x - 2x + 100 - 21\quad\quad =$

$(x^2 + 18x + 79)$ sq ft

4.7 Introduction to Factoring

Earlier we learned how to multiply a variety of polynomials to obtain products. In this section, we explore the concept of multiplication from the reverse position. We begin with a product and then determine which factors, or components, were multiplied to arrive at the product. For example, we learned that multiplying the monomial x by the binomial $(x + 3)$ yields the product $x^2 + 3x$. In this example, x and $(x + 3)$ are called the factors of the product $x^2 + 3x$. When we begin with the product and reverse the process, we refer to this as factoring. Thus, if we are asked to factor a polynomial, we have to discover which factors, when multiplied together, yield (or give us) the same polynomial expression as the one we started with.

Let's simplify this procedure for now by using only a number with no variables. Take the number 7, for example, and factor it. Which number times another number equals 7? The solution is 1 and 7, because these two numbers multiplied together equal 7. So we say that 1 and 7 are factors of 7. In this example, 1 and 7 are the only possible factors, because 7 is a prime number.

However, many numbers can be factored in more than one way. For instance, we can factor 12 as the positive integers 1×12, or 2×6, or 3×4, or $2 \times 2 \times 3$. Thus, when you think of factors, visualize them as "factory workers" arranged in special assembly lines that can all make the same product. The "1 and 12 team" manufactures the product 12, as does the "2 and 6 team," the "3 and 4 team," and the "2, 2, and 3 team." Moreover, our mathematical factory might have yet another assembly line section that "employs" only negative integer "workers" to produce the number 12, such as the "−6 and −2 team." When we factor polynomials that contain variables, we apply the same concept as the one we've just discussed for factoring the number 12.

Example 23

Factor: $12x^2$

◆ **Step 1**   Think of this monomial as the "finished product" from the "math factory," but we need to know how it was "made." How many different types of "manufacturing teams" could have made the same product $12x^2$? Some are listed here:

$12x^2 = (3x)(4x)$

$$12x^2 = (6x)(2x)$$

$$12x^2 = (x)(12x)$$

$$12x^2 = (2)(6x^2)$$

$$12x^2 = (-2x)(-6x)$$

Write in the margin the other factor combinations that are also possible.

Example 24

Write three factorizations of $9y^3$.

$$9y^3 = (y)(9y^2)$$

$$9y^3 = (3y^2)(3y)$$

$$9y^3 = (-3)(-3y^3)$$

Can you think of others?

4.8 The Greatest Common Factor

A common factor is one that is shared by two or more terms. For example, 4 is a factor of 8, but 4 is also a factor of 12. Thus, 4 is a common factor of both 8 and 12. What is the greatest common factor (GCF)? Of all the factors common to a list of integers, for example, the greatest common factor is, as its name states, the largest one. So, not only is 4 a common factor of 8 and 12 (other common factors are 1 and 2), but 4 is also the greatest common factor of 8 and 12. Table 4.1 lists all

Table 4.1: Factors of Positive Integers

Positive integer	Possible factors	Common factors	Greatest common factor
4	**1, 2, 4**		
8	**1, 2, 4**, 8	**1, 2, 4**	**4**
16	**1, 2, 4**, 8, 16		
24	**1, 2**, 3, **4**, 6, 8, 12, 24		

the possible positive integer factors of 4, 8, 16, and 24. It also shows which of the factors are common (shared by all), and which one is the greatest common factor of this list of integers.

Finding the Greatest Common Factor

When factoring polynomials, we often want to find the greatest common factor of two or more numbers. We proceed in this way:

1. Write each number in the list as a product of its prime factors. A prime number is a number that can be divided by only itself and the number 1. For instance, both 3 and 4 are factors of 12, but of these two factors, only 3 is a prime factor, because 4 is also divisible by 2.

2. Write down each prime factor that is common to all the numbers in the list.

3. Count how many times each common prime factor appears in the factored form of each number in the list. For example, imagine that we have factored 8 and 16 into their primes:

$$8 = 2 \times 2 \times 2$$

$$16 = 2 \times 2 \times 2 \times 2$$

4. Notice that the number 2 is the prime factor common to both 8 and 16. It appears three times in the factored form of 8, but four times in the factored form of 16. We find the GCF by choosing the factored form in which the common prime factors appear in all lists. Thus, we select the factored form of $2 \times 2 \times 2 = 8$. We have found that the GCF of the two numbers 8 and 16 is 8. If there are no common prime factors, such as for 7 and 10, the GCF is 1, because 1 is a factor of every number.

Example 25

Find the GCF of 15 and 30.

◆ **Step 1** Write each number in the list as a product of its prime factors by dividing each number by the smallest possible prime number until you reach the number 1. The prime factors of 15 are 3 and 5, since $(3 \times 5) = 15$, and the prime factors of 30 are 2, 3, and 5, since $(2 \times 3 \times 5) = 30$.

◆ **Step 2**   Write down the prime factors that are common to 15 and 30. They are 3 and 5.

◆ **Step 3**   Multiply the prime factors to yield the GCF.

$3 \times 5 = 15$

> The GCF of 15 and 30 is 15.

The GCF need not be one of the numbers in question, as shown in example 26.

Example 26

> Find the GCF of 6, 10, and 18.

◆ **Step 1**   Write down the prime factors of each number.

$6 = 2 \times 3$

$10 = 2 \times 5$

$18 = 2 \times 3 \times 3$

Compare the prime factored form of each number. Which number stands out as common to all three integers? It is the number 2. Notice that 2, the common prime factor, appears once in the factored form of each number in the list, but there are no other common primes for all three numbers.

> Therefore, the GCF of 6, 10, and 18 is 2.

Example 27

> What is the GCF of 30 and 45?

◆ **Step 1**   Write down the prime factors of each number.

$30 = 2 \times 3 \times 5$

$45 = 3 \times 3 \times 5$

◆ **Step 2**   Notice which factors are common. They are 3 (but only once) and 5. Multiply to find the GCF.

$3 \times 5 = 15$

The GCF of 30 and 45 is 15.

Example 28

Find the greatest common factor of $16x^4$, $20x^6$, and $-18x^3$.

◆ **Step 1**   Write each term as a product of its prime factors.

$16x^4 = 2 \cdot 2 \cdot 2 \cdot 2 \cdot x \cdot x \cdot x \cdot x$

$20x^6 = 2 \cdot 2 \cdot 5 \cdot x \cdot x \cdot x \cdot x \cdot x \cdot x$

$-18x^3 = -1 \cdot 2 \cdot 3 \cdot 3 \cdot x \cdot x \cdot x$

The numerical value of the GCF is 2 (the only number common to all terms). The GCF will also contain the variables that appear in all the terms in the list. For example, the factor x appears three times in each term, so x^3 is the GCF of the three.

◆ **Step 2**   Multiply 2 and x^3 to obtain the GCF.

$2 \times x^3 =$

$2x^3$ is the GCF.

Example 29

What is the GCF of $a^2b^3c^5$, a^3b^5c, and a^2b^4?

◆ **Step 1**   Factor the terms.

$a^2b^3c^5 = a \cdot a \cdot b \cdot b \cdot b \cdot c \cdot c \cdot c \cdot c \cdot c$

$a^3b^5c = a \cdot a \cdot a \cdot b \cdot b \cdot b \cdot b \cdot b \cdot c$

$$a^2b^4 = a \cdot a \cdot b \cdot b \cdot b \cdot b$$

◆ **Step 2**   The common factors are a (twice) and b (three times), or a^2 and b^3. Multiply to obtain the GCF. The solution:

a^2b^3

Note that the exponents in the GCF are the smallest exponents of each variable that appears in every term. So the GCF in example 29 could have been found by noticing that a^2 and b^3 are the lowest powers of a and b, and that c doesn't appears in the third monomial at all. Thus, the GCF is a^2b^3.

Factoring Out the GCF

Polynomials can be factored in several ways. One method involves factoring out the greatest common factor. For example, the polynomial $3x + 15$ is the sum of two terms, $3x$ and 15 (whose greatest common factor is 3). By using the distributive property, we can express the original polynomial, $3x + 15$, not as the sum of its two terms but rather as the product of its GCF (3) and the binomial $x + 5$.

$$3x + 15 = 3 \cdot x + 3 \cdot 5 =$$

$$3(x + 5)$$

Thus, 3, the GCF, is factored out of the polynomial $3x + 15$.

Example 30

Factor out the GCF: $x^4 + x^2 + x$

◆ **Step 1**   Write down the variable with the smallest exponent. It is x, the GCF.

◆ **Step 2**   Write each term as a product with x as one factor.

$x(x^3 + x + 1)$

If you want to check your answer, multiply the GCF x and the trinomial $x^3 + x + 1$.

$x(x^3 + x + 1) = x^4 + x^2 + x$

4.9 Factoring by Grouping

Factoring by grouping is another method for factoring polynomials. It works best with four-term polynomials. This method involves grouping the terms of the polynomial and looking within each group for common factors, which are then factored out to yield a product.

Example 31

Factor by grouping: $2x + 4 + xy + 2y$

◆ **Step 1**   Arrange the terms into two groups.

$2x + 4$ $xy + 2y$

◆ **Step 2**   What is the common factor in the first group?

$2x = 2 \cdot x$

$4 = 2 \cdot 2$

The common factor is 2. Factor out the 2. Thus:

$2x + 4 = 2(x + 2)$

◆ **Step 3**   Find the common factor in the second group.

$xy = x \cdot y$

$2y = 2 \cdot y$

The common factor is y. Factor out the y. Thus:

$xy + 2y = y(x + 2)$

◆ **Step 4**   Look closely at the results. There is a common factor, $(x + 2)$, in both groups.

Factor out this binomial $(x + 2)$.

The other factor is $(2 + y)$.

$$2(x + 2) + y(x + 2) \ =$$

$$(2 + y)$$

The solution is the product of the common factor binomial $x + 2$ and the binomial factor $2 + y$.

$$(x + 2)(2 + y)$$

Example 32

Factor by grouping: $12 - 3b + 2ab - 8a$

◆ **Step 1**   Make two groups and look for common factors.

$$12 - 3b \ = 3(4 - b)$$

$$2ab - 8a = 2a(b - 4)$$

◆ **Step 2**   Notice that there are no common factors, so rearrange the polynomial into two other groups.

$$2ab - 3b \ = b(2a - 3)$$

$$-8a + 12 = -4(2a - 3)$$

Now we have a common factor $(2a - 3)$. The other binomial factor is $b - 4$. The solution:

$$(2a - 3)(b - 4)$$

4.10 Factoring Trinomials, Part 1

In previous examples, we were able to factor polynomials by finding common factors. Sometimes, however, we are required to factor trinomials that have no common factors. In this section, we focus on trinomials that belong to the following four categories of polynomials, in which the coefficient of the squared term is 1 ($1x^2 = x^2$).

1. $x^2 + bx + c$

2. $x^2 - bx + c$

3. $x^2 + bx - c$

4. $x^2 - bx - c$

Let's begin this section with trinomials of the type $x^2 + bx + c$, where the sign of the constant c (the last term of the trinomial) is always positive. We learned that the FOIL method provided an easy way of multiplying two binomials. When we factor polynomials, such as $x^2 + 7x + 12$, we thus have to reverse our FOIL steps to search for the two binomial factors whose product is the trinomial we started with. If we want to factor $x^2 + 7x + 12$, for example, we know that our two factors must both contain the variable x, because $x \cdot x = x^2$. Furthermore, because there are only positive signs in this trinomial, there will only be positive signs in our two factors. Using our knowledge of FOIL, we can start to build the binomial factors like this:

$(x + ?)(x + ?)$	F	Multiply the first terms: $x \cdot x = x^2$

At this point, we know that the first term of both binomial factors is x. What we need to discover is which two numbers that when multiplied yield a product that equals 12 (the last term of the trinomial $x^2 + 7x + 12$) and that when added yield a sum that equals $7x$ (the middle term of the trinomial). Take the last term 12 and find as many pairs of factors as you can. Then add each pair of factors to yield a sum.

Factors of 12	Sum of the factors
1×12	13
2×6	8
3×4	7

Recall that the middle term of the trinomial is $7x$. Which two factors of 12 listed above add up to 7? The factors 3 and 4. Let's substitute them into the two binomial factors $(x + ?)(x + ?)$ that we have begun to build to get $(x + 3)(x + 4)$ as our factors. To check our result, by using all the FOIL steps, we should end up with the original trinomial, $x^2 + 7x + 12$.

$(x + 3)(x + 4)$	F	x^2
$(x + 3)(x + 4)$	O	$4x$
$(x + 3)(x + 4)$	I	$3x$
$(x + 3)(x + 4)$	L	12

FOIL yields the product $x^2 + 4x + 3x + 12 = x^2 + 7x + 12$. So, $x^2 + 7x + 12 = (x + 3)(x + 4)$.

Example 33

Factor: $x^2 - 11x + 10$

◆ **Step 1**   We know that the first term of both binomial factors is x. Thus, write down

$(x + ?)(x + ?)$

◆ **Step 2**   Factor the last term 10, and then add the factors. Because the coefficient of the middle term is negative (-11), we must write down only negative factors.

Negative factors of 10	Sum of the factors
-1×-10	-11
-2×-5	-7

◆ **Step 3**   The trinomial's middle term is $-11x$, so we select the factors -1 and -10, whose sum is -11.

$(x - 1)(x - 10)$

◆ **Step 4**   Check your work by multiplying the binomials.

$(x - 1)(x - 10) = x^2 - 11x + 10$

The factorization is correct.

$x^2 - 11x + 10 = (x - 1)(x - 10)$

To this point, we have worked with polynomials whose constant (the last term of the polynomial) was positive. Let's work now with polynomials whose constant is negative, such as the categories $x^2 + bx - c$ and $x^2 - bx - c$. When we factor polynomials with negative constants, we search for two numbers whose product is negative and whose sum is equal to the coefficient b of the middle term. To yield a product whose sign is negative, we know that one of the two numbers must be positive, and the other must be negative.

Example 34

Factor: $z^2 + 4z - 5$

◆ **Step 1**   We know that the first term of each binomial factor is z, so write down

$(z + ?)(z + ?)$

◆ **Step 2**   Write down the factors of -5 and their sums.

Factors of -5	Sum of the factors
1×-5	-4
-1×5	$+4$

◆ **Step 3**   The trinomial's middle term is $4z$, so select the factors -1 and 5, since $5z - 1z = 4z$.

Write down the two binomial factors.

$(z - 1)(z + 5)$

Example 35

Factor: $y^2 - 21y - 72$

◆ **Step 1**   We know that the first term of each binomial factor is y, so write down

$(y + ?)(y + ?)$

◆ **Step 2**   Write down factors of -72 and their sums.

Factors of -72	Sum of the factors
1×-72	-71
2×-36	-34
3×-24	-21
4×-18	-14
6×-12	-6
8×-9	-1

Notice that the factors 3 and -24 when added equal -21, which is the numerical coefficient of the trinomial's middle term. Note also that there are six more factors of -72 (-1×72, for example), but once we found two that equal -21 when added, we really could have stopped there.

◆ **Step 3**   Write down the two binomial factors.

$$(y + 3)(y - 24)$$

4.11   Factoring Trinomials, Part 2

In this section, we factor trinomials that fit into these categories:

- Factoring a trinomial by first rearranging the terms

- Factoring a trinomial when the coefficient of the squared term is not equal to 1

- Factoring a trinomial with a greatest common factor

Factoring by First Rearranging the Terms

Sometimes trinomials need to be rewritten before they can be factored, because their terms are not arranged in an order that makes the factoring process easy.

Example 36

Factor: $t^2 + 8 - 9t$

◆ **Step 1**   Look carefully at this polynomial. It is not expressed in descending order. Always check the problem carefully, and rearrange the terms if necessary.

Rewrite as $t^2 - 9t + 8$.

◆ **Step 2**   Write down $(t + ?)(t + ?)$. Since the middle term is negative and the constant is positive, both factors of 8 must be negative. The trinomial's middle term is $-9t$, so select the factors -1 and -8 (product is 8, sum is -9) to complete the process.

$$(t - 1)(t - 8)$$

When the Coefficient of the Squared Term Is Not Equal to 1

Not all trinomials are like the ones we have worked on to this point. In some trinomials, the coefficient of the squared term is greater than 1.

Example 37

Factor: $2a^2 + 7a + 3$

◆ **Step 1**   We can see that the numerical coefficient of the squared term is greater than 1. (It is 2.) Proceed in this case by finding two numbers whose product is $2 \times 3 = 6$ (the 2 and 3 come from the first and last terms of the trinomial) and whose sum is 7, the coefficient of the middle term. The answer is 1 and 6, since $1 \times 6 = 6$, and $1 + 6 = 7$.

◆ **Step 2**   Select the numbers 1 and 6 and rewrite the middle term, $7a$ as $1a + 6a$.

$2a^2 + 7a + 3 \qquad =$

$2a^2 + 1a + 6a + 3 =$

◆ **Step 3**   Rearrange the polynomial $2a^2 + 1a + 6a + 3$ into two groups, as we did for factoring by grouping.

$2a^2 + 1a$ and $6a + 3$

◆ **Step 4**   Now factor by grouping.

$2a^2 + 1a = a(2a + 1)$

$6a + 3 \quad = 3(2a + 1)$

Notice that the common factor is $(2a + 1)$. The other factor:

$$a(2a+1)+3(2a+1)$$

$$(a+3)$$

◆ **Step 5**   Write down the two binomial factors.

$$(2a+1)(a+3)$$

Factoring with a Greatest Common Factor

Some trinomials look very complicated, containing terms with large coefficients and variables raised to powers greater than 2. To work with complicated trinomials, we first take out the greatest common factor (GCF), if possible, factor again what remains, and then include the GCF in the final result.

Example 38

Factor: $15x^4 - 39x^3 + 18x^2$

◆ **Step 1**   Factor out the GCF.

$$15x^4 \;\; = 3 \cdot 5 \cdot x^2 \cdot x^2$$

$$-39x^3 = 3 \cdot -1 \cdot 13 \cdot x^2 \cdot x$$

$$18x^2 \;\; = 3 \cdot 2 \cdot 3 \cdot x^2$$

The GCF is $3x^2$. Thus:

$$15x^4 - 39x^3 + 18x^2 = 3x^2(5x^2 - 13x + 6)$$

◆ **Step 2**   Factor the trinomial $5x^2 - 13x + 6$. Find two integers whose product is $5 \times 6 = 30$ and whose sum is -13.

Factors of 30	Sum of the factors
-1×-30	-31
-2×-15	-17
-3×-10	-13
-5×-6	-11

◆ **Step 3**   Using the two integers -3 and -10, rewrite the middle term of the trinomial $5x^2 - 13x + 6$ as

$$5x^2 - 10x - 3x + 6$$

◆ **Step 4**   Arrange the terms into two groups.

$$5x^2 - 10x \text{ and } - 3x + 6$$

◆ **Step 5**   Factor the first group.

$$5x^2 - 10x = 5x(x - 2)$$

◆ **Step 6**   Factor the second group.

$$-3x + 6 = -3(x - 2)$$

The common factor is the binomial $(x - 2)$, and the other factor is $(5x - 3)$. Thus, $5x^2 - 13x + 6 = (x - 2)(5x - 3)$.

◆ **Step 7**   Finish writing down the solution by reintroducing the GCF $3x^2$ that was factored out in step 1 above.

$$15x^4 - 39x^3 + 18x^2 = 3x^2(x - 2)(5x - 3)$$

4.12 Introduction to Rational Expressions

Rational expressions (also known as fractional expressions or algebraic fractions) are quotients of two polynomials. For example, both $\dfrac{7}{x+14}$ and $\dfrac{x^2+x-6}{2x+3}$ are rational expressions.

Simplifying Rational Expressions

Simplifying rational expressions is similar to reducing ordinary fractions. For example, we may reduce or simplify the fraction $\dfrac{6}{8}$ by factoring both the numerator and the denominator, separating the common factor or factors, rewriting the original fraction as a product of two fractions, and then removing a factor of 1.

◆ **Step 1**   Factor the numerator and the denominator.

$$\frac{6}{8} = \frac{2 \cdot 3}{2 \cdot 2 \cdot 2} =$$

$$\frac{2}{2} \cdot \frac{3}{2 \cdot 2} =$$

◆ **Step 2**   Separate the common factor 2 and rewrite the original fraction as a product of two fractions. Note that $\frac{2}{2} = 1$.

$$1 \cdot \frac{3}{2 \cdot 2} =$$

◆ **Step 3**   Multiply the factors in the denominator, and then remove a factor of 1.

$$1 \cdot \frac{3}{4} = \frac{3}{4}$$

> Thus, $\frac{6}{8}$ can be simplified as $\frac{3}{4}$.

We can use this basic method to simplify rational expressions, as the following examples show.

Example 39

> Simplify the rational expression: $\dfrac{4x^2}{8x}$

◆ **Step 1**   Factor the numerator and the denominator.

$$\frac{4x^2}{8x} = \frac{2 \cdot 2 \cdot x \cdot x}{2 \cdot 2 \cdot 2 \cdot x}$$

◆ **Step 2**   Separate the common factors $(2 \cdot 2 \cdot x = 4x)$ and rewrite the original rational expression as a product of two rational expressions.

$$\frac{4x}{4x} \cdot \frac{x}{2} =$$

$$1 \cdot \frac{x}{2} =$$

$$\frac{x}{2}$$

Example 40

Simplify: $\dfrac{y^2 - 25}{y^2 + 6y + 5}$

◆ **Step 1**   Factor both the numerator and the denominator.

$$y^2 - 25 \quad = (y + 5)(y - 5)$$

$$y^2 + 6y + 5 = (y + 5)(y + 1)$$

Note that $y^2 - 25$ is the difference of two squares, which readily factors into the sum and difference of the square roots. Thus,

$$\frac{y^2 - 25}{y^2 + 6y + 5} = \frac{(y + 5)(y - 5)}{(y + 5)(y + 1)}$$

◆ **Step 2**   Separate the common factor $y + 5$, and rewrite as a product of two rational expressions.

$$\frac{y + 5}{y + 5} \cdot \frac{y - 5}{y + 1}$$

◆ **Step 3**   Remove a factor of 1. Remember that $\dfrac{y + 5}{y + 5} = 1$.

$$\frac{y^2 - 25}{y^2 + 6y + 5} = \frac{y - 5}{y + 1}$$

Example 41

Simplify: $\dfrac{3x^2 + 7x + 2}{x^2 - 4}$

◆ **Step 1**   Factor the rational expression.

$$\frac{3x^2 + 7x + 2}{x^2 - 4} = \frac{(3x + 1)(x + 2)}{(x - 2)(x + 2)}$$

◆ **Step 2**   Cancel out a factor of 1.

$$\frac{(x + 2)}{(x + 2)}$$

$$\frac{3x^2 + 7x + 2}{x^2 - 4} = \frac{3x + 1}{x - 2}$$

4.13 Adding and Subtracting Rational Expressions

We begin by adding rational expressions that have the same denominators. This is a straightforward process, because all we have to do is to add the numerators and, if necessary, simplify as we did in the previous section.

Example 42

Add: $\dfrac{y}{y - 2} + \dfrac{2}{y - 2}$

◆ **Step 1**   Both rational expressions have the same denominator, so just add the numerators.

$$\frac{y}{y - 2} + \frac{2}{y - 2} =$$

$$\frac{y + 2}{y - 2}$$

When we add rational expressions that have different denominators, before we can add the numerators, we first have to rewrite the expressions so that they have the same denominators. To do this, we have to determine the least common denominator (LCD) of the rational expression. For example, to add $\dfrac{1}{5}$ and $\dfrac{1}{10}$, we must find the LCD of the numbers 5 and 10. It is 10, the smallest number that is divisible by both 5 and 10. So, $\dfrac{1}{5} = \dfrac{1 \cdot 2}{5 \cdot 2} = \dfrac{2}{10}$, and thus $\dfrac{1}{5} + \dfrac{1}{10} = \dfrac{2}{10} + \dfrac{1}{10} = \dfrac{3}{10}$.

Example 43

Add: $\dfrac{1}{3} + \dfrac{x}{5}$

◆ **Step 1**   Determine the LCD of these two rational expressions. It is 15.

◆ **Step 2**   Rewrite each term as a fraction with the LCD of 15 as a denominator.

Three goes into 15 five times, so multiply 5 by 1, the numerator of the first expression. Enter the number 5 as the numerator of the new first expression.

$$\frac{1}{3} = \frac{?}{15}$$

$$\frac{1}{3} = \frac{5}{15}$$

The denominator of the second rational expression is 5. Five goes into 15 three times, so multiply the numerator of the second expression, x, by 3. Enter the product $3x$ as the numerator of the new second expression.

$$\frac{x}{5} = \frac{?}{15}$$

$$\frac{x}{5} = \frac{3x}{15}$$

◆ **Step 3**   Add the two new fractions.

$$\frac{5}{15} + \frac{3x}{15} = \frac{5 + 3x}{15}$$

The method for subtracting rational expressions that have the same denominator is similar to the one used to add them, except we subtract the numerators.

Example 44

Subtract: $\dfrac{x+y}{2} - \dfrac{y}{2}$

◆ **Step 1**   Both rational expressions have the same denominators, so subtract the numerators.

$$\frac{x+y}{2} - \frac{y}{2} =$$

$$\frac{x + y - y}{2} =$$

$$\frac{x}{2}$$

Example 45

Subtract: $\frac{4}{7} - \frac{b}{2}$

◆ **Step 1**   The denominators are different, so write down the LCD. In this case, it is 14.

◆ **Step 2**   Rewrite the terms as fractions with 14 as the denominator. The denominator of the first rational expression is 7. Seven goes into 14 twice, so multiply the numerator by 2. The denominator of the second expression is 2. Two goes into 14 seven times, so multiply the numerator b by 7.

$$\frac{4}{7} = \frac{8}{14}$$

$$\frac{b}{2} = \frac{7b}{14}$$

◆ **Step 3**   Write down a new rational expression whose numerator is the difference $8 - 7b$ and whose denominator is 14, the LCD.

$$\frac{8}{14} - \frac{7b}{14} =$$

$$\frac{8 - 7b}{14}$$

4.14 Multiplying and Dividing Rational Expressions

We multiply rational expressions by multiplying the numerators, multiplying the denominators, and simplifying if possible.

Example 46

Multiply: $\frac{x - 2}{x + 3} \cdot \frac{x + 1}{x + 5}$

◆ **Step 1**   Place parentheses around the grouped terms. Since none of the grouped terms are the same, nothing cancels out.

$$\frac{(x-2)}{(x+3)} \cdot \frac{(x+1)}{(x+5)} =$$

◆ **Step 2**   Multiply the numerators and the denominators.

$$\frac{(x-2)(x+1)}{(x+3)(x+5)} =$$

◆ **Step 3**   Use FOIL to express as a fraction of trinomials, if necessary.

$$\frac{x^2 - x - 2}{x^2 + 8x + 15}$$

Example 47

Multiply: $\dfrac{x^2 - 25}{x^2 - 4x + 3} \cdot \dfrac{x - 1}{x + 5}$

◆ **Step 1**   Factor the rational expressions before multiplying to check for identical terms that can cancel out.

$$\frac{x^2 - 25}{x^2 - 4x + 3} \cdot \frac{x - 1}{x + 5} =$$

$$\frac{(x-5)(x+5)}{(x-1)(x-3)} \cdot \frac{x-1}{x+5} =$$

◆ **Step 2**   Place parentheses around the terms and cancel out where possible.

$$\frac{(x-5)\cancel{(x+5)}}{\cancel{(x-1)}(x-3)} \cdot \frac{\cancel{(x-1)}}{\cancel{(x+5)}} =$$

$$\frac{x - 5}{x - 3}$$

When we divide rational expressions, we must first invert or turn upside down the divisor, and then multiply as we did above. For example, to perform the operation $\dfrac{x}{x-2} \div \dfrac{x}{x+5}$, we invert the divisor $\dfrac{x}{x+5}$ before multiplying.

Example 48

Divide: $\dfrac{x}{x-2} \div \dfrac{x}{x+5}$

◆ **Step 1** Invert the divisor $\frac{x}{x+5}$ so that it becomes $\frac{x+5}{x}$ and change to multiplication.

$$\frac{x}{x-2} \cdot \frac{x+5}{x} =$$

◆ **Step 2** Group terms.

$$\frac{x(x+5)}{(x-2)x} =$$

$$\frac{x(x+5)}{x(x-2)} =$$

◆ **Step 3** Cancel terms if possible.

$$\frac{\cancel{x}(x+5)}{\cancel{x}(x-2)} =$$

$$\boxed{\dfrac{x+5}{x-2}}$$

Problems

1. Evaluate the polynomial: $x^3 + x^2 - 5$, where $x = 3$

2. Subtract: $(-6b + 2) - (b^2 + b - 3)$

3. Subtract: $(5a^2b - 2ab + 9ab^2) - (8a^2b + 13ab + 12ab^2)$

4. Multiply: $(-5x^4)(-9x^7)$

5. Multiply: $(5x^3y^2z^2)(3x^3yz)$

6. Multiply: $3z(8 - 6z + 12z^3)$

7. Multiply: $(2y^2 + y - 2)(-2y^2 + 4y - 5)$

8. Divide: $\dfrac{3x^4y^2 - 15x^3y + 6x}{6x^2y^3}$

9. Factor out the GCF: $13x^6 - 26x^5 + 39x^2$

10. Factor: $x^2 + 10x + 21$

11. Add: $\dfrac{x-5}{6} + \dfrac{x}{6}$

12. Subtract: $\dfrac{x-4}{x} - \dfrac{x+4}{x}$

13. Factor by grouping: $7b^2 + 14b - ab - 2a$

14. Simplify: $\dfrac{z^2 + 5z + 4}{z^2 - 1}$

15. Divide: $\dfrac{x^2 - 12x + 32}{x^2 - 6x - 16} \div \dfrac{x^2 - x - 12}{x^2 - 5x - 24}$

Focus on English

Grammar

Whose

Whose indicates possession but is often confused with, or spelled as, "who's," which is the contracted form of "who is." Complete the following examples, using either *whose* or *who is*.

1. There is a book on the table. _____ book is it?

2. _____ our math teacher?

3. _____ apple is this?

4. _____ our president?

5. _____ slide rule is this?

Contractions

Contractions are often used in conversations. For example, *we are students* is contracted to *we're students*. In contractions, ' stands for a missing letter—for example, *'m* is the contracted form of *am*. Look at the following examples of contractions.

Present Tense of the Verb "To Be"

Full form	Contraction
I am your friend.	I'm your friend.
You are in my math class.	You're in my math class.
He is Kwan.	He's Kwan
She is Maria.	She's Maria.
It is a math book.	It's a math book.
We are math students.	We're math students.
You are in classroom 24.	You're in classroom 24.
They are instructors.	They're instructors.

Present Tense Verb "To Be" in the Negative Form

Full form	Contraction
I am not Swedish.	I'm not Swedish.
You are not Filipino.	You're not Filipino.
He/She/It is not Italian.	He/She/It isn't Italian.
We are not Spanish.	We're not Spanish.
You are not British.	You're not British.
They are not Jamaican	They're not Jamaican

Write the sentences, using contractions.

1. I cannot come tomorrow evening.

2. John is a mathematician.

3. You are in class 3.

4. It is not working.

5. They are going to France this summer.

A, An, The, Some, Any

A and *an* are called indefinite articles, and we use them with singular nouns. Use *a* with a noun beginning with a consonant, and use *an* with a noun beginning with a vowel (a, e, i, o, u). For example, *a book, an apple.* Use *the* (the definite article) when we know which noun we are referring to. For example, *the* book. There are two kinds of nouns in English, countable and uncountable. Countable are things you can count, and countable nouns can be either singular or plural. For example, *one penny, two pennies, three pennies.* Uncountable nouns are things you can't count, such as butter, cheese, or rice. Here are some rules:

Use *a* or *an* with singular countable nouns.

Use *some* with plural countable nouns and with uncountable nouns in positive sentences.

Use *any* with plural countable nouns and with uncountable nouns in negative sentences or questions.

Look at the following examples:

	Countable	Uncountable
Positive sentence		
We need	an orange.	some cheese.
We need	some oranges.	some milk.
Negative sentence		
We don't need	an apple.	any rice.
We don't need	any apples.	any butter.
Question		
Do we need	a tomato?	any milk?
Do we need	any tomatoes?	any sugar?

Furthermore, Moreover

Furthermore and *moreover* are called logical connectors. They are used to signal to the reader that the discussion is continuing. Sometimes, students use the word *plus* instead of, for example, *moreover* to inform the reader of additional information. *Plus* used in this context is incorrect. Write a paragraph about any topic you wish, and try to use logical connectors to improve the quality of your writing.

 Improving Mathematical Vocabulary

Pronunciation

There are no set rules for pronouncing English words. The best way to tackle pronouncing mathematical words is to check with your teacher and practice saying the words out loud. In the following examples, the stressed part of the word is underlined, such as

mon<u>o</u>mial

bin<u>o</u>mial

Underline the stressed syllable or syllables in the following math vocabulary:

1. trinomial

2. polynomial

3. square of a binomial

4. difference of squares

5. divisor

6. dividend

7. remainder

8. greatest common factor

9. rational expression

10. degree

 ## Dictionary Work

Define the following words, and practice using them in writing samples.

extract. The dentist extracted one of David's wisdom teeth.

invert

substitute

facilitate

Chapter 5
Graphing

In chapter 3, we graphed inequalities in one variable. In this chapter, we will learn how to graph linear equations in two variables.

5.0 Linear Equations in Two Variables

We recognize a linear equation containing two variables by the following form:

$$ax + by = c,$$

where a, b, and c are all real numbers,

$a \neq 0$ and $b \neq 0$, and x and y are the variables.

For example, to solve the equation $4x - 3y = 5$, we have to obtain values for both x and y. If we let $x = 2$ and $y = 1$, the equation is true, or we say those values satisfy the equation.

$$4x - 3y = 5$$

$$4(2) - 3(1) = 5$$

$$8 - 3 = 5$$

Rather than writing a solution for the above equation as $x = 2$ and $y = 1$, we can simply write (2, 1). The numbers inside the parentheses are called an ordered pair, and the value of x (or the first letter alphabetically if we are using variables other than x and y) is always written down before the value of y (or the other variable). Thus, it is very important to remember that the ordered pairs (2, 1) and (1, 2) do not represent the same solution for an equation, because the ordered pair (2, 1) means that $x = 2$ and $y = 1$, but the ordered pair (1, 2) means that $x = 1$ and $y = 2$.

Sometimes, we are given the first or second value in an ordered pair and are asked to complete the pair that satisfies a given equation.

Example 1

Does the ordered pair (4, 1) satisfy the equation $3x - 13y = -1$?

◆ **Step 1** The ordered pair tells us that the value of $x = 4$ and that of $y = 1$. Insert these values into the given equation and solve.

$$3x - 13y = -1$$

$$3(4) - 13(1) = -1$$

$$12 - 13 = -1$$

$$-1 = -1$$

The ordered pair (4, 1) satisfies the equation.

Example 2

Complete the ordered pair (5, y) for the equation $y = -3x + 9$.

◆ **Step 1** We know that $x = 5$. Insert this value into the equation and solve for y.

$$y = -3x + 9$$

$$y = -3(5) + 9$$

$$y = -15 + 9$$

$$y = -6$$

The ordered pair is (5, -6).

Example 3

Complete the ordered pairs for the equation $y = 5x + 3$.

a. $(-1, y)$

b. $(x, 23)$

c. $(0, y)$

◆ **Step 1**   a. Insert $x = -1$ into the equation and solve for y.

$y = 5x + 3$

$y = 5(-1) + 3$

$y = -5 + 3$

$y = -2$

The first ordered pair is $(-1, -2)$

◆ **Step 2**   b. Insert $y = 23$ into the equation and solve for x.

$y \quad = 5x + 3$

$23 \quad = 5x + 3$

$23 - 3 = 5x + 3 - 3$

$20 \quad = 5x$

$\dfrac{20}{5} \quad = \dfrac{5x}{5}$

$4 \quad = x$

The second ordered pair is $(4, 23)$

◆ **Step 3**   c. Let $x = 0$ and solve for y.

$y = 5x + 3$

$y = 5(0) + 3$

$y = 0 + 3$

$y = 3$

The third ordered pair is $(0, 3)$.

x	y
−1	−2
4	23
0	3

Figure 5.1: Vertical Table of Values

x	−1	4	0
y	−2	23	3

Figure 5.2: Horizontal Table of Values

In example 3, we found several solutions for the given equation $y = 5x + 3$. We can present these three ordered pairs in a table of values. The table can be presented either vertically or horizontally, as figures 5.1 and 5.2 illustrate.

Example 4

Complete the table of values for the equation $y = 4x + 2$.

x	y
−3	
	0
8	

◆ **Step 1**   Insert the known values from the table above for either *x* or *y* and solve.

Let $x = -3$.

$y = 4x + 2$

$y = 4(-3) + 2$

$y = -12 + 2$

$y = -10$

◆ **Step 2**   Let $y = 0$.

$$y \quad = 4x + 2$$
$$0 \quad = 4x + 2$$
$$4x + 2 \quad = 0$$
$$4x + 2 - 2 = 0 - 2$$
$$4x \quad = -2$$
$$\frac{4x}{4} \quad = \frac{-2}{4}$$
$$x \quad = -\frac{1}{2}$$

◆ **Step 3**   Let $x = 8$.

$$y = 4x + 2$$

$$y = 4(8) + 2$$

$$y = 32 + 2$$

$$y = 34$$

◆ **Step 4**   Complete the table.

x	y
-3	-10
$-\dfrac{1}{2}$	0
8	34

5.1 Graphing Linear Equations in Two Variables

Figure 5.3 shows a coordinate system that consists of two number lines, one displayed horizontally and the other vertically. The horizontal line is called the x-axis, and the vertical line is called the y-axis. The origin, whose coordinates are $(0, 0)$, is the point at which the x-axis and y-axis meet. Each ordered pair corresponds to a point in the coordinate system. When we plot ordered pairs, the numbers of each pair become the coordinates of the point.

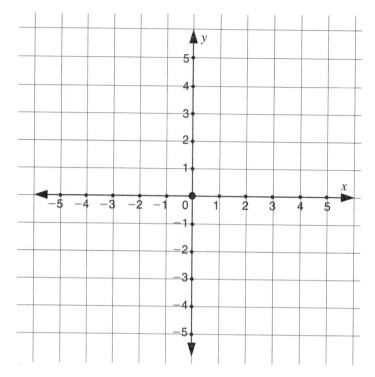

Figure 5.3: A Rectangular Coordinate System

How do we plot the ordered pair (3, 4)? Remember that the first number represents the value of *x,* and the second number represents the value of *y.* Starting at the origin (0, 0), illustrated by the large dot in figure 5.3, go toward the right along the *x*-axis until you reach 3. Then, from this point, go up the *y*-axis until you reach 4 (see fig. 5.4). Place a dot to mark the point whose coordinates are (3, 4).

Example 5

Plot the ordered pairs: (−2, −3) and (−2, 3)

◆ **Step 1**   From the origin (0, 0), go toward the left along the *x*-axis to −2, and then down along the *y*-axis to −3.

◆ **Step 2**   For the second ordered pair, go toward the left along the *x*-axis to −2, and then up along the *y*-axis to 3 (see fig. 5.5).

Now that we understand how to plot ordered pairs that satisfy an equation, we can illustrate this equation by drawing a graph. Suppose we have an equation

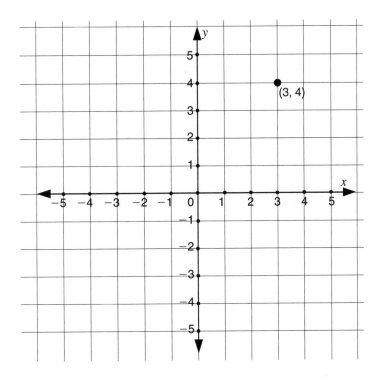

Figure 5.4: Plotting the Ordered Pair (3, 4)

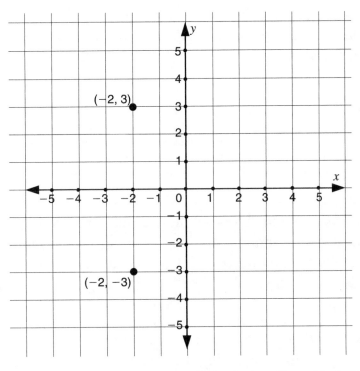

Figure 5.5: Plotting the Ordered Pairs (−2, −3) and (−2, 3)

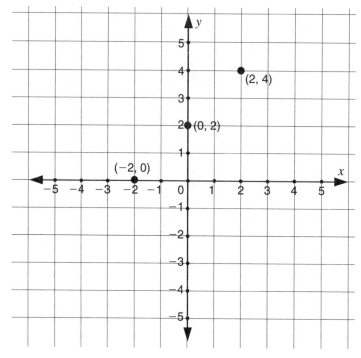

Figure 5.6: Plotting the Ordered Pairs (0, 2), (−2, 0), (2, 4)

$y = x + 2$, and the incomplete ordered pairs $(0, y)$, $(x, 0)$, and $(2, y)$. We can use this information to complete a table of values, plot the points, and draw the graph (see fig 5.6). Here is the completed table of values for the equation $y = x + 2$.

x	0	−2	2
y	2	0	4

Figure 5.7 shows that when we draw a line through the plotted points, we find they are located on a straight line whose two arrowheads indicate that the line extends indefinitely in both directions. Thus, we can state that the line or graph of any linear equation in two variables is a straight line, and every point on that line satisfies the equation.

Suppose we are asked to graph the equation $y = -x + 3$ but are not provided with any information regarding the graph's coordinates. We can still create a table of values by simply letting $x = 0$ and solving for y and then letting $y = 0$

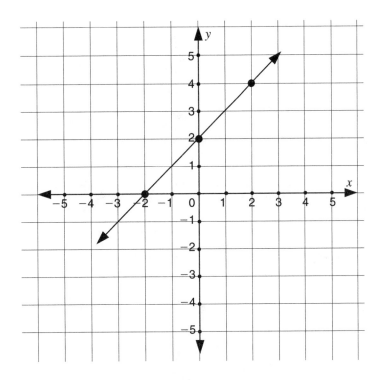

Figure 5.7: Graphing the Equation $y = x + 2$

and solving for x. Although we need only two points to draw a graph, it's always a good idea to have a third point to make sure they are all in a line. (If they are not, that means at least one of the points is incorrect. This is a good check of your math.) How do we find the third point? We assign some other number to either x or y and then solve.

Example 6

Graph the equation: $y = -x + 3$

◆ **Step 1**   Construct a table of values by letting $x = 0$ and solving for y; by letting $y = 0$ and solving for x; and by letting $x = 1$ and solving again for y.

x	0	3	1
y	3	0	2

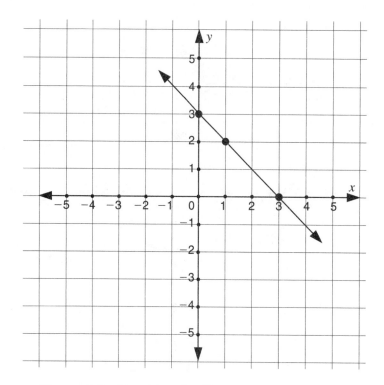

Figure 5.8: Graphing the Equation $y = -x + 3$

◆ **Step 2**   Plot the points, and draw a line through them (see fig. 5.8).

Graphing Linear Equations of the Type $y = mx$

Some linear equations are presented in the form $ax + by = 0$, where both a and b are real numbers. Equations of this type may also be expressed as $y = mx$, where $m = -\frac{a}{b}$, so that $3x + y = 0$ can be written as $y = -3x$. If $x = 0$, then we can see that $y = 0$, too. Similarly, if $y = 0$, then x is also equal to 0. Thus, our first two ordered pairs would be (0, 0) and (0, 0). We cannot draw a graph with only these coordinates, so we need to try other values for both x and y (see example 7).

Example 7

Graph the equation: $2x - y = 0$

◆ **Step 1**   Let $x = 1$ and $y = 4$ for the first two points, and then let $x = -1$ for the third point.

◆ **Step 2**   Compile a table of values.

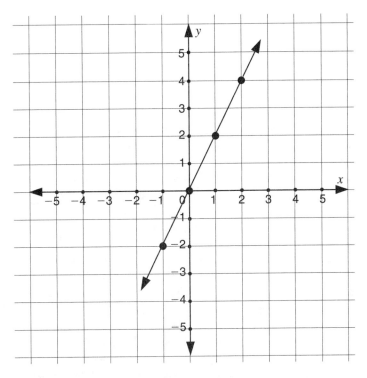

Figure 5.9: Graphing the Equation $2x - y = 0$

x	1	2	-1
y	2	4	-2

◆ **Step 3**   Plot the points and draw a line through them (see fig. 5.9).

Notice that the graph of the equation $2x - y = 0$ passed through the origin. This is true for all linear equations of the form $ax + by = 0$ or $y = mx$.

Graphing Linear Equations of the Type $x = k$

The equation $x = 4$ can also be expressed as $x + 0y = 4$. No matter which value we assign to y in this equation, x always equals 4. We write this type of equation as $x = k$, where k is a constant number.

Example 8

Graph the equation: $x = 4$

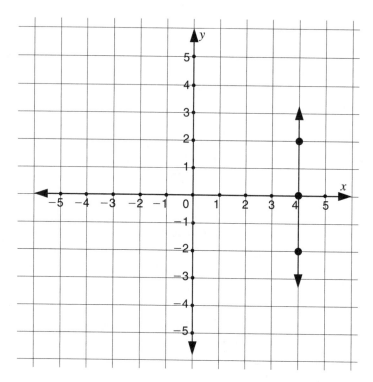

Figure 5.10: Graphing the Equation $x = 4$

◆ **Step 1**   Remember that x must equal 4. Choose any value for y to compile a table of values.

x	4	4	4
y	-2	0	2

◆ **Step 2**   Plot the points and draw the graph (see fig. 5.10).

As figure 5.10 illustrates, the graph of an equation $x = k$ is a vertical line.

Graphing Linear Equations of the Type $y = k$

Similarly, the equation $y = 3$ can be written as $0x + y = 3$. Again, no matter which number we choose for x, y always equals 3 in this equation. This type of equation is expressed as $y = k$, where k is a constant number.

Example 9

Graph the equation: $y = 3$

◆ **Step 1**   Remember that y must equal 3. Choose any value for x to complete a table of values.

x	-2	1	3
y	3	3	3

◆ **Step 2**   Plot the points and draw the graph (see fig. 5.11).

Figure 5.11 illustrates that the graph of the equation $y = k$ is a horizontal line.

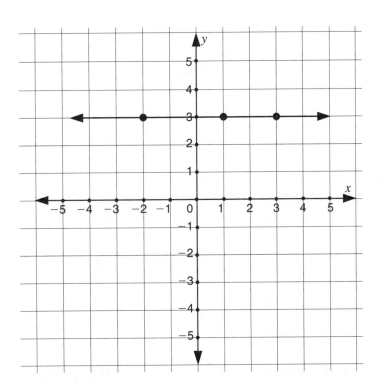

Figure 5.11: Graphing the Equation $y = 3$

5.2 The Distance Between Two Points

In this section, we learn how to calculate the distance between two points. We know that if the two points are located on a vertical line, they have identical x coordinates; and if the points are positioned on a horizontal line, their y coordinates are the same. How do we find the distance between the points shown in figure 5.12?

When points have identical x coordinates, we subtract the value of the first y coordinate from the second y coordinate. If the result is a negative number, use the absolute value of this number $|y_2 - y_1|$. What are the coordinates of the two points shown in figure 5.12? $(x_1, y_1) = (3, 3)$ and $(x_1, y_2) = (3, -3)$. To find the distance between the two points, perform the following operation, where $y_1 = 3$ and $y_2 = -3$:

$$|y_2 - y_1| =$$
$$|-3 - (3)| =$$
$$|-3 - 3| =$$
$$|-6| = 6$$

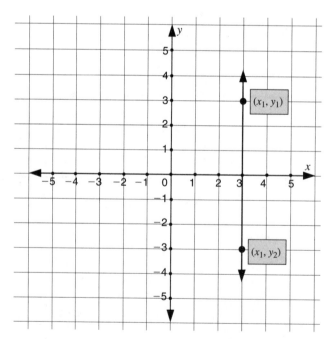

Figure 5.12: Finding the Distance Between Two Points on a Vertical Line

The distance between the two points is 6 units.

Example 10

Find the distance between the points shown in figure 5.13.

◆ **Step 1**   When the points have identical *y* coordinates, we subtract the value of the first *x* coordinate from the second *x* coordinate. If the result is a negative number, use the absolute value of the number $|x_2 - x_1|$.

◆ **Step 2**   Determine the coordinates of the two points shown in figure 5.13. They are $(x_1, y_1) = (-3, 2)$ and $(x_2, y_1) = (3, 2)$.

◆ **Step 3**   To find the distance between the two points, perform the absolute value operation where $x_1 = -3$, and $x_2 = 3$.

$$|x_2 - x_1| =$$

$$|3 - (-3)| =$$

$$|3 + 3| =$$

$$|6| = 6$$

The distance between the two points is 6 units.

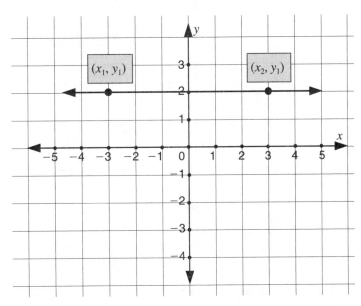

Figure 5.13: Finding the Distance Between Two Points on a Horizontal Line

The Pythagorean Theorem

The majority of the equations that we have graphed so far are straight lines located at various angles from both the x and y axes (the plural form of *axis*). Figure 5.14 illustrates the graph of the equation $y = x + 1$ with two points $(x_1, y_1) = (0, 1)$ and $(x_2, y_2) = (3, 4)$.

As figure 5.14 shows, we can draw a vertical line downward from point (x_2, y_2) until it meets a horizontal line drawn across from point (x_1, y_1). We can label the point where the two dotted lines meet (x_2, y_1) or $(3, 1)$. The three line segments (the diagonal one and the two dotted ones) form a right triangle. Using the Pythagorean theorem, we can calculate the length of one side of a triangle if we know the lengths of the other two sides. Figure 5.15 shows a right triangle with sides a, b, and c, and angles A, B, and C. The side c opposite the right angle C is called the hypotenuse. The hypotenuse is the longest side, and the other two sides are called the legs.

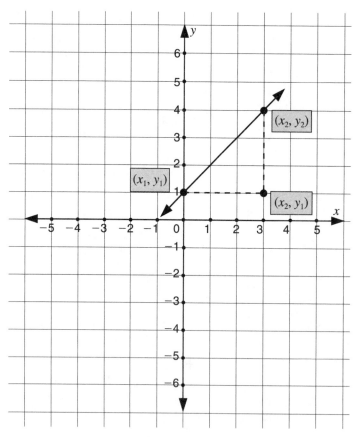

Figure 5.14: The Pythagorean Theorem and the Distance Between Two Points

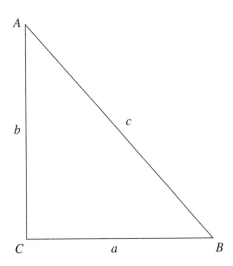

Figure 5.15: A Right Triangle

The Pythagorean theorem states that $a^2 + b^2 = c^2$ for all right triangles. If side $a = 3$ units and side $b = 4$ units, we can calculate the length in units of side c by using the Pythagorean formula:

$$a^2 + b^2 = c^2$$
$$3^2 + 4^2 = c^2$$
$$9 + 16 = c^2$$
$$25 = c^2$$
$$\sqrt{25} = \sqrt{c^2}$$
$$5 = c$$

The length of side c is 5 units.

With this knowledge, we can now find the distance between the two points in figure 5.14 as shown in example 11.

Example 11

Find the distance between the two large points in figure 5.14.

◆ **Step 1** Draw a diagram that illustrates the problem (fig. 5.16).

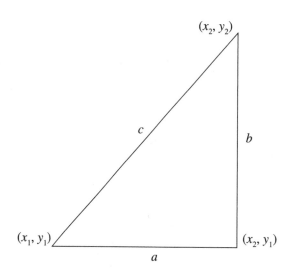

Figure 5.16: Diagram for Distance Between Points

◆ **Step 2**   Find the distance between points (x_1, y_1) and (x_2, y_1). To do this
we subtract x_1 from x_2. Figure 5.14 shows that $x_1 = 0$ and $x_2 = 3$.
Now perform the operation $\lvert x_2 - x_1 \rvert$.

$\lvert 3 - 0 \rvert =$

$\lvert 3 \rvert =$

3

Thus, side $a = 3$ units.

◆ **Step 3**   Find the distance between points (x_2, y_2) and (x_2, y_1) shown in the
diagram as side b. To do this, we subtract y_1 from y_2. The figure
shows that $y_1 = 1$ and $y_2 = 4$. Perform the operation $\lvert y_2 - y_1 \rvert$.

$\lvert 4 - (1) \rvert =$

$\lvert 4 - 1 \rvert \quad =$

$\lvert 3 \rvert \qquad =$

3

Side $b = 3$ units.

◆ **Step 4**   We know that side $a = 3$ and side $b = 3$, so we can find side c by using the Pythagorean theorem. The result represents the distance between the two large points (0, 1) and (3, 4).

$$a^2 + b^2 = c$$

$$3^2 + 3^2 = c^2$$

$$9 + 9 = c^2$$

$$18 = c^2$$

$$\sqrt{18} = \sqrt{c^2}$$

$$\sqrt{9}\sqrt{2} = 3\sqrt{2} = c$$

Side c $= 3\sqrt{2}$ units

The distance between the two large points in figure 5.14 is $3\sqrt{2}$ units. Although $3\sqrt{2}$ is an irrational number, we can have a sense of its value as being between $3\sqrt{1} = 3$ and $3\sqrt{4} = 3 \times 2 = 6$, using two perfect squares that we know from chapter 1.

The Distance Formula

We can also calculate the distance between two points (x_1, y_1) and (x_2, y_2) by using the distance formula, which is just the Pythagorean formula stated in a different way.

$$d = \sqrt{(x_2 - x_1)^2 + (y_2 - y_1)^2}$$

Example 12

Find the distance between points (x_1, y_1), whose coordinates are $(-3, -2)$, and (x_2, y_2), whose coordinates are $(3, 4)$.

◆ **Step 1**   Use the distance formula $d = \sqrt{(x_2 - x_1)^2 + (y_2 - y_1)^2}$ where $x_2 = 3$, $x_1 = -3$, $y_2 = 4$, and $y_1 = -2$.

$$d = \sqrt{(3-(-3))^2 + (4-(-2))^2}$$

$$d = \sqrt{(3+3)^2 + (4+2)^2}$$

$$d = \sqrt{(6)^2 + (6)^2}$$

$$d = \sqrt{36+36}$$

$$d = \sqrt{72}$$

$$d = \sqrt{36}\sqrt{2}$$

$$d = 6\sqrt{2}$$

The distance between the two points is $6\sqrt{2}$ units.

5.3 The Midpoint

In the previous section, we learned how to find the distance between two points on a line. In this section, we will work with a line segment, which is the part of a line between two points, called endpoints. We will discover here how to calculate the midpoint of a line segment, which is located halfway between the two endpoints (see fig. 5.17). To find the coordinates of the midpoint of a line segment, we use the midpoint (M) formula, where (x_1, y_1) and (x_2, y_2) are the endpoints.

$$M = \left(\frac{x_1 + x_2}{2}, \frac{y_1 + y_2}{2} \right)$$

Example 13

Find the midpoint of the line segment joining points (x_1, y_1) and (x_2, y_2) in figure 5.17.

♦ **Step 1**   Let $(x_1, y_1) = (0, 1)$ and $(x_2, y_2) = (3, 4)$.

♦ **Step 2**   Use the midpoint formula, where $x_1 = 0$; $x_2 = 3$; $y_1 = 1$; $y_2 = 4$, and $M = $ midpoint.

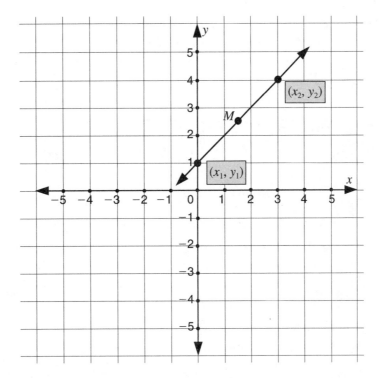

Figure 5.17: A Graph Showing the Midpoint of a Line Segment

$$M = \left(\frac{x_1 + x_2}{2}, \frac{y_1 + y_2}{2} \right)$$

$$M = \left(\frac{0 + 3}{2}, \frac{1 + 4}{2} \right)$$

$$M = \left(\frac{3}{2}, \frac{5}{2} \right)$$

The midpoint coordinates are $\left(\frac{3}{2}, \frac{5}{2} \right)$.

5.4 The Slope of a Line

The steepness of a line is known as its slope (designated by m). We measure the slope of a line by using the following formula:

$$m = \frac{y_2 - y_1}{x_2 - x_1}, \text{ where } x_2 \neq x_1$$

The vertical change $(y_2 - y_1)$ is known as the rise, and the horizontal change $(x_2 - x_1)$ is called the run (see fig. 5.18).

Example 14

Find the slope of the line passing through points (x_1, y_1) and (x_2, y_2) in figure 5.18.

◆ **Step 1**   The ordered pairs are (0, 1) and (3, 4).

◆ **Step 2**   Use the formula $m = \frac{y_2 - y_1}{x_2 - x_1}$, where $x_1 = 0$; $x_2 = 3$; $y_1 = 1$; and $y_2 = 4$.

$$m = \frac{4 - 1}{3 - 0}$$

$$m = \frac{3}{3}$$

$$m = 1$$

The slope of the line is 1.

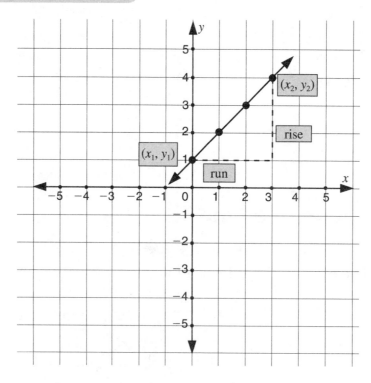

Figure 5.18: The Rise and Run of a Slope

Example 15

Find the slope of the line passing through points $(-1, 5)$ and $(1, 1)$.

◆ **Step 1**   Use the formula $m = \frac{y_2 - y_1}{x_2 - x_1}$, where $x_1 = -1$; $x_2 = 1$; $y_1 = 5$; and $y_2 = 1$.

$$m = \frac{1 - (5)}{1 - (-1)}$$

$$m = \frac{-4}{2}$$

$$m = -2$$

The slope of the line is -2.

There are four important facts to remember about slopes:

- A line with positive slope rises from left to right.

- A line with negative slope falls from left to right.

- The slope of a vertical line is undefined.

- The slope of a horizontal line equals zero.

Finding the Slope of a Line from Its Equation

It is easy to find the slope of a line from its equation. Rewrite the equation as $y = mx + b$ by solving the equation for y. The coefficient of x gives us the slope m, and b is a number. We will discuss the usefulness of the equation $y = mx + b$ in section 5.6.

Example 16

Find the slope of the line that represents the equation $-6x + 4y = 4$.

◆ **Step 1**   Solve for y.

$$-6x + 4y \quad = 4$$

$$6x - 6x + 4y = 4 + 6x$$

$$4y \quad\quad = 4 + 6x$$

$$\frac{4y}{4} \quad\quad = \frac{4}{4} + \frac{6x}{4}$$

$$y \quad\quad = 1 + \frac{6x}{4}$$

$$y \quad\quad = 1 + \frac{3}{2}x$$

◆ **Step 2**   Rearrange the equation.

$$y = \frac{3}{2}x + 1$$

◆ **Step 3**   Note that slope m is the coefficient of x.

$$m = \frac{3}{2} = \text{slope}$$

5.5 The *x*-Intercept and the *y*-Intercept

Figure 5.19 shows the graph of the equation $y = -2x + 3$ with two points $(-1, 5)$ and $(1, 1)$.

Notice that the straight line crosses, or intercepts, both the *x*-axis and the *y*-axis. The point where the graph crosses the *x*-axis is called the *x*-intercept (note that $y = 0$ at that point, because it is right on the *x*-axis). By looking at figure 5.19, we can see that the coordinates of that point are $\left(\frac{3}{2}, 0\right)$. The point where the graph crosses the *y*-axis is known as the *y*-intercept (and similarly, $x = 0$ there, because it is right on the *y*-axis). The figure shows that its coordinates are $(0, 3)$. Linear equations can be graphed if we know both the *x*-intercept and the *y*-intercept. To find the *x*-intercept, we let $y = 0$ in our given equation and solve for x. Similarly, we find the *y*-intercept by letting $x = 0$ and solving for y.

Example 17

Given the equation $3x + y = 3$, find the *x*-intercept and the *y*-intercept.

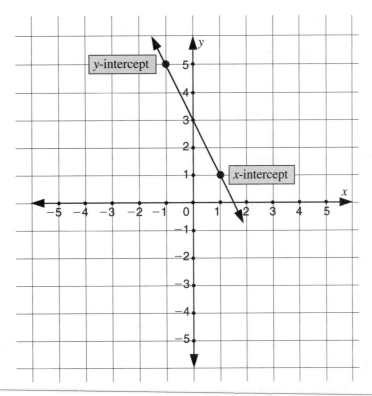

Figure 5.19: The *x*-Intercept and the *y*-Intercept

◆ **Step 1**   To find the *x*-intercept, let $y = 0$, and solve for *x*.

$$3x + y = 3$$
$$3x + 0 = 3$$
$$3x = 3$$
$$\frac{3x}{3} = \frac{3}{3}$$
$$x = 1$$

◆ **Step 2**   To find the *y*-intercept, let $x = 0$, and solve for *y*.

$$3x + y = 3$$
$$3(0) + y = 3$$
$$0 + y = 3$$
$$y = 3$$

◆ **Step 3**   Write down the x-intercept and the y-intercept as ordered pairs.

> The x-intercept is (1, 0), and the y-intercept is (0, 3).

Finally, there are two important facts to remember about intercepts:

- The second coordinate of the x-intercept is always zero (0).

- The first coordinate of the y-intercept is always zero (0).

5.6 The Slope-Intercept Equation

We already know that the coefficient of x in the equation $y = mx + b$ gives us the slope of a line. Furthermore, we learned that the first coordinate of the y-intercept is always 0. This knowledge helps us to understand the slope-intercept equation, which allows us to find the slope of a line and its y-intercept. The slope-intercept equation, where m (the coefficient of x) is the slope of a line, and b represents the y-intercept, whose coordinates can be expressed as $(0, b)$:

$$y = mx + b$$

Example 18

> Find the slope and y-intercept of the line whose equation is $y = 2x + 1$.

◆ **Step 1**   Make sure that the equation is written in slope-intercept form: $y = mx + b$.

◆ **Step 2**   Find the slope from the equation. Since slope m is the coefficient of x, $m = 2$.

◆ **Step 3**   Determine the y-intercept. We know that the first coordinate of the y-intercept is always 0, and its second coordinate is b. In this equation $b = 1$, so the y-intercept is (0, 1).

> Thus, given the equation $y = 2x + 1$, the slope is 2, and the y-intercept is the ordered pair (0, 1).

Example 19

Find the slope and *y*-intercept of the line whose equation is $4x - 3y = -9$.

◆ **Step 1** Rewrite the equation in slope-intercept form, by solving for *y*.

$$4x - 3y = -9$$

$$4x - 3y - 4x = -9 - 4x$$

$$-3y = -9 - 4x$$

$$-3y = -4x - 9$$

$$\frac{-3y}{-3} = \frac{-4x}{-3} + \frac{-9}{-3}$$

$$y = \frac{4}{3}x + 3$$

◆ **Step 2** The slope *m* equals the coefficient of *x*.

$$m = \frac{4}{3}$$

◆ **Step 3** Determine the *y*-intercept. We know that the first coordinate of *y* is always 0 and its second coordinate equals *b* in the slope-intercept formula.

Since $b = 3$ in this problem, the *y*-intercept is (0, 3).

5.7 The Point-Slope Equation

In this section, we learn how to graph and write the equation of a line when we know the slope of the line and any point through which the line passes.

Example 20

Graph the line with slope $m = \frac{1}{2}$ passing through point $(-4, 2)$. Then identify the coordinates of a second point on the line.

◆ **Step 1**   Plot the given point $(-4, 2)$ (see fig. 5.20).

◆ **Step 2**   From this point, go up 1 unit (rise) and then go 2 units to the right (run), since slope $m = \frac{1}{2}$ (positive) to find a second point.

◆ **Step 3**   Write down the coordinates of the second point. They are $(-2, 3)$.

◆ **Step 4**   Graph the line.

We can also write an equation of a line given its slope and any point on the line. To do this, we use the point-slope equation, where (x, y) represents any point on the line, m is the slope of the line, and (x_1, y_1) are the coordinates of a given point.

$$y - y_1 = m(x - x_1)$$

This is a variation of the equation for the slope of a line, given in section 5.4.

Example 21

For a line with slope $m = -2$ passing through point $(3, -10)$, write an equation in point-slope form. Also write it in slope-intercept form.

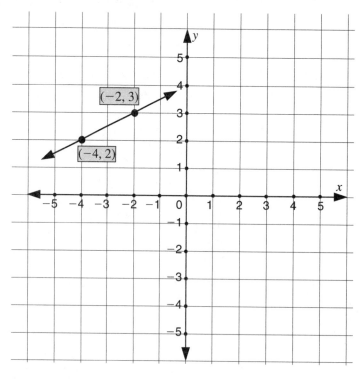

Figure 5.20: Graphing the Line with Slope $m = \frac{1}{2}$ Passing Through Point $(-4, 2)$

◆ **Step 1** Use the equation $y - y_1 = m(x - x_1)$, where $y_1 = -10$; $x_1 = 3$; and $m = -2$.

$y - (-10) = -2(x - 3)$ is point-slope form.

$y + 10 \quad = -2x + 6$

$y \qquad = -2x - 4$ is slope-intercept form.

5.8 Graphing Linear Inequalities in Two Variables

We will conclude this chapter by learning how to graph linear inequalities in two variables.

Example 22

Graph the inequality: $2x + 3y \geq -9$

◆ **Step 1** *Temporarily* remove the inequality sign and replace it with an equal sign. Solve for y in the resulting equation.

$$2x + 3y \quad = -9$$
$$3y + 2x - 2x = -9 - 2x$$
$$3y \qquad = -2x - 9$$
$$\frac{3y}{3} \qquad = \frac{-2x}{3} - \frac{9}{3}$$
$$y \qquad = \frac{-2x}{3} - 3$$

The equation is now in the form of a slope-intercept equation.

◆ **Step 2** Graph the equation, using information from the slope-intercept equation. Thus, plot the y-intercept $(0, -3)$. The slope $m = -\frac{2}{3}$ is negative, so from the y-intercept, go *down* the y-axis 2 units, and then across to the right 3 units.

◆ **Step 3**   If the inequality contains either the ≤ symbol or the ≥ symbol, draw a solid line connecting the points to show that the ordered pairs that satisfy the "equal to" part of the inequality are *located on the line itself.* (If the inequality contains either the < symbol or the > symbol, draw a dashed line [- - - -] to indicate that points along this line are *not* solutions of the inequality.)

◆ **Step 4**   The line drawn serves as a boundary dividing the plane into two sections. Note the location of the line. The two half planes can be located either *above or below* the line, or *to the right or to the left* of the line. Shade the half plane that contains solutions of the inequality. We know which section to shade by selecting any point that is *not* on the line (called a test point). Insert the coordinates (ordered pair) for that point into the inequality and determine whether the point is a possible solution. If it is, shade the half plane that contains the *test point.* If it is not, shade the other half plane. For example, if a test point is a possible solution and is located on the right side of the boundary line, shade the right side. If it is not, shade the left side of the line (see fig. 5.21). Let's choose point (2, 3). Insert these values for x and y into the original inequality and determine whether the point is a possible solution.

Let $x = 2$ and $y = 3$.

$2x + 3y \geq -9$

Is $2(2) + 3(3) \geq -9$?

Is $4 + 9 \geq -9$?

Is $13 \geq -9$? Yes.

Our selected test point satisfies the inequality, so point (2, 3) is a possible solution.

◆ **Step 5**   Shade the section above the line that contains the point (see fig. 5.22).

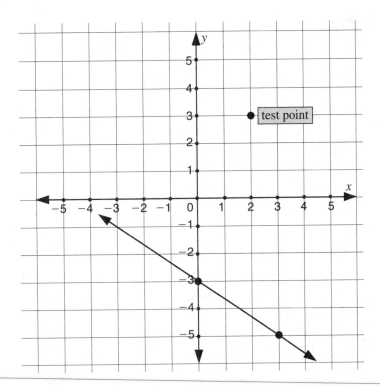

Figure 5.21: Graphing Inequalities—a Test Point

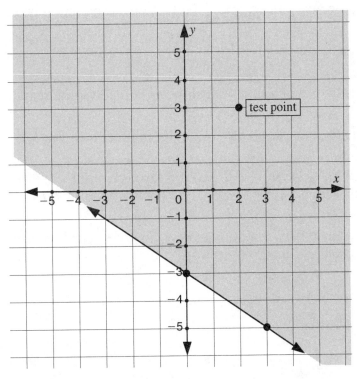

Figure 5.22: Graphing the Inequality $2x + 3y \geq -9$

Problems

1. Does the ordered pair $(5, 3)$ satisfy the equation $3x + 4y = 27$?

2. Complete the ordered pair $(x, 3)$ for the given equation: $4y = 8x + 2(5 - 3)$

3. Complete the table of values for the equation: $3y = 6x + 9$

4. Plot the ordered pair: $(-3, 2)$

5. Graph the equation $3y - x = 6$, given the following information: $(0, y)$; $(x, 1)$; and $(3, y)$.

6. Graph the equation: $2y = x - 4$

7. Find the slope of the line from the equation: $3y = 4x - 7$

8. Given the equation $4x - y = 8$, find the x-intercept and the y-intercept.

9. Find the slope and y-intercept of the line whose equation is $4x + 2y = 8$.

10. Graph the equation: $y = -3x$

11. Write the equation of a line with slope $m = 0$ and y-intercept $(b) = (0, 5)$.

12. Draw a line that has slope $m = -\dfrac{3}{4}$ and y-intercept $(0, 5)$.

13. For a line with slope $m = -2$ passing through point $(3, -10)$, write an equation in point-slope form.

14. Find the distance between points (x_1, y_1) whose coordinates are $(-3, -2)$ and (x_2, y_2) whose coordinates are $(3, 4)$.

15. Graph the inequality: $x \geq 3$

Focus on English

Grammar

Can, Cannot, Can't

Can has different meanings. For example, *I can play tennis* means that I know how to play tennis. *I can come* means that it is possible for me to come. *Can you help me?* means "Please help me." Never use *to* after *can*. For example, *I can dance* not *I can to dance*. We can express the negative form of can in two ways—*cannot* and its contraction, *can't*.

Positive sentences	
I	
You	
He/She/It	can dance.
We	
You	
They	

Negative sentences	
I	
You	
~~He/She/It~~	can't swim.
We	
You	
They	

Positive questions						
Can	I			Yes,	I	can.
	you				you	
	he/she/it	help?			he/she/it	
	we				we	
	you				you	
	they				they	

Negative questions						
Can	I			No,	I	can't.
	you				you	
	he/she/it	help?			he/she/it	
	we				we	
	you				you	
	they				they	

Complete the sentences with *can* or *can't*.

1. I can dance but I _____ swim.

2. _____ I smoke here?

    No, it's a no-smoking café.

3. I _____ speak German but not English.

4. _____ you help me? This box is very heavy.

5. I _____ come tonight. I have too much homework to do.

6. I'm sorry. I _____ remember your name.

Vertically, Horizontally

Vertically and *horizontally* are adverbs. We use adverbs to say how people do things, and adverbs usually go after the verb. For example, *she drives carefully*. We make adverbs from adjectives. Here are the following rules:

Adjective	Adverb
	+ ly
careful	carefully
quick	quickly
horizontal	horizontally
bad	badly
aggressive	aggressively
quiet	quietly
	Consonant + y > ily
healthy	healthily
easy	easily
	Irregular
good	well
fast	fast
hard	hard

Adjective or adverb? Cross out the wrong word.

Example: Her Japanese is perfect/~~perfectly~~.

1. The food was very good/well.

2. Drive careful/carefully!

3. My mother dresses very good/well.

4. The boss likes her because she works hard/hardly.

5. Everything happened very quick/quickly.

6. The table can be presented vertical/vertically.

 ## Improving Mathematical Vocabulary: Spelling

Read the following e-mail and circle the words that are misspelled.

To: [mikesmith@zenmail.com]

From: [daveadams@zenmail.com]

Hi Mike!

I'm studeying for my math test. The test is on graffing. Theirs lots of things we need to know. For example, we need to know what the hypotenus is. Right now, I'm working on the distence formela. Also, our teacher wants us to know various eqwasuns such as the slope-intersept and point-slope eqwasuns. I hope I pass. See you Friday night.

Dave

 ## Dictionary Work

Define the following words:

vertical

horizontal

Chapter 6
Geometry

In chapter 2, we worked with squares and rectangles. In this chapter, we will study other geometric figures, as well as three-dimensional objects.

6.0 Lines and Angles

Earlier, we had the opportunity to draw many lines that passed through points on a rectangular coordinate system. Lines continue indefinitely in both directions, but have no width and no depth. For example, in figure 6.1, line *XY* is located in the plane *A*. We can visualize a plane as a flat surface that has width and length, but no depth.

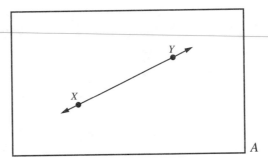

Figure 6.1: Line *XY* in Plane *A*

As stated in chapter 5, a line segment is the part of a line that consists of two delineating points, such as *E* and *F*, and all points in between. Mathematicians use another symbol to indicate a line segment. For example, line segment *EF* can also be written as $\overline{EF}$ Moreover, the midpoint of the line segment usually designated *M*, as in chapter 5, divides the segment into two equal parts (see fig. 6.2).

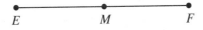

Figure 6.2: Line Segment *EF* with Midpoint *M*

Figure 6.3 illustrates a part of a line called a ray. Point *C* is called the endpoint, which is always named first, followed by one other point on the ray. In figure 6.3, the ray is called ray *CD*, with point *D* identified as the second point.

Figure 6.3: Ray *CD*

An angle is a geometric figure that is formed by two rays that meet at a common endpoint called the vertex of the angle. The symbol for angle is ∠. Figure 6.4 shows ∠*XYZ*. The middle letter (*Y* in this angle) always denotes the vertex. The value of an angle is its measure (*m*). For example, the measure of a right angle, labeled *ABC*, is 90°, or in mathematical symbols $m\angle ABC = 90°$.

Types of Angles

There are four general types of angles, illustrated in figures 6.5 to 6.8:

Acute: An acute angle is greater than zero degrees (0°), but is less than 90°.

Right: A right angle measures exactly 90°.

Obtuse: An obtuse angle is greater than 90°, but is less than 180°.

Straight: A straight angle measures 180°.

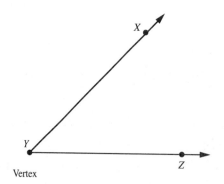

Figure 6.4: The Vertex of an Angle *XYZ*

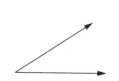

Figure 6.5: An Acute Angle

Figure 6.6: A Right Angle

Figure 6.7: An Obtuse Angle   **Figure 6.8:** A Straight Angle

Two angles are complementary if they add up to 90° (see fig. 6.9), and two angles are supplementary if the sum of the angles is 180° (see fig. 6.10).

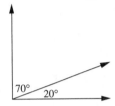

Figure 6.9: Complementary Angles

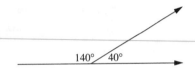

Figure 6.10: Supplementary Angles

Example 1

Find the supplement of a 60° angle.

◆ **Step 1**   If m is the measure of an angle, then its supplement $= 180 - m$.

◆ **Step 2**   Subtract 60 from 180.

$180 - 60 = 120$

The supplement of the 60° angle is 120°.

Example 2

Find the complement of a 25° angle.

◆ **Step 1**   If *m* is the measure of an angle, then its complement = 90 − *m*.

◆ **Step 2**   Subtract 25 from 90.

90 − 25 = 65

The complement of the 25° angle is 65°.

Example 3

Find the measure of an angle whose supplement is ten times the measure of its complement.

◆ **Step 1**   Let *m* equal the angle we are looking for. The supplement of this angle can be represented as 180 − *m*, and the complement of this angle can be written as 90 − *m*. In this problem, the supplement of the angle, 180 − *m*, is ten times its complement, 90 − *m*.

◆ **Step 2**   Write the equation and solve for *m*.

$$180 - m = 10(90 - m)$$
$$180 - m = 900 - 10m$$
$$180 - m + 10m = 900 - 10m + 10m$$
$$180 + 9m = 900$$
$$180 - 180 + 9m = 900 - 180$$
$$9m = 720$$
$$\frac{9m}{9} = \frac{720}{9}$$
$$m = 80$$

The measure of the angle is 80°.

In figure 6.11, we see two intersecting lines *AB* and *CD*. Notice that the formation of these lines creates four angles (∠*AVC*, ∠*CVB*, ∠*BVD*, and ∠*DVA*) that share a common vertex (*V*).

When two angles are next to each other and share a common vertex, we say that they are adjacent. Moving clockwise, ∠*AVC* is adjacent to ∠*CVB*, and ∠*CVB*

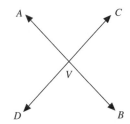

Figure 6.11: Adjacent Angles

is adjacent to ∠BVD. In turn, ∠BVD is adjacent to ∠DVA, and ∠DVA is adjacent to ∠AVC. The sum of adjacent angles located on a straight line is 180°. For example, $m∠AVC + m∠CVB = 180°$.

Figure 6.12 illustrates that when two lines intersect, in addition to the pairs of adjacent angles, two pairs of angles—called vertical angles—are formed. Vertical angles are the angles across from each other when two lines cross.

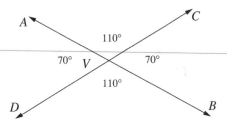

Figure 6.12: Vertical Angles

It is important to remember that vertical angles always have the same measure. In other words, if $m∠AVC$ is 110°, then the measure of its paired vertical angle (in fig. 6.12 ∠BVD) is also equal to 110°. Two angles that have the same measure are called congruent angles.

Example 4

Examine figure 6.13, and then find $m∠BZY$.

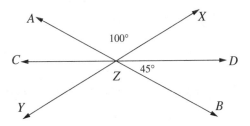

Figure 6.13

◆ **Step 1**   Find ∠*BZY* in figure 6.13. ∠*BZY* and ∠*AZX* are vertical (opposite) angles, so they have the same measure.

Thus, if *m*∠*AZX* = 100°, then *m*∠*BZY* is also 100°.

Example 5

In figure 6.13, find *m*∠*XZD*.

◆ **Step 1**   Look at the figure again and note that ∠*AZX*, ∠*XZD*, and ∠*DZB* together form a straight angle whose measure is 180°. Since *m*∠*AZX* = 100°, and *m*∠*DZB* = 45°, then *m*∠*XZD* =

180 − (100 + 45) =

180 − 145   =

35

m∠*XZD* = 35°

Angles Formed by Two Parallel Lines and a Transversal Line

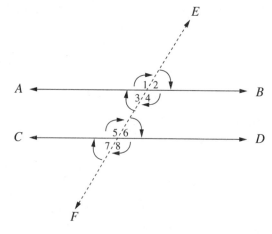

Figure 6.14: Angles Formed by Parallel Lines and a Transversal Line

Figure 6.14 shows a transversal line *EF* intersecting two parallel lines, *AB* and *CD*, in the same plane. Several different angles are formed when a transversal line cuts across two parallel lines:

Alternate interior angles: When a transversal line intersects two parallel lines in the same plane, the vertical angles on opposite sides of the transversal (thus, "alternate") in the area between the parallel lines (thus, "interior") are known as alternate interior angles. These angles have the same measure. In figure 6.14, the two pairs of alternate interior angles are as follows:

$\angle 3$ and $\angle 6$
$\angle 4$ and $\angle 5$

Alternate exterior angles: When a transversal line intersects two parallel lines in the same plane, the angles on opposite sides of the transversal (thus, "alternate") outside the parallel lines (thus, "exterior") are known as alternate exterior angles. These angles have the same measure. In figure 6.14, the two pairs of alternate exterior angles are as follows:

$\angle 1$ and $\angle 8$
$\angle 2$ and $\angle 7$

Corresponding angles: If two parallel lines are intersected by a transversal line, the angles on the same side of the transversal and in the corresponding locations in relation to the parallel lines are called corresponding angles. Notice that one will always be outside the parallel lines (exterior) and the other one inside the lines (interior). These angles have the same measure. Figure 6.14 shows four pairs of corresponding angles.

$\angle 1$ and $\angle 5$
$\angle 2$ and $\angle 6$
$\angle 3$ and $\angle 7$
$\angle 4$ and $\angle 8$

Supplementary interior angles: When two parallel lines are cut by a transversal, the two interior angles on the same side of the transversal are supplementary. That means that the sum of their measures is equal to 180°. Figure 6.14 shows two pairs of supplementary interior angles:

$\angle 3$ and $\angle 5$
$\angle 4$ and $\angle 6$

Supplementary exterior angles: When two parallel lines are cut by a transversal, the two exterior angles on the same side of the transversal are also supplementary. Figure 6.14 shows two pairs of supplementary exterior angles:

$\angle 1$ and $\angle 7$
$\angle 2$ and $\angle 8$

Example 6

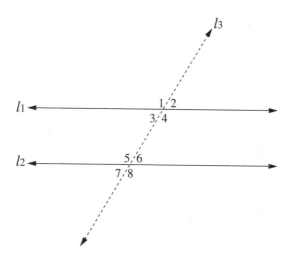

Figure 6.15

Figure 6.15 shows two parallel lines l_1 and l_2, cut by the transversal line l_3. What is the measure of $\angle 6$ if $m\angle 1 = 100°$?

◆ **Step 1**   Angles 1 and 2 together form a straight angle whose measure = 180°. Thus, if $m\angle 1 = 100°$, then $m\angle 2 = 80°$.

◆ **Step 2**   Since $\angle 2$ and $\angle 6$ are corresponding angles, they have the same measure.

Thus, $m\angle 6 = 80°$.

6.1 Triangles

In this section, we examine various types of triangles (three-sided figures) and how to work with their interior angles. Note that triangles are named by their vertices. The triangle below is $\triangle ABC$. It could also be called $\triangle BCA$ or $\triangle CAB$.

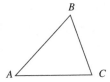

Acute triangle: An acute triangle is formed by three acute angles. An acute angle is less that 90°.

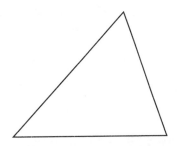

Figure 6.16: An Acute Triangle

Obtuse triangle: An obtuse triangle has one obtuse angle. An obtuse angle is greater than 90° but less than 180°.

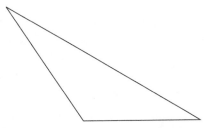

Figure 6.17: An Obtuse Triangle

Right triangle: A right triangle has one right angle, whose measure is 90°. The longest side opposite the right angle is called the hypotenuse.

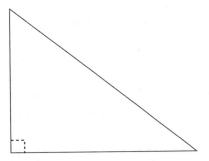

Figure 6.18: A Right Triangle

Equilateral triangle: An equilateral triangle is one whose three sides are the same length. The three angles are also equal, so sometimes this is called an equiangular triangle. Each angle is 60°.

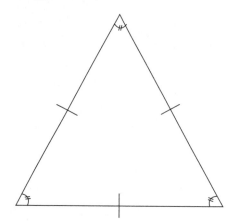

Figure 6.19: An Equilateral Triangle

Isosceles triangle: An isosceles triangle has two sides of equal length. The two angles at the base (the third side) of the triangle are equal.

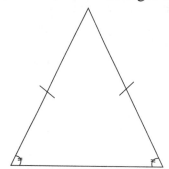

Figure 6.20: An Isosceles Triangle

Scalene triangle: A scalene triangle has three sides of different lengths. Furthermore, all of its angles are different.

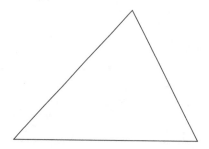

Figure 6.21: A Scalene Triangle

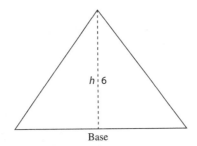

Figure 6.22: Triangle with Height *h*

The following important facts are true for all triangles:

- The sum of the three angles of a triangle = 180°.

- The perimeter formula for triangles is $P = a + b + c$ where *a*, *b*, and c are the three sides of the triangle.

- The area formula for triangles is $A = \frac{1}{2}bh$, where *b* is the length of the triangle's base and *h* is the triangle's height. The height of a triangle does not have to be the length of one of its sides. It is actually the vertical distance from the vertex across from the base to the base.

Example 7

Figure 6.22 shows a triangle with height *h* = 6 units and area = 24 square units. What is the length of the base?

◆ **Step 1** Use the formula $A = \frac{1}{2}bh$, where *A* = 24, and *h* = 6. Solve for *b*.

$$24 = \frac{1}{2}b(6)$$
$$24 = 3b$$
$$\frac{24}{3} = \frac{3}{3}b$$
$$8 = b$$

The base of the triangle is 8 units.

Example 8

Find the perimeter of a triangle with sides *a* = 5 units, *b* = 6 units, and *c* = 7 units.

◆ **Step 1**   Use the perimeter formula of a triangle $P = a + b + c$. We don't need to know the height of the triangle to solve this problem.

◆ **Step 2**   Add the sides a, b, and c.

$5 + 6 + 7 =$

$11 + 7 \quad =$

18 units

Example 9

The perimeter of an equilateral triangle is 24 inches. Find the length of each side.

◆ **Step 1**   We know that an equilateral triangle has three sides of equal length. Thus, to find the length of each side, divide the perimeter by 3.

$$\frac{24}{3} = 8$$

The length of each side is 8 inches.

Example 10

Figure 6.23 shows $\triangle DBC$ within a larger $\triangle ABC$. Find the measure of $\angle 1$ and $\angle 2$.

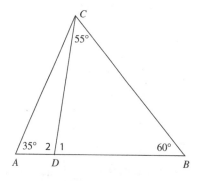

Figure 6.23

◆ **Step 1**   We know that the three angles of a triangle = 180°. If $m\angle BCD =$ 55° and $m\angle DBC = 60°$, then

$m\angle 1 = 180 - (55 + 60)$

$m\angle 1 = 180 - 115$

$m\angle 1 = 65$

> The measure of $\angle 1$ is 65°.

◆ **Step 2**   Angles 1 and 2 together form the straight angle ADB, whose measure is 180°. Since we now know that $m\angle 1 = 65°$, we find $m\angle 2$ by subtracting 65° from 180°.

$180 - 65 = 115$

> The measure of $\angle 2$ is 115°.

Example 11

> Figure 6.24 shows $\triangle ABC$ and $\triangle DBE$, which is an equilateral triangle. Find $m\angle EDB$ and $m\angle DAB$.

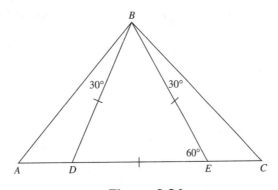

Figure 6.24

◆ **Step 1**   Since $\triangle DBE$ is an equilateral triangle, which has all equal sides and angles, $m\angle EDB = 60°$. Write this on figure 6.24.

◆ **Step 2**   Since ∠*EDB* and ∠*BDA* form the straight angle *ADE,* whose measure is 180°, then *m*∠*BDA* = 180 − 60 = 120°. Write this on the figure.

◆ **Step 3**   If *m*∠*BDA* = 120° and *m*∠*ABD* = 30°, then *m*∠*DAB* =

180 − (120 + 30) =

180 − 150   =

30

Thus, *m*∠*DAB*   = 30°.

6.2 Quadrilaterals

Rectangles, squares, parallelograms, rhombuses, and trapezoids are quadrilaterals, which means they have four sides. This section discusses each of these and their unique properties.

Rectangles

A rectangle is a quadrilateral whose four angles are right angles and whose opposite sides are parallel (see fig. 6.25). Furthermore, the opposite sides of a rectangle are of equal length, and the diagonals are also of equal length.

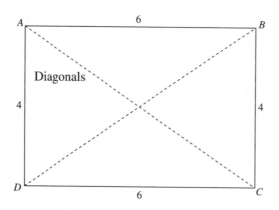

Figure 6.25: A Rectangle

Example 12

Figure 6.26 shows rectangle *ABCD*. What is the measure of ∠1?

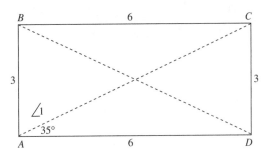

Figure 6.26

◆ **Step 1**   Since figure 6.26 shows a rectangle, we know that $m\angle BAD = 90°$.
If $m\angle CAD = 35°$, then

$m\angle 1 = 90 - 35 = 55$.

Thus, $m\angle 1 = 55°$.

Parallelograms

A parallelogram is a quadrilateral whose opposite sides are parallel and of the same length. Its diagonals bisect each other. Moreover, the opposite angles of a parallelogram are equal in measure. In figure 6.27, *AD* is called the base, and *EB* represents the parallelogram's height (vertical distance between the base and its parallel side). Since the diagonals of a parallelogram bisect each other, $\overline{BF} = \overline{FD}$ and $\overline{AF} = \overline{FC}$.

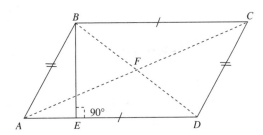

Figure 6.27: A Parallelogram

To find the area of a parallelogram, use the formula $A = bh$, where A refers to the area of the parallelogram, b is the measure of the base, and h is the height.

Example 13

Find the height of a parallelogram whose base is 7 inches and whose area is 21 square inches.

◆ **Step 1**   Use the formula $A = bh$, where $A = 21$ and $b = 7$.

$$21 = 7(h)$$

$$\frac{21}{7} = \frac{7h}{7}$$
$$3 = h$$

The height of the parallelogram is 3 inches.

To find the perimeter of a parallelogram, use the formula $P = 2a + 2b$, where $a =$ the side of a parallelogram and $b =$ the base.

Example 14

Figure 6.28 shows a parallelogram with side $a = 2$ feet and base $b = 4$ feet. Find the perimeter of the parallelogram.

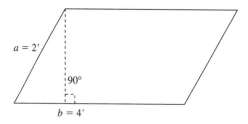

Figure 6.28

◆ **Step 1**   Use the formula $P = 2a + 2b$, where a is 2 feet and b is 4 feet.

$$P = 2(2) + 2(4)$$

$$P = 4 + 8$$

$P = 12$

The perimeter of the parallelogram is 12 feet.

Example 15

Figure 6.29 is a parallelogram *ABCD*. Find the measure of angle 1.

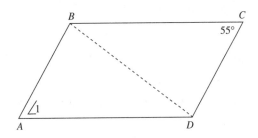

Figure 6.29

◆ **Step 1**   Examine the figure. Since *ABCD* is a parallelogram, its opposite angles have the same measure.

If $m\angle BCD = 55°$, then $m\angle 1$ is also 55°.

Rhombuses

A rhombus (plural: *rhombuses* or *rhombi*) is a quadrilateral whose four sides are of equal length and whose opposite sides are parallel. Furthermore, the opposite angles are equal, the diagonals are perpendicular to each other, and the diagonals bisect the rhombus's angles, or divide them into two equal angles.

Example 16

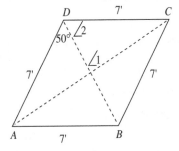

Figure 6.30: A Rhombus

Figure 6.30 is a rhombus. Find the measures of ∠1 and ∠2.

◆ **Step 1**   Since the diagonals of a rhombus are perpendicular, the measure of angle 1 is 90°.

◆ **Step 2**   Diagonal *DB* bisects ∠*ADC* into two equal angles.

Since *m*∠*ADB* = 50°, then *m*∠2 also equals 50°.

Squares

A square is a quadrilateral whose four sides are of the same length and whose opposite sides are parallel. Furthermore, the four angles of a square are right angles. The diagonals are of equal length, are perpendicular to each other, and bisect the angles (see fig. 6.31).

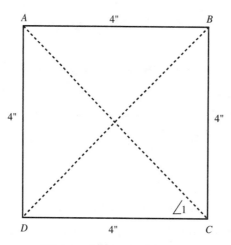

Figure 6.31: A Square

Example 17

Figure 6.31 illustrates a square with side = 4 inches. Find the measure of ∠1.

◆ **Step 1**   Since the figure is a square, *m*∠*BCD* = 90°. We also know that the diagonal bisects ∠*BCD*.

Thus, the measure of ∠1 is $\frac{90}{2} = 45°$.

Trapezoids

A trapezoid is a quadrilateral with only two parallel sides, called bases. The nonparallel sides are known as legs. An isosceles trapezoid is one whose legs are of equal length and whose base angles have the same measure (see fig. 6.32), but not all trapezoids are isosceles.

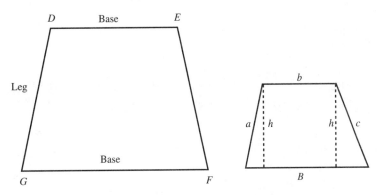

Figure 6.32: A Trapezoid

The following formula, where A is the area of the trapezoid, B and b are the bases, and h is the height, is used to calculate the area of a trapezoid:

$$A = \frac{1}{2}(B + b)h$$

Here, again, the height is the vertical distance between the bases, not the lengths of the legs.

Example 18

Find the area of a trapezoid whose base B = 5 inches, base b = 4 inches, and height h = 6 inches.

◆ **Step 1**   Use the formula $A = \frac{1}{2}(B + b)h$, inserting the known values for B, b, and h.

$A = \frac{1}{2}(5 + 4)6$

$A = \frac{1}{2}(9)6$

$A = \frac{1}{2}(54)$

$A = 27$ square inches

Calculating the perimeter of a trapezoid is straightforward. The formula, where P is the perimeter of the trapezoid, b and B are the two bases, and a and c are the two legs, is as follows:

$$P = a + b + c + B$$

Example 19

Find the length of leg c of a trapezoid whose perimeter is 50 inches, leg $a = 14$ inches, base $b = 8$ inches, and base $B = 16$ inches.

◆ **Step 1**   Use the perimeter formula $P = a + b + c + B$, and solve for c.

50          $= 14 + 8 + c + 16$

50          $= 38 + c$

$50 - 38 = 38 - 38 + c$

12          $= c$

The leg c measures 12 inches.

Example 20

Figure 6.33 shows an isosceles trapezoid with $m\angle 1 = 60°$. Find the measure of $\angle 2$.

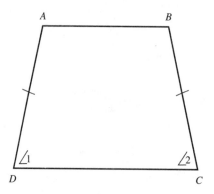

Figure 6.33

◆ **Step 1**   Since the figure is an isosceles trapezoid, the measure of angle 1 is the same as the measure of angle 2.

Thus, $m\angle 2 = 60°$

Example 21

Figure 6.34 shows an isosceles trapezoid with $m\angle 1 = 48°$. Find the measure of $\angle 2$.

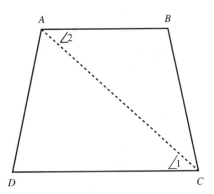

Figure 6.34

◆ **Step 1**   Notice that AB is parallel to DC, so AC is a transversal line that intersects AB and DC. Thus, $\angle 1$ and $\angle 2$ are alternate interior angles, so they have the same measure.

Thus, $m\angle 2 = 48°$.

6.3 Circles

Figure 6.35 shows a circle and some of its various parts. The diameter $\overline{AOE}$ is a line segment that passes through the center, and radius $\overline{OF}$ is a line segment drawn from the center to any point on the circle. Chord $\overline{BD}$ is a line segment joining any two points on the circle, and arc $\overset{\frown}{BC}$ is the part of the circle from point B to point C. If an arc traces half of the circle, as $\overset{\frown}{AFE}$ does here, it is called a semicircle.

To calculate the area of a circle, we use this formula, where the letter r is the radius of the circle and the Greek letter π (*pi*, pronounced "pie") is approximately 3.14, or $\frac{22}{7}$:

$$A = \pi r^2$$

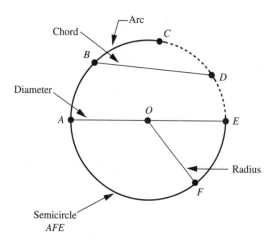

Figure 6.35: A Circle and Its Parts

The value of π is the same value for all circles. It is the ratio of a circle's perimeter (called its circumference) to its diameter.

Example 22

Find the area of a circle with radius = 7 meters.

◆ **Step 1**   Using the formula $A = \pi r^2$, insert the known values and solve for A.

$$A = \frac{22}{7}(7^2)$$

$$A = \frac{22}{7}(49)$$

$$A = 22 \cdot 7$$

$A = 154$ square meters

The diameter of a circle can be found by using the following simple formula, since the diameter is made up of two radii (the plural of radius) placed end to end:

$$d = 2r$$

As figure 6.35 shows, the diameter of a circle is a line that touches the circle twice and passes through the center.

Example 23

If the radius of a circle is 3.5 feet, what is its diameter?

◆ **Step 1**   Use the formula $d = 2r$ and insert the known values.

$d = 2(3.5)$

$d = 7$

The diameter of the circle is 7 feet.

The circumference of a circle can be found using either of the following two formulas:

$$C = 2\pi r$$

$$C = \pi d$$

Example 24

If the circumference of a circle = 88 inches, what is its radius?

◆ **Step 1**   Use the formula $C = 2\pi r$, and insert the known values.

$$88 = 2\left(\frac{22}{7}\right)r$$

$$88 = \frac{44}{7}r$$

$$88\left(\frac{7}{44}\right) = \frac{44}{7}r\left(\frac{7}{44}\right)$$

$$\frac{616}{44} = r$$

$$14 = r$$

The radius is 14 inches.

Circles and Angles

Various angles may be formed within a circle itself, such as central angles and inscribed angles. As figure 6.36 shows, a central angle is one whose vertex is the center of the circle and whose sides are radii.

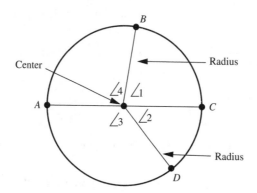

Figure 6.36: Central Angles

It is very important to remember the following: The sum of the measures of the central angles of a circle = 360°. If we examine the central angles shown in figure 6.36, we see that they intercept four arcs of the circle. Angle 1 intercepts arc $\widehat{BC}$; $\angle 2$ intercepts arc $\widehat{CD}$; $\angle 3$ intercepts arc $\widehat{DA}$; and $\angle 4$ intercepts arc $\widehat{AB}$. The measure of each of these arcs in degrees is the same as the measure of each of their respective central angles. Thus, if the measure of $\angle 2 = 60°$, the measure of arc $\widehat{CD}$ is also 60°. Remember, then, that the measure of an arc in degrees is the same as the measure of the central angle that intercepts it, and the measure of the arc of a complete circle is 360°.

Example 25

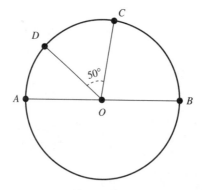

Figure 6.37: A Circle with $m \angle COD = 50°$

Figure 6.37 shows a circle with $m\angle COD = 50°$. What is the measure of arc $\overset{\frown}{CD}$?

◆ **Step 1** Note that $\angle COD$ is a central angle. The $m\angle COD = 50°$.

The measure of its intercepted arc $\overset{\frown}{CD}$ is also 50°.

An inscribed angle is one whose sides are chords of a circle and whose vertex is a point on the circle (see fig. 6.38). In the figure, inscribed $\angle 1$ intercepts arc $\overset{\frown}{BC}$. It is important to know that the measure of an inscribed angle is half the measure of the arc it intercepts.

Example 26

In figure 6.38, if arc $\overset{\frown}{BC}$ measures 70°, find the measure of $\angle 1$.

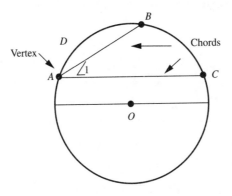

Figure 6.38: An Inscribed Angle

◆ **Step 1** Notice that $\angle 1$ is an inscribed angle. If arc $\overset{\frown}{BC}$ measures 70°, then the measure of $\angle 1$ is half the measure of arc $\overset{\frown}{BC}$.

$$m\angle 1 = \frac{70}{2}$$
$$m\angle 1 = 35$$

The measure of $\angle 1$ is 35°.

Circles and Tangents

A tangent is a line that touches a circle at only one point, called the point of tangency. When a radius meets a point of tangency, it is perpendicular to the tangent. Furthermore, if two tangents meet at a point outside the circle, the tangents are of equal length (see fig. 6.39), in which $\overline{CD} = \overline{ED}$.

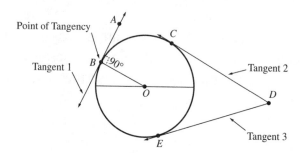

Figure 6.39: Tangents

Finally, the measure of an angle created by a tangent and a chord is half the measure of the arc it intercepts (see fig. 6.40, in which arc $\widehat{BC} = 100°$, but $\angle ABC = 50°$).

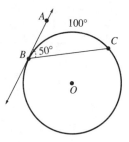

Figure 6.40: A Tangent and a Chord

Example 27

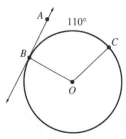

Figure 6.41

Figure 6.41 shows a circle with center *O* and tangent *AB*. What is the measure of angle *ABO*?

◆ **Step 1** $\overline{BO}$ is a radius. We know that when a radius meets a point of tangency, it is perpendicular to the tangent.

Thus, $m\angle ABO$ is 90°.

Example 28

What is the measure of angle *CAB* in figure 6.42?

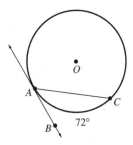

Figure 6.42

◆ **Step 1**   Since $\angle CAB$ is formed by tangent *AB* and chord $\overline{AC}$, its measure is half the measure of the arc $\overset{\frown}{AC}$.

Since, $\overset{\frown}{AC} = 72°$, then $m\angle CAB = \dfrac{72}{2} = 36°$.

6.4 Surface Area and Volume

In this section, we will study three-dimensional objects that occupy space, such as rectangular solids, cubes, and right-circular cylinders.

Rectangular Solids and Cubes

Figure 6.43 shows a rectangular solid. We can find the surface area of the figure by adding the areas of the six faces (sides) and noticing that opposite faces are equal. Thus, we use the following formula, where S = surface area, l = length, w = width, and h = height:

$$S = 2lw + 2wh + 2lh$$

In most problems, the length is given first, followed by the width, and then the height. For example, a packing box may be described by a moving company as 4 feet by 3 feet by 2 feet, which indicates it is 4 feet long, 3 feet wide, and 2 feet high.

Example 29

Imagine that the object in figure 6.43 is a brick measuring 9 inches by 5 inches by 7 inches. What is the brick's surface area?

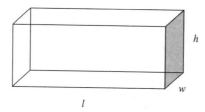

Figure 6.43: A Rectangular Solid

◆ **Step 1** Use the formula $S = 2lw + 2wh + 2lh$ where $l = 9$, $w = 5$, and $h = 7$.

$S = 2(9)(5) + 2(5)(7) + 2(9)(7)$

$S = (18)(5) + (10)(7) + (18)(7)$

$S = 90 + 70 + 126$

$S = 286$ square inches

If we were asked to calculate the volume of the rectangular solid shown in figure 6.43, we use the following formula, which says that volume is the area of one face times the height. V is the volume in cubic units, l is the length of the solid, w is the width, and h is the height.

$$V = lwh$$

Example 30

What is the volume of a brick that measures 9 inches by 5 inches by 3 inches?

◆ **Step 1** Use the formula $V = lwh$ where $l = 9$, $w = 5$, and $h = 3$.

$V = (9)(5)(3)$

$V = 45(3)$

$V = 135$ cubic inches

A cube is a rectangular solid whose length, width, and height are equal (see fig. 6.44).

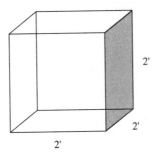

Figure 6.44: A Cube

To find the surface area of a cube, we use this formula, where S is the surface area in square units and s is the length of the side of the cube:

$$S = 6s^2$$

The volume of a cube may be found by using the following formula, $V = lwh$, where $l = w = h = s$. V equals volume in cubic units and s is the length of the side of the cube:

$$V = s^3$$

Example 31

Marcie's car has two red and green dice hanging from the rearview mirror. If the side of each die (the singular of *dice*) measures 2 inches, find the total surface area of the two dice and the total volume of the dice.

◆ **Step 1**   To find the surface area of a die, use the formula $S = 6s^2$, where $s = 2$.

$S = 6(2)^2$

$S = 6(4)$

$S = 24$ square inches

If one die has a surface area of 24 square inches, then both dice together have a total surface area twice that.

The total surface area of the dice is 48 square inches.

◆ **Step 2**   We find the volume of one die by using the formula $V = s^3$ where $s = 2$.

$V = 2^3$

$V = (2)(2)(2)$

$V = (4)(2)$

$V = 8$ cubic inches

If the volume of one die $= 8$ cubic inches, both dice together have a total volume of 2×8 cubic inches $= 16$ cubic inches.

Right-Circular Cylinders

A right-circular cylinder is shown in figure 6.45.

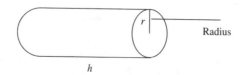

Figure 6.45: A Right-Circular Cylinder

To find the surface area of this object, think of it as a rectangle rolled up with two circles at the ends. The area of a rectangle is length times width. The length is h and the width is the circumference of the circular edge, or $2\pi r$, so the area of the rectangular part is $(2\pi r)h$. For the circles, each has area πr^2, so both have area $2(\pi r^2)$. Thus, the surface area of a right-circular cylinder is shown as follows, where S = surface area in square units, r = the radius of the circular part of the cylinder, $\pi = \frac{22}{7}$ (or approximately 3.14), and h = the height of the cylinder:

$$S = 2\pi rh + 2\pi r^2$$

To calculate the volume of a right-circular cylinder, we use the area of a circular face πr^2 times the height of the cylinder h, where V is the volume in cubic units, $\pi = \frac{22}{7}$ (or approximately 3.14), and h is the height of the cylinder:

$$V = \pi r^2 h$$

Example 32

If the radius of a right-circular cylinder is 7 feet and its height is 14 feet, what is its volume?

◆ **Step 1**   Use the volume formula $V = \pi r^2 h$ where $r = 7$ and $h = 14$.

$V = \dfrac{22}{7}(7)^2(14)$

$V = \dfrac{22}{7}(49)(14)$

$V = \dfrac{22}{\cancel{7}}(^7\cancel{49})(14)$

$V = 22(7)(14)$

$V = 154(14)$

$V = 2{,}156$

The volume of the right-circular cylinder is 2,156 cubic feet.

Problems

1. Find the measure of an angle whose supplement is three times the measure of its complement.

2. In figure 6a, find the measure of $\angle BGE$.

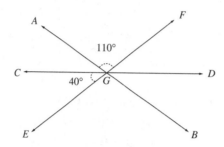

Figure 6a

3. In figure 6b, l_1 is parallel to l_2. Both lines are cut by the transversal l_3. Find the measures of $\angle 6$, $\angle 2$, and $\angle 5$.

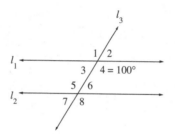

Figure 6b

4. The perimeter of an equilateral triangle is 45 cm. Find the length of one side.

5. Find the measure of angles CDB, BCD, and ACB in figure 6c.

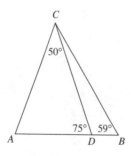

Figure 6c

6. Figure 6d is a rectangle *ABCD*. Find the measure of ∠1.

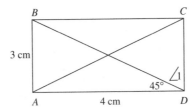

Figure 6d

7. In figure 6d, find the length of $\overline{AC}$.

8. Figure 6e is a rhombus *ABCD*. Find the measures of ∠1 and ∠2.

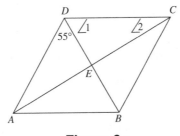

Figure 6e

9. In figure 6e, if $\overline{DE} = 6''$ and $\overline{EC} = 8''$, what is the length of $\overline{CD}$?

10. Figure 6f shows a circle with chord *AB*. If arc $\overset{\frown}{BAC} = 215°$ and $m\angle COD = 55°$, what is the measure of arc $\overset{\frown}{CD}$ and the measure of arc $\overset{\frown}{DB}$?

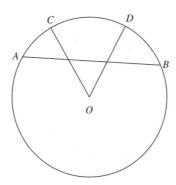

Figure 6f

11. Find the measure of ∠*BAC* in figure 6g.

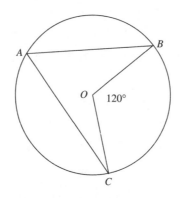

Figure 6g

12. In figure 6h, line *AB* is parallel to line *CD*. What is the corresponding angle to ∠*EGB*?

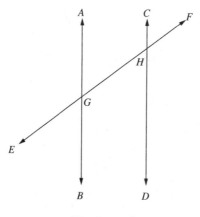

Figure 6h

13. In figure 6i, *ABCD* is a parallelogram. Find the measures of ∠1 and ∠2.

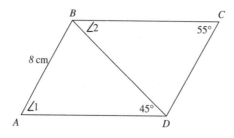

Figure 6i

14. In figure 6i, what is the length of $\overline{CD}$?

15. Fred plans to build a small platform made out of a wooden cube with side = 6 feet. How many square yards of wood does Fred need if he decides to include a base for his platform? (Use the formula $S = 6s^2$.)

Focus on English

Grammar

Draw

Draw is an irregular verb whose past tense is *drew*. We use the past simple tense for actions that have ended. Here are the spelling rules for regular verbs in the past simple.

Infinitive	Past simple	Spelling
to play	played	*add* -ed
to live	lived	*add* -ed
to stop	stopped	*one vowel + one consonant = double consonant*
to study	studied	*consonant* + y > ied

Past Simple Irregular Verbs

Here is a list of irregular verbs in the past simple. The best way to remember them is to read and write in English as much as you can.

Infinitive	Past
to go	went
to see	saw
to have	had
to leave	left
to buy	bought
to drive	drove
to wear	wore
to do	did
to get	got
to come	came
to meet	met
to find	found
to read	read (pronounced *red*)
to speak	spoke
to think	thought
to take	took

It is important to remember that verbs are only irregular in positive sentences. For example, *I saw the movie last night.* In negative sentences we use the regular verb, such as *I didn't see the movie last night.*

I	
You	
He/She/It	didn't *buy* a new car
We	
You	
They	

To, Two, and Too

To, *two*, and *too* sound the same but are spelled differently and have different meanings. For example, *two* is the number 2. *Too* is another word for also, such as *I'm a student in Professor Lin's class too*. *To* can also be a preposition, as in the following example, *I'm going to California this summer.*

Fill in the blanks with either *two, too,* or *to.*

1. The last four digits of my social security number are three, _____, five, six.

2. I'm a dancer _____.

3. Can you come _____ the house tonight?

4. I'm going to France _____.

5. There are _____ keys on the key ring.

 Improving Mathematical Vocabulary: Pronunciation

Underline the stressed syllable or syllables in the following words (for example, <u>ver</u>tex).

1. congruent

2. transversal

3. perpendicular

4. bisect

5. tangent

6. adjacent

Write down a definition of each of the words listed above.

 ## Dictionary Work

Use a dictionary to find out the difference between the words in each pair.

chord	cord
complement	compliment
interior	exterior

Chapter 7
Data Analysis, Logic, and Probability

7.0 Interpreting Graphs and Charts

Standardized math tests often include one or more graphs, figures, or charts that require interpretation or analysis. These problems include the following:

- Bar graphs

- Pie charts

- Line graphs

- Tables

Bar Graphs

A bar graph, shown in figure 7.1, is an effective way to present data for easy comparison.

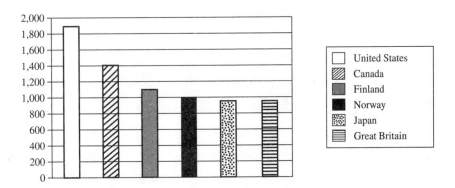

Figure 7.1: 1990 Per Capita Production of Household Garbage (in Pounds)

Figure 7.1 shows the amount of household garbage in pounds that each person ("per capita") produced in 1990 in six countries. Notice that the bars are arranged along the horizontal, or *x*-axis, in the following order: the United States, Canada, Finland, Norway, Japan, and Great Britain. Located along the vertical, or *y*-axis, is the scale divided by a number of tiny horizontal lines, called ticks. The scale ranges from 0 pounds of garbage and continues upward to a maximum of 2,000 pounds. Before you read the scale, it is important to check the interval represented by each tick—in this figure, it is 200 pounds.

How do we interpret the data? We can see at a glance that the taller the bar, the more garbage per capita is produced. This allows us to make quick comparisons between two countries or among several of them.

Example 1

In figure 7.1, which country produced the most garbage per capita in 1990?

◆ **Step 1**   Examine the bar graph and find which bar is the tallest. It is the United States.

Therefore, the United States produced the most garbage per capita in 1990.

Example 2

In figure 7.1, which two countries produced the same amount of garbage per capita in 1990?

◆ **Step 1**   Look at the figure again and find the two bars that are equal in height. The two countries are Japan and Great Britain.

Therefore, Japan and Great Britain produced the same amount of garbage per capita in 1990.

Example 3

In figure 7.1, what is the approximate difference in production between the United States and Finland?

◆ **Step 1** The United States produced approximately 1,900 pounds of garbage per capita and Finland produced approximately 1,100 pounds of garbage per capita.

Thus, the approximate difference is 1,900 − 1,100 = 800 pounds.

Example 4

In figure 7.2, in which month did the paint company sell the most white paint?

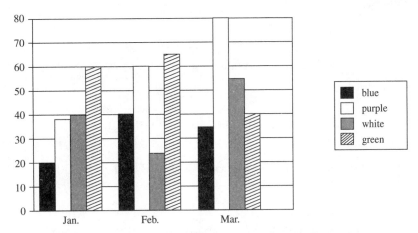

Figure 7.2: Paint Sold (in Thousands of Gallons)

◆ **Step 1** Look at the bars representing white paint sold and find the tallest bar.

◆ **Step 2** Look at the horizontal axis and find the month. It is March.

The paint company sold the most white paint in the month of March.

Example 5

According to figure 7.2, what is the total number of gallons of purple paint sold in the period January through March?

◆ **Step 1**   Study the bar graph to determine how many gallons of purple paint were sold for each month.

January: 38,000

February: 60,000

March: 80,000

◆ **Step 2**   Add the numbers for the months.

The total—178,000 gallons of purple paint—is the amount of purple sold.

Example 6

According to figure 7.2, in which month did the paint company sell the least paint?

◆ **Step 1**   Add the total paint sales for each month.

January paint sales: 20,000 + 38,000 + 40,000 + 60,000 = 158,000 gallons

February paint sales: 40,000 + 60,000 + 25,000 + 65,000 = 190,000 gallons

March paint sales: 35,000 + 80,000 + 55,000 + 40,000 = 210,000 gallons

◆ **Step 2**   Compare the numbers.

The paint company sold the least paint in January.

Pie Charts

We can also display data in a pie chart in which the size of each "slice" represents a certain amount of a type of information. Figure 7.3 displays the amount in dollars of part of a monthly household budget. Each month, $50 is spent on parking, $250 is spent on utilities, $300 is spent on food, and $500 is spent on rent.

Example 7

According to figure 7.3, how much is spent each month on utilities and parking?

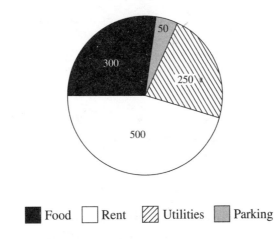

■ Food ☐ Rent ▨ Utilities ▨ Parking

Figure 7.3: Part of a Monthly Household Budget in U.S. Dollars

◆ **Step 1** Examine the pie chart and add the amounts for utilities and parking.

The total cost is $250 + $50 = $300.

Example 8

According to figure 7.3, the cost of food and utilities is what percent of the total monthly expenses?

◆ **Step 1** To find the total monthly expenses, add the amounts represented by each "slice" of the pie chart.

The total monthly expenses = $1,100.

◆ **Step 2**   Calculate the total cost of food and utilities.

The total cost = $550.

◆ **Step 3**   Express the cost of food and utilities as a percentage of the total monthly costs:

$$\frac{550}{1,100} \cdot 100 =$$

$$\frac{55,000}{1,100} = 50$$

The cost of food and utilities is 50% of the total monthly expenses.

Line Graphs

When we construct a line graph, we plot points (which represent data) in relation to the x-axis and the y-axis (see fig. 7.4).

How do we read line graphs? Figure 7.4 is a line graph showing the annual revenue of Two-K Corporation, expressed in four quarters. To find the income for the third quarter, first locate the third quarter on the x-axis, and then go up the y-axis. That point represents the revenue for the third quarter: $90 million (that is, ninety million dollars).

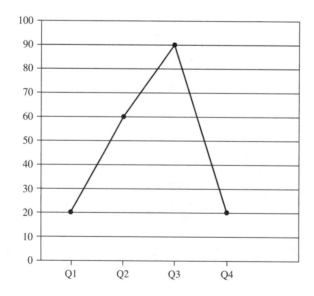

Figure 7.4: Annual Revenue of Two-K Corporation (in Millions of Dollars)

Example 9

In which two quarters were revenues for Two-K Corporation the same (see fig. 7.4)?

◆ **Step 1**   Examine the line graph to see which two quarters are the same.

Two-K Corporation's revenues were the same for the first and the fourth quarters.

Example 10

According to figure 7.4, between which two quarters did the company experience the sharpest decline in revenues?

◆ **Step 1**   Examine the line graph and note where the line fell the most.

The company experienced the sharpest decline in revenues between the third and the fourth quarters.

Tables

The compilation of tables represents an excellent method of organizing and presenting data for many purposes, such as displaying nutritional facts on food labels, indicating ideal height-weight proportions, and showing returns on investments. Table 7.1 lists data on Vitapep's high-potency multivitamin and mineral bottles. (*Note*: The data have been contrived for the sole purpose of practicing analytical skills and must not be used as part of a wellness program.)

Example 11

If Maricelo's health-care provider recommends that he take two Vitapep capsules every day, how many micrograms (mcg) of vitamin B_{12} will the capsules provide, according to table 7.1?

◆ **Step 1**   Table 7.1 states that one capsule provides 30 mcg of vitamin B_{12}.

Two capsules will provide 30 mcg $\times$ 2 = 60 mcg of vitamin B_{12}.

Table 7.1: Multivitamin and Mineral Content of Vitapep Capsules

One capsule provides	Amount	% U.S. RDA*
Vitamin C	150 mg	300
Vitamin A	8,000 IU	150
Vitamin D	120 IU	30
Vitamin E	120 IU	400
Vitamin B_1	30 mg	2,000
Vitamin B_2	30 mg	2,000
Vitamin B_6	30 mg	1,500
Vitamin B_{12}	30 mcg	500
Niacinamide	30 mg	150
Pantothenic acid	30 mg	300
Biotin	30 mcg	10
Folic acid	120 mcg	33
PABA	30 mg	No RDA established
Calcium	500 mg	50
Iodine	50 mcg	30
Magnesium	35 mg	10
Zinc	10 mg	60

*RDA = recommended daily allowance

Example 12

If Donna's health-care provider recommends that every day she take one multivitamin and mineral pill that provides her with at least 150% of the U.S. RDA of vitamin A and niacinamide, at least 5 mg of zinc, and no more than 30 mg each of vitamin B_1, vitamin B_2, vitamin B_6, and PABA, would Vitapep's brand of vitamin and mineral capsules be a suitable choice for Donna, according to table 7.1?

◆ **Step 1**   Check the table to see whether Vitapep's capsules provide the necessary nutrients within the stated limits set by the health-care provider.

Based on the data shown in table 7.1, Vitapep's brand would be a suitable choice.

7.1 Inductive Reasoning

When we use inductive reasoning, we draw conclusions based on specific observations. Imagine, for instance, that little green and purple beings were secretly observing the traffic patterns at several busy intersections in a city, and their conversation went something like this:

FARGON: Have you noticed, Zaxx, that these earthlings stop their transportation devices every time the strange hanging lights turn red?

ZAXX: I have, Fargon, but I have also observed that the earthlings' vehicles move again every time the hanging lights turn green. What have you seen, Zorox?

ZOROX: I have observed the same pattern, Zaxx and Fargon, but I have also documented that once in a while, one of the earthlings' vehicles will fail to stop when the strange lights turn red and that when this happens, a terrible honking noise comes from their transportation devices. We can induce from our observations that all transportation devices are expected to stop when the hanging lights turn red and can proceed when the suspended lights turn green. But those who do not conform to the red- and green-light pattern must endure the honking noises that come from their transportation devices.

When the imaginary Fargon, Zaxx, and Zorox were engaged in inductive reasoning, they were dealing with patterns—specifically patterns about earthlings' behavior. In math, we also look for patterns, such as the patterns found in various types of numerical or alphabetical sequences or series.

Increasing Pattern

In an increasing pattern, the elements of the sequence continually increase by some amount that we have to recognize in order to determine the next element in the sequence. For example, the numerical sequence 1, 2, 3, 4, 5, 6, 7 reveals an increasing pattern in which 1 is added to each element in the sequence to find the next element. What comes after 7? Simply add 1 to 7, and we can quickly determine that the next element in the sequence is 8.

Example 13

What is the next number in the following sequence? 1, 4, 7, 10, 13 . . .

◆ **Step 1**   Note that 3 is added to each element in the sequence. Thus, add 3 to 13.

$$3 + 13 = 16$$

The next number in the sequence is 16.

Decreasing Pattern

Similarly, a decreasing pattern is one in which the elements of the sequence continually decrease by some amount that we have to ascertain in order to find the next element in the sequence. For example, the numerical sequence 8, 7, 6, 5 shows a decreasing pattern in which 1 is subtracted from each element in the sequence to find the next element. Thus, what number comes after 5? Subtracting 1 from 5 gives us 4, the next number in the sequence.

Example 14

What is the next number in the following sequence?
26, 20, 14, 8 . . .

◆ **Step 1**   Notice that each subsequent number in the sequence decreases by 6. Thus, subtract 6 from 8.

$$8 - 6 = 2$$

Alternating Pattern

In an alternating pattern, numbers in a sequence are subjected to one or more alternating features or conditions. In the sequence 2, 7, 6, 11, 10, the value 5 is added to the first number (2) to obtain the second (7), and then 1 is subtracted from the second number (7) to arrive at the third number (6). The alternating pattern continues when 5 is added to the third number (6) to give us 11, and then when 1 is subtracted from this fourth number (11) to give us 10, the fifth number. Based on this pattern, the sixth number in the sequence is $10 + 5 = 15$ (see fig. 7.5).

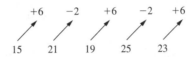

Figure 7.5: An Alternating Pattern

Example 15

What are the next two numbers in the following sequence?
15, 21, 19, 25, 23 . . .

◆ **Step 1** Decide what type of pattern is shown. It is an alternating one.

$$+6 \quad -2 \quad +6 \quad -2 \quad +6$$
$$15 \quad\quad 21 \quad\quad 19 \quad\quad 25 \quad\quad 23$$

Figure 7.6: Another Alternating Pattern

◆ **Step 2** Calculate the sixth and seventh numbers in the sequence.

23 + 6 = 29

29 − 2 = 27

The next two numbers in the sequence are 29 and 27.

Circular Pattern

A circular pattern is revealed when the elements of a sequence are subjected to a distinct set of changes that repeat throughout the sequence. For example, the sequence 1, 2, 5, 3, 4, 7, 5 is subject to a circular pattern, as figure 7.7 shows.

The circular pattern that repeats throughout the sequence is +1, +3, −2. Thus, we add 1 to the first number to get 2. We add 3 to the second number (2) to get 5. Then we subtract 2 from the third number (5) to arrive at 3. At this point, the pattern repeats itself. We add 1 to the fourth number (3) to give us 4. Then we add 3 to 4, which is 7 (the sixth number), and subtracting 2 from this number gives us 5. What is the next number in the sequence? The pattern is about to repeat itself, so we add 1 to 5, which gives us 6.

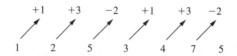

Figure 7.7: A Circular Pattern

Example 16

What is the next number in the sequence? 1, 3, 1, 5, 7, 5, 9 . . .

◆ **Step 1**   The pattern in this sequence is a circular one: +2, −2, +4.

The next number in the sequence is 9 + 2 = 11

Example 17

What are the seventh and tenth numbers in the sequence? 3, 1, 5, 6, 4, 8 . . .

◆ **Step 1**   Draw a diagram to identify the pattern (see fig. 7.8).

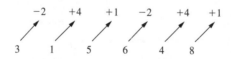

Figure 7.8

The pattern is a circular one: −2, +4, +1

The seventh number in the sequence is 8 + 1 = 9.

The eighth number is 9 − 2 = 7.

The ninth number is 7 + 4 = 11.

The tenth number is 11 + 1 = 12.

The seventh and tenth numbers are 9 and 12.

Letters in a Sequence

Sometimes we are asked to find specific letters in a sequence. The easiest way to do this is to assign numbers to letters of the alphabet and then use the numbers to discover which pattern is hidden within the sequence. For example, let A = 1, B = 2, C = 3, D = 4, E = 5, F = 6, G = 7, and so on.

Example 18

> What is the next letter in the sequence B, D, F, H . . . ?

◆ **Step 1**   Let A = 1, B = 2, C = 3, and so on.

◆ **Step 2**   Draw a diagram to find the pattern (see fig. 7.9).

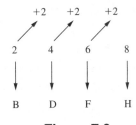

Figure 7.9

◆ **Step 3**   The next number is 8 + 2 = 10. If A = 1, B = 2, and so on, then 10 = J.

> The next letter in the sequence is J.

7.2 Deductive Reasoning

When we use deductive reasoning, we move from the general to the specific. For example, if we know that the sum of the measures of the central angles of any (general) circle is 360°, then we know that the sum of the measures of the central angles of a *specific* circle is also 360°. Deductive reasoning problems present a set of facts that we cannot violate. In other words, as we proceed step-by-step, we must make sure that each of our statements or assumptions is *true* according to the stated facts. For instance, if we are working with a problem whose facts state that Jim *always* sits between Mary and Meg every time their friend Bob invites them to dinner, then we cannot build a scenario in which Jim is seated next to Bob.

Example 19

The history department at a college is making up its fall schedule. All the instructors named below have to teach two sections of U.S. History and one additional section of any field of history, including Texas History, that must be taught during the fall semester.

Professor Smith always teaches World History and U.S. History.

Professor Cole will teach anything but Mexican-American History.

Professor Thomas wants to teach only Native American History and U.S. History.

Professor Boyd refuses to teach anything but Women's History and U.S. History.

Professor Moreno was hired to teach only U.S. History and Mexican History.

Who is available to teach Texas History?

◆ **Step 1**   Make up a chart like the one in table 7.2, using the first initial of each professor's last name. As you read through the facts presented, cross off a professor's initial if he or she is not available or is not willing to teach a certain class.

Professor Smith always teaches World History, so she is not available to teach any of the other classes listed in the table. Thomas wants to teach only Native American History and U.S. History. Other than U.S. History, Boyd will teach only Women's History, so we can cross her off for the other classes. Moreno was hired to teach U.S. History and Mexican History, so he is unavailable to teach Texas History. That leaves us with Professor Cole, who will teach anything but Mexican History.

Thus, Professor Cole is available to teach Texas History.

Table 7.2

World History	Mexican History	Native American History	Women's History	Texas History
S̶	S̶	S̶	S̶	S̶
C̶	C̶	C̶	C̶	C
T̶	T̶	T	T̶	T̶
B̶	B̶	B̶	B	B̶
M̶	M	M̶	M̶	M̶

Example 20

Marcie, Leandro, Jim, and Esther meet at the local diner for breakfast. They park their vehicles side by side. Marcie's truck is between Leandro's sedan and Esther's station wagon. The sedan is not next to Jim's coupe, which is parked on the left end. Whose vehicle is parked on the right end?

◆ **Step 1**   Before drawing a diagram of the parking lot, assign letters to each vehicle.

Let MT = Marcie's truck; LS = Leandro's sedan; ES = Esther's station wagon, and JC = Jim's coupe. Draw a trial diagram based on the above facts.

JC	LS	MT	ES

Does this diagram satisfy all the conditions? No, because LS is *not* supposed to be parked next to JC. We need to revise the diagram.

JC	ES	MT	LS

Does this diagram satisfy all the conditions? Yes, so Leandro's sedan is parked on the right end.

7.3 Sets and Subsets

A set, which is a collection of clearly defined things, is made up of items called elements or members. Mathematicians use special symbols (set notation) when working with sets and subsets. For example, the set containing the numbers 4 and 7 is expressed in set notation as $\{4, 7\}$. If we want to state that 4 is a member or an element of the set containing 4 and 7, we write $4 \in \{4, 7\}$. (The symbol $\in$ means "is a member of.") If an item is not an element of a set, we use the symbol $\notin$ ("is not a member of"). Thus $6 \notin \{4, 7\}$ indicates that 6 is not an element of the set $\{4, 7\}$. We can also label sets using capital letters. $S = \{4, 7\}$. Thus, $4 \in S$, but $6 \notin S$. Two or more sets are considered equal sets if the sets contain all of the same elements. Thus, if $A = \{1, 3, 5, 7\}$ and $B = \{7, 3, 5, 1\}$, then $A = B$. Sometimes a set contains no elements and is called an empty set or a null set. We use the symbols { } or ∅ to indicate the empty set. For example, if S = {all human beings taller than thirty feet}, then $S = \varnothing$.

Example 21

Express in set notation the set containing all whole numbers between 1 and 6.

The solution is {2, 3, 4, 5}

Example 22

If S = {2, 4, 6}, express in set notation that 8 is not an element of S.

$8 \notin S$

Universal Sets

A universal set is labeled U and refers to the set that includes all the elements that are relevant to a particular situation. For example, if we were discussing all the people who have so far walked on the moon, the universal set contains all the astronauts who have accomplished this feat.

Infinite Sets

The set of all positive integers is an example of an infinite set, because we cannot include within it a final number in the sequence. We write three ellipsis dots in the set to show that the sequence continues indefinitely: {1, 2, 3, 4, 5, 6, 7, ...}. This is similar to the use of three dots to indicate that an irrational decimal, such as 2.637189..., goes on forever, as shown in chapter 1.

Finite Sets

A finite set has a finite number of elements within it (including 0). For example, the set of all days in the week beginning with the letter T is a finite set, because T = {Tuesday, Thursday}.

Subsets

If all the elements of a set A are also elements of a set B, then A is a subset of B. We write this as $A \subset B$. For example, if $A = \{0, 4\}$ and $B = \{0, 1, 2, 3, 4\}$, then $A \subset B$. If set $C = \{2, 8\}$ is *not* a subset of set $D = \{1, 3, 5, 7\}$, we express this as $C \not\subset D$. We can find the total number of subsets of any finite set by using the following rule:

> A set with n elements contains 2^n subsets.

Example 23

How many subsets does $B = \{1, 2\}$ have?

◆ **Step 1**   Use the rule 2^n, where $n = 2$ (the number of elements in set B).

$2^2 = 4$
We can list the subsets as follows:
$\{1, 2\}$ The set is a subset of itself.
$\{1\}$
$\{2\}$
$\{\ \}$ The empty set is a subset of any set.

7.4 Set Operations

We can perform several operations involving sets, such as finding the union of two sets or finding the intersection of two sets.

Union of Two Sets

The union of two sets X and Y, expressed as $X \cup Y$, is the set of all elements included in X *and* all elements included in Y. Thus, if $X = \{1, 3, 4\}$ and $Y = \{4, 5, 6\}$, then $X \cup Y = \{1, 3, 4, 5, 6\}$. We can see that 4 is an element that belongs to both X and Y, but we do not duplicate the number when performing the set operation $X \cup Y$.

Example 24

Perform the operation $X \cup Y$ if $X = \{2, 4\}$ and $Y = \{5, 6\}$.

◆ **Step 1**   What is the union of sets X and Y? $X = \{2, 4\}$ and $Y = \{5, 6\}$, so the following is true:

$X \cup Y = \{2, 4, 5, 6\}$

Intersection of Two Sets

The intersection of two sets Y and Z is the set of all members that are common to both sets Y and Z. We express the intersection of Y and Z as $Y \cap Z$. For example, if $Y = \{a, b, c\}$ and $Z = \{c, d, e\}$, then $Y \cap Z = \{c\}$.

Example 25

Perform the operation $A \cap B$ if $A = \{2, 7, 8\}$ and $B = \{7, 9\}$.

◆ **Step 1**   The only element common to both sets A and B is 7.

$A \cap B = \{7\}$

Example 26

If $A = \{0, 4, 6\}$ and $B = \{7, 1\}$, find $A \cap B$.

◆ **Step 1**   Which elements of A are also contained in B?

There are none.

$A \cap B = \varnothing$

Example 27

If $A = \{3, 4, 5, 8, 9\}$, $B = \{8, 9, 11\}$, and $C = \{9, 11\}$, perform the operation $(A \cap B) \cap C$.

◆ **Step 1**   Examine sets A and B and perform the operation $A \cap B$. (Perform the operation within the parentheses first.)

$A \cap B = \{8, 9\}$

◆ **Step 2**   Perform the operation $(A \cap B) \cap C$. Which number is present in all three sets? It is 9.

$(A \cap B) \cap C = 9$

Example 28

If $A = \{3, 4, 5, 6\}$, $B = \{4, 5, 8, 9, 10\}$, and $C = \{5, 7, 9, 10\}$, perform the operation $(A \cap B) \cup C$.

◆ **Step 1**   Find $A \cap B$. It is particularly important here to perform the operation within the parenthesis first. Which numbers are common to both sets A and B?

$A \cap B = \{4, 5\}$

◆ **Step 2**   Find $(A \cap B) \cup C$. We know that $A \cap B = \{4, 5\}$, what is the union with set C?

$(A \cap B) \cup C = \{4, 5, 7, 9, 10\}$

7.5 Probability

Many standardized mathematics tests include questions based on the counting principle. For example, Mary is deciding what to wear to her birthday party.

She takes out of her closet three sweaters (pink, red, and white) and three skirts (gray, black, and navy). If she selects one sweater and one skirt, how many different outfit combinations are possible? We can solve this problem by constructing a tree diagram (see fig. 7.10). The diagram is a visual presentation of all the different combinations of options Mary has when she chooses one sweater and one skirt. On the left side of the tree diagram are listed the three sweater options. As we follow along the "tree branches," we find that Mary can combine each different color sweater with one of three skirts (gray, black, or navy). On the right side of the diagram, we list each of the possible sweater-and-skirt combinations.

Count and list the number of possible sweater-and-skirt combinations shown on the right side of the diagram: PG, PB, PN, RG, RB, RN, WG, WB, WN = 9

Thus, Mary has nine possible outfit combinations. The tree diagram illustrates the counting principle, which states that if one choice is made from each group of options, the following is true:

> The total number of possible combinations or outcomes = the product of the number of choices available for each option.

In the above example, Mary selected one from three sweater colors and one from three skirt colors: (3)(3) = 9

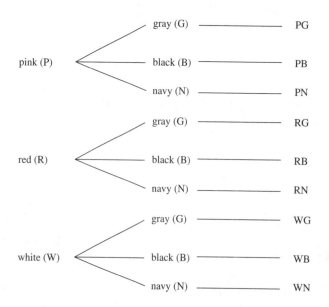

Figure 7.10: A Tree Diagram

Example 29

At a Chinese restaurant, diners can choose a three-course meal composed of one appetizer, a bowl of soup, and an entrée. Diners are asked to select one out of three appetizers (egg roll, fried wonton, or shrimp toast), one out of three soups (egg drop, wonton, or hot and sour), and one out of four entrées (Kung Pao Chicken, Szechuan Beef, Tzau Lhiou Eggplant, or Pork Lo Mein). How many possible dinner combinations are available to diners?

◆ **Step 1**   Determine the maximum number of appetizers, soups, and entrées. Three appetizers, three soups, and four entrées is the maximum number, so we need to multiply.

(3)(3)(4) = 36 possible combinations

Example 30

Yen-Hua went to the local printer to order wedding invitations. The printer showed her several options listed in table 7.3. If she selects one from each column, how many different invitations are possible?

The total number of different invitations equals the product of the number of choices available for each option. There are four font choices, four different card stock colors, and three sizes.

The total number of possible invitations is (4)(4)(3) = 48

Table 7.3

Font choices	Colors of card stock	Available sizes
Arial	Beige	3×5 in.
Brush Script	Blush Pink	4×6 in.
Desdemona	Champagne	5×8 in.
Matura MT	Ivory	

Understanding Probability

The study of probability enables us to make predictions about the likelihood that a certain event will occur. In order to make observations or measurements, mathematicians design and implement experiments. For example, when a two-sided coin is tossed in the air, theoretically there is a 50% chance that it will fall "heads-up."

An outcome is one of the possible observations or measurements that can be made as a result of conducting an experiment. Thus, if a coin is tossed in the air and falls "tails-up," this is one outcome of the experiment. Favorable outcomes of an experiment are those that satisfy the conditions or requirements of a specific event. If we roll a die, one possible event is obtaining an even number. We can write this as follows: $E = \{2, 4, 6\}$.

Theoretical probability is a real number between 0 and 1 that indicates the likelihood that an outcome will occur. On one extreme, a probability of 0 means that the event is impossible. On the other extreme, a probability of 1 means that the event will always take place. For instance, no matter how much we try to extend life, death is a certainty for all of us. To determine the theoretical probability of an event E [which we write as $P(E)$], we use the following formula:

$$P(E) = \frac{\text{number of favorable outcomes}}{\text{number of possible outcomes}}$$

If two dice are rolled once, how many possible outcomes are there? Table 7.4 indicates that there are 36 possible outcomes when two dice are rolled once.

Example 31

If two dice are rolled once, what is the probability that the sum of the numbers appearing on the top of the dice is 8?

Table 7.4

1 and 1	2 and 1	3 and 1	4 and 1	5 and 1	6 and 1
1 and 2	2 and 2	3 and 2	4 and 2	5 and 2	6 and 2
1 and 3	2 and 3	3 and 3	4 and 3	5 and 3	6 and 3
1 and 4	2 and 4	3 and 4	4 and 4	5 and 4	6 and 4
1 and 5	2 and 5	3 and 5	4 and 5	5 and 5	6 and 5
1 and 6	2 and 6	3 and 6	4 and 6	5 and 6	6 and 6

◆ **Step 1** Write down the total number of possible outcomes. Table 7.4 illustrates there are 36.

◆ **Step 2** Determine how many outcomes are favorable to the event. In other words, the sum of the numbers of the two dice must equal 8.

There are five outcomes favorable to the event.

◆ **Step 3** Calculate the probability using this formula:

$$P(E) = \frac{\text{number of favorable outcomes}}{\text{number of possible outcomes}},$$ where the number of favorable outcomes = 5, and the number of possible outcomes = 36.

$$P(E) = \frac{5}{36}$$

The probability of obtaining a sum of 8 when two dice are rolled is $\frac{5}{36}$.

Example 32

The letters that spell the names of two states, Mississippi and Missouri, are written on separate cards. If the cards are placed in a box and one card is drawn at random, what is the probability that the card has the letter *S* on it?

◆ **Step 1** Determine the number of possible outcomes by counting the total number of letters in *Mississippi* and *Missouri*. The result is 19.

◆ **Step 2**   Determine the number of outcomes favorable to the event by counting how many cards have the letter *S* on them. There are six—four in *Mississippi* and two in *Missouri.*

◆ **Step 3**   Calculate the probability by using the formula

$$P(E) = \frac{\text{number of favorable outcomes}}{\text{number of possible outcomes}},$$ where the number of favorable outcomes = 6, and the number of possible outcomes is 19.

> The probability of drawing a card with an *S* on it is $\frac{6}{19}$.

7.6   Mean, Median, Mode, and Range

Mean, median, and mode are all referred to as measures of central tendency, or how values cluster in a number of events. Range is a related concept.

Mean

Mean, or average, enables us to make comparisons. For example, the average annual temperature of International Falls, Minnesota, is 36.4°F, whereas the average temperature of Key West, Florida, is 77.7°F. We calculate the mean of a set of numbers by adding the value of each number and then dividing by how many numbers are in the set. We can express this as follows, where $\bar{x}$ is the symbol for mean; x_1 represents the values of the numbers; Σ (summation) is the sum of the values; and n equals how many numbers are in the set:

$$\bar{x} = \frac{\Sigma x_1}{n}$$

Example 33

> What is the mean of the following set of numbers?
> {4, 8, 11, 18, 19, 24}

◆ **Step 1**   Determine how many numbers are in the set. There are six.

◆ **Step 2**   Calculate the sum of all the numbers in the set.

$$4 + 8 + 11 + 18 + 19 + 24 = 84$$

◆ **Step 3:** Divide the sum by how many numbers are in the set.

$$\frac{84}{6} = 14$$

The mean, or average, is 14.

Note that the mean does not have to be an element of the set.

Example 34

Four students (Rafael, Mike, Janine, and Bob) received the result of their last Art History exam. Mike earned 20 points, Rafael earned three times as many points as Mike, and Janine received as many points as Rafael. If the mean, or average, of the students' scores is 55 points, what was Bob's score?

◆ **Step 1** Organize the data.

Mike's score: 20

Rafael's score: $20(3) = 60$

Janine's score $= 60$

Bob's score $= x$

◆ **Step 2** Add up all the scores.

$20 + 60 + 60 + x = 140 + x$

◆ **Step 3** There are four students and the mean is 55, so we write the equation:

$$\frac{140 + x}{4} = 55$$

◆ **Step 4** Multiply both sides by 4.

$$4\left(\frac{140+x}{4}\right) = 55(4)$$

$$140 + x = 220$$

$$140 - 140 + x = 220 - 140$$

$$x = 80$$

Bob earned 80 points.

Median

If there is an odd number of numbers in a set arranged in either ascending or descending order, the median is the middle number in the set. If there is an even number of numbers in a set, the median is the average of the two middle numbers. There are as many numbers above (greater than) the median as there are below (less than) the median.

Example 35

What is the median of the following numbers?
{6, 3, 2, 1, 7, 15, 18, 20, 4}

◆ **Step 1** Rearrange the numbers in ascending order.

{1, 2, 3, 4, 6, 7, 15, 18, 20}

◆ **Step 2** Identify the middle number.

It is 6. (There are four numbers less than 6 and four greater than 6.)

Example 36

What is the median of the following numbers?
{8, 2, 4, 1, 9, 7, 15, 18}

◆ **Step 1** Rearrange the numbers in ascending order.

{1, 2, 4, 7, 8, 9, 15, 18}

◆ **Step 2**   There is an even number of numbers in the set, so we need to find the two middle numbers.

They are 7 and 8.

◆ **Step 3**   Find the average, or mean, of these two numbers.

$$\frac{7+8}{2} = \frac{15}{2} = 7.5$$

The median is 7.5. (There are four numbers less than 7.5 and four greater than 7.5.)

Example 37

During the last six games, the local high school football team scored the following points: 24, 31, 10, 9, 46, 27. What is the median of the scores?

◆ **Step 1**   Rearrange the scores in ascending order.

9, 10, 24, 27, 31, 46

◆ **Step 2**   There is an even number of scores, so we need to find the two middle scores.

24 and 27

◆ **Step 3**   Calculate the mean of these two scores.

$$\frac{24+27}{2} = \frac{51}{2} = 25.5$$

The median of the scores is 25.5.

Mode

In a list of numbers, the mode is simply the number that appears most frequently.

Example 38

Find the mode in the following set of numbers:
{4, 8, 6, 9, 0, 1, 13, 9, 5, 4, 18, 4}

◆ **Step 1**   It is easier to identify the mode if we rearrange the numbers in ascending order.

{0, 1, 4, 4, 4, 5, 6, 8, 9, 9, 13, 18}

◆ **Step 2**   Find the number that appears most frequently.

The mode is the number 4.

Example 39

Table 7.5 shows the number of hours worked in one week by six employees at the neighborhood store. What is the mode of the hours worked?

Table 7.5: The Number of Hours Worked by Employees

Employee	Hours worked
Roberta	40
Caroline	35
Michael	40
Juan	35
Sarah	30
Kim	35

◆ **Step 1**   Examine the table and find the number that appears the most often.

The mode is 35.

Range

In a list of numbers, the range is the difference between the smallest and the largest numbers.

Example 40

What is the range of the following list of numbers?
5, 2, 1, 8, 4, 9, 10, 12, 3

◆ **Step 1**   Rearrange the numbers in ascending order.

1, 2, 3, 4, 5, 8, 9, 10, 12

◆ **Step 2**   Subtract the smallest number from the largest number.

$12 - 1 = 11$

The range is 11.

Problems

To answer questions 1–4, see figure 7a.

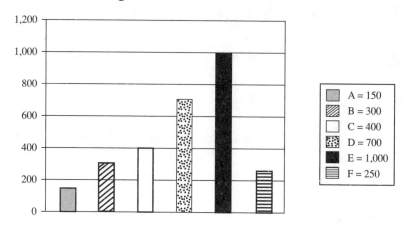

Figure 7a: 1995–2000 Production of Pencils (in Millions) by Companies A–F

1. Which company produced the fewest pencils between 1995 and 2000?

2. Which company produced the most pencils between 1995 and 2000?

3. Company D's production is what percentage of the total production of companies A–F?

4. Which company manufactured as much as the sum of the production of companies B and C?

To answer questions 5–7, see figure 7b.

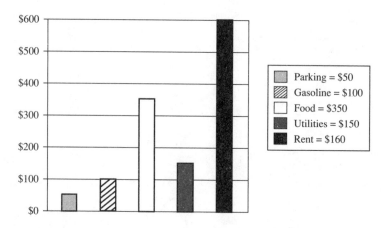

Figure 7b: Household Budget per Month

5. What is the total cost for gasoline and parking?

6. What percentage of the household budget is spent on food?

7. If the landlord raises the rent by 15% (and all other expenses remain the same), what will be the new total monthly budget?

To answer questions 8 and 9, see figure 7c.

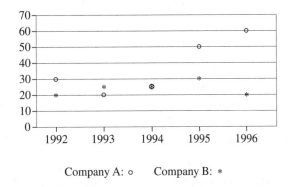

Company A: ○   Company B: *

Figure 7c: Annual Revenue (Millions of Dollars) of Companies A and B

8. In which year did company A and company B report the same revenues?

9. In what year did the two companies report the greatest difference in revenues?

10. Complete the data in table 7a.

Table 7a

Item	Unit price	Quantity	Total price
Math textbook	$60.00	3	
Graphing calculator		4	$360.40
Ballpoint pens	$0.75		$8.25
File folders		5	$6.15
Package of paper	$0.99		$3.96

11. What is the next number in the sequence?

3, 9, 15, 21, 27, 33, . . .

12. What are the next two numbers in the sequence?

    28, 21, 14, 7, . . .

13. What are the next two numbers in the sequence?

    18, 24, 22, 28, 26, . . .

14. What is the mean of the following numbers?

    10, 13, 12, 16, 19, 18, 22

15. Eight people are seated at a dinner table. Three sit along one side, and three sit along the other side. Two people sit opposite each other at the ends of the table. Two men cannot sit next to each other, and there has to be at least one female seated at one of the ends of the table. Frank sits opposite Mark, and Jane sits between Frank and Robert. Arthur sits to the right of Katy, and Robert sits to the left of Katy. Susan refuses to sit next to Arthur. Where does Candace sit?

Focus on English

Grammar

Capital Letters

Use CAPITAL letters for the pronoun *I* and for the initial (first) letter of names, languages, cities, nationalities, countries, days, and months. For example, *I'm American.* In the following paragraph, circle the letters that should be capitalized.

> i am Diego and i'm from mexico. i have traveled to three countries—the united states, france, and spain. I liked paris very much. i'm a student and I will graduate in august. I like my morning classes, but on tuesday my first class starts at 8:00 a.m.

Imperatives

An imperative is a command telling us to do or not to do something. There are only two forms—one positive and the other negative.

Infinitive	Positive imperative	Negative imperative
to look	Look at figure 7!	Don't look at figure 7!

Fill in the blanks with the correct imperative.

1. (to open) _____ the door! (positive)

2. (to turn on) _____ the light! (positive)

3. (to fill in) _____ that form! (negative)

4. (to answer) _____ the question! (positive)

5. (to look) _____ at me! (negative)

Improving Mathematical Vocabulary

1. What is the difference between a bar graph and a pie chart?

2. What is an empty, or null, set?

3. What is the difference between mean, median, and mode?

 Dictionary Work

The following groups of words sound alike but are spelled differently and have different meanings. Use a dictionary to find the differences.

their	there
feat	feet
sea	see
pie	pi
wring	ring
road	rode
rote	wrote
made	maid

Chapter 8

Systems of Linear Equations

8.0 Systems of Linear Equations in Two Variables

In chapter 5, we discussed linear equations that contain two variables. We recognize this type of equation by the form $ax + by = c$, where a, b, and c are all real numbers and $a \neq 0$, and $b \neq 0$. We know that a solution of an equation in two variables is an ordered pair that satisfies the equation. In this chapter, we will work with systems of linear equations in two variables. A system of linear equations is made up of two or more linear equations that all contain the same variables. See, for example, the following system of linear equations in two variables, x and y:

$$2x - y = 8$$

$$x + 3y = 11$$

The solution of a system in two variables is any ordered pair that makes *both* equations in the *same* system true.

Example 1

Is the ordered pair (3, 2) a solution for the following linear system?
$3x - y = 7$
$2x + 2y = 10$

◆ **Step 1**   Substitute 3 for x and 2 for y in both equations.

$3x - y = 7$	$2x + 2y = 10$
Does $3(3) - 2 = 7$?	Does $2(3) + 2(2) = 10$?
$9 - 2 = 7$	$6 + 4 = 10$
Yes	Yes

Both equations are true, so the ordered pair (3, 2) is a solution for the system.

Example 2

Is the ordered pair $(2, -4)$ a solution for the following linear system?

$4x - 3y = 20$

$2x + 3y = 8$

◆ **Step 1**   Substitute 2 for x and -4 for y in both equations.

$4x - 3y = 20$	$2x + 3y = 8$
Does $4(2) - 3(-4) = 20$?	Does $2(2) + 3(-4) = 8$?
$8 + 12 = 20$	$-8 \neq 8$
Yes	No

Only one of the equations is true, so the ordered pair $(2, -4)$ is not a solution for the system.

Example 3

If the ordered pair $(2, 4)$ satisfies the system of equations, complete the second equation in the system.

$3x + 2y = 14$

$4x + y = ?$

◆ **Step 1**   Check to see that $(2, 4)$ satisfies the first equation.

Does $3(2) + 2(4) = 14$?

$6 + 8 = 14$

Yes

◆ **Step 2**   Substitute 2 for x and 4 for y in the second equation.

$4(2) + 4 = ?$

$8 + 4 = 12$

The second equation in the system is $4x + y = 12$.

Example 4

> If the ordered pair $(-3, 5)$ satisfies the system of equations below, complete both equations in the system.
>
> $4x - 2y = ?$
>
> $x + 5y = ?$

◆ **Step 1**   Substitute -3 for x and 5 for y to solve both equations.

$4x - 2y = ?$	$x + 5y = ?$
$4(-3) - 2(5) = ?$	$-3 + 5(5) = ?$
$-12 - 10 = -22$	$-3 + 25 = 22$

The complete system of equations is as follows:

$4x - 2y = -22$
$x + 5y = 22$

8.1   Solving by Graphing

We can solve systems of linear equations in two variables by graphing. We do this by graphing on the same plane the lines of the equations in the system and then locating the point where the two lines intersect. We find the solution of the system of equations by reading the coordinates of that point.

Example 5

> Solve the system of equations by graphing.
> $2x + y = 6$
> $x + y = 4$

◆ **Step 1**   Construct a table of values for each equation by letting $x = 0$, $y = 0$, and $x = 1$ for both equations.

Equation $2x + y = 6$ Table of Values

x	0	3	1
y	6	0	4

Equation $x + y = 4$ Table of Values

x	0	4	1
y	4	0	3

◆ **Step 2**   Plot the points for each equation and draw a line through each set of points (see fig. 8.1).

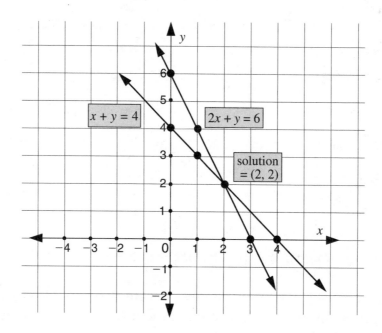

Figure 8.1: Solving the System of Equations $2x + y = 6$ and $x + y = 4$

◆ **Step 3**   Find the point where the two equations intersect.

The ordered pair (2, 2) is the solution to the system of equations.

Example 6

Solve the system of equations by graphing.
$2x + 3y = 6$
$4x + 6y = 12$

◆ **Step 1**   Construct a table of values for each equation by letting $x = 0$, $y = 0$, and $y = 1$ for both equations.

Equation $2x + 3y = 6$ Table of Values

x	0	3	1.5
y	2	0	1

Equation $4x + 6y = 12$ Table of Values

x	0	3	1.5
y	2	0	1

◆ **Step 2**　　Plot the points for each equation and draw a line through each set of points (see fig. 8.2).

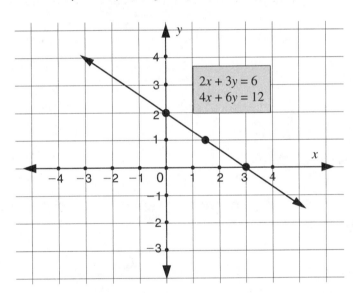

Figure 8.2: Solving the System of Equations $2x + 3y = 6$ and $4x + 6y = 12$

We can see from the graph that the two equations have the same points. Thus, the graphs of the two equations in the system are the same line. The graph in figure 8.2 has an infinite number of solutions, because every point along the line is a solution of the system of equations.

Let's look closely at the two equations in the system:

$$2x + 3y = 6$$

$$4x + 6y = 12$$

We see that the second equation can be found by multiplying both sides of the first equation by 2. In other words, the two equations in the system are simply different forms of the *same* equation. That is why they have the same graph.

Note that if the graphs of two equations are parallel lines, they will never intersect, and there is no solution.

8.2 Solving by Substitution

Graphing is just one of several methods we can use to solve systems of linear equations. In this section, we will learn how to use the substitution method, which requires us to isolate one of the two variables in the system. Because this method involves several steps, it is easier to discuss it by working through a few examples.

Example 7

Solve the system:
(1) $4x + y = 6$
(2) $2x + 3y = 8$

♦ **Step 1** Choose the variable to be isolated. Let's select y in equation (1). Solve for y.

$$4x + y = 6$$

$$y + 4x - 4x = 6 - 4x$$

$$y = 6 - 4x$$

Let's label this equation (1a).

♦ **Step 2** Substitute equation (1a) for y in equation (2).

$$2x + 3y = 8$$

$$2x + 3(6 - 4x) = 8$$

$$2x + 18 - 12x = 8$$

$$-10x + 18 \quad = 8$$

$$-10x + 18 - 18 = 8 - 18$$

$$-10x \qquad\quad = -10$$

$$\frac{-10x}{-10} \qquad = \frac{-10}{-10}$$

$$x \qquad\qquad = 1$$

◆ **Step 3** In order to find the value of y, substitute the value of x into either equation (1) or equation (2). It's always a good idea to use the simpler equation, so let's work with equation (1). Let $x = 1$ in equation $4x + y = 6$, and solve for y.

$$4x + y \quad = 6$$

$$4(1) + y \quad = 6$$

$$4 + y \quad = 6$$

$$y + 4 - 4 = 6 - 4$$

$$y = 2$$

◆ **Step 4** Write down the ordered pair that is the solution of the system. We know that $x = 1$ and $y = 2$. Thus, the ordered pair is (1, 2).

◆ **Step 5** We can check our solution by inserting the values of x and y into the system of equations.

(1) $4x + y = 6$	(2) $2x + 3y = 8$
$4(1) + 2 = 6$	$2(1) + 3(2) = 8$
$4 + 2 = 6$	$2 + 6 = 8$
True	True

Example 8

Solve the system:

(1) $4x + 2y = -2$

(2) $x = 13 - 5y$

◆ **Step 1**   In this example, x is already isolated in equation (2), so substitute $13 - 5y$ for x in equation (1) and solve for y.

(1) $4x + 2y = -2$

$4(13 - 5y) + 2y = -2$

$52 - 20y + 2y = -2$

$52 - 18y = -2$

$52 - 52 - 18y = -2 - 52$

$-18y = -54$

$\dfrac{-18y}{-18} = \dfrac{-54}{-18}$

$y = 3$

◆ **Step 2**   Find the value of x by substituting $y = 3$ into one of the two original equations. Let's select equation (1) and solve for x.

(1) $4x + 2y = -2$

$4x + 2(3) = -2$

$4x + 6 = -2$

$4x + 6 - 6 = -2 - 6$

$4x = -8$

$\dfrac{4x}{4} = \dfrac{-8}{4}$

$x = -2$

◆ **Step 3**   Write down the ordered pair that is the solution to the system $(-2, 3)$. Check by inserting the values of x and y into equations (1) and (2).

(1) $4x + 2y = -2$	(2) $x = 13 - 5y$
$4(-2) + 2(3) = -2$	$-2 = 13 - 5(3)$
$-8 + 6 = -2$	$-2 = 13 - 15$
$-2 = -2$	$-2 = -2$
True	True

Example 9

Solve the system:

(1) $x + 2y = 6$

(2) $x + 2y = 4$

◆ **Step 1**   Let's begin with equation (1).

(1) $x + 2y = 6$

$x + 2y - 2y = 6 - 2y$ (equation 1a)

$x = 6 - 2y$

◆ **Step 2**   Substitute $6 - 2y$ for x in equation (2) and solve for y.

(2) $x + 2y = 4$

$6 - 2y + 2y = 4?$

$6 = 4?$

False

Note that the variable y dropped out of the equation, leaving us with a false statement. When this occurs, we say that the system of equations has no solution, which we write as $\varnothing$. If we were to graph these two equations, the lines would be parallel and would never intersect.

8.3 Solving by Elimination

We can also solve systems of linear equations by using the elimination method, which involves eliminating a variable in order to isolate another. The following examples show how we implement this method.

Example 10

Solve the system of equations:

(1) $3x + y = 7$

(2) $2x - y = 3$

◆ **Step 1**   The variable y in equation (1) and the variable y in equation (2) are opposites. In other words, one is positive and the other is negative, and they have the same coefficients. This means that when we add y and $-y$, the result is zero, and variable y has been eliminated.

◆ **Step 2**   Arrange equations (1) and (2) in separate rows and add vertically on both sides of the equations.

(1) $3x + y = 7$

(2) $2x - y = 3$
_____

$5x + 0 = 10$

◆ **Step 3**   Solve for x.

$5x = 10$

$\dfrac{5x}{5} = \dfrac{10}{5}$

$x = 2$

◆ **Step 4**   Let $x = 2$ in either equation (1) or (2) and solve for y. Let's select equation (1).

(1) $3x + y = 7$

$3(2) + y = 7$

$6 + y = 7$

$6 - 6 + y = 7 - 6$

$y = 1$

The solution is the ordered pair (2, 1).

◆ **Step 5**   Check the solution by inserting the values for x and y into the system of linear equations.

(1)	$3x + y = 7$	(2)	$2x - y = 3$
	$3(2) + 1 = 7$		$2(2) - 1 = 3$
	$6 + 1 = 7$		$4 - 1 = 3$
	True		True

The ordered pair (2, 1) satisfies the system of equations.

Example 11

Solve the system of equations:

(1) $2x + 4y = 10$

(2) $-4x + 2y = 10$

◆ **Step 1**   We cannot add at this stage, because neither the x variables nor the y variables are opposites. However, if we multiply equation (1) by 2, we can eliminate x.

◆ **Step 2**   Multiply equation (1) by 2.

(1) $2x + 4y = 10$

$2x(2) + 4y(2) = 10(2)$

$4x + 8y = 20$

Let's call this equation (1a).

◆ **Step 3**   Notice that the $4x$ in equation (1a) is now the opposite of the $-4x$ in equation (2). We can now add vertically to eliminate x and solve for y.

(1a) $4x + 8y = 20$

(2) $\underline{-4x + 2y = 10}$

$0 \; + 10y = 30$

$$\frac{10y}{10} = \frac{30}{10}$$

$y \; = 3$

◆ **Step 4**   Insert 3 for y in equation (1) or (2), but not (1a), and solve for x. Let's use equation (1).

(1) $2x + 4y \quad\;\; = 10$

$2x + 4(3) \quad = 10$

$2x + 12 \quad\;\; = 10$

$2x + 12 - 12 = 10 - 12$

$2x \quad\quad\quad\;\; = -2$

$$\frac{2x}{2} \quad\quad\;\; = \frac{-2}{2}$$

$x \quad\quad\quad\;\; = -1$

The solution is the ordered pair $(-1, 3)$.

Example 12

Solve the system of equations:
(1) $-3x - 2y = -4$
(2) $2x - 5y \;\; = 9$

◆ **Step 1**   Again, we cannot add, because neither the x variables nor the y variables are opposites. However, if we multiply the entire equation (1) by 2, and multiply the entire equation (2) by 3, we can later eliminate x.

(1) $-3x - 2y \quad = -4$

$-3x(2) - 2y(2) = -4(2)$

$-6x - 4y \quad = -8$

Let's call this equation (1a).

(2) $2x - 5y \quad = 9$

$2x(3) - 5y(3) = 9(3)$

$6x - 15y \quad = 27$

Let's call this equation (2a).

◆ **Step 2**   We can now add equation (1a) and equation (2a).

(1a) $-6x - 4y = -8$

(2a) $\underline{6x - 15y = 27}$

$0 \; -19y = 19$

$$\frac{-19y}{-19} = \frac{19}{-19}$$

$y \quad = -1$

◆ **Step 3**   Substitute -1 for y in equation (2) or equation (1) and solve for x. Let's use equation (2).

(2) $2x - 5y \quad = 9$

$2x - 5(-1) = 9$

$2x + 5 \quad = 9$

$2x + 5 - 5 = 9 - 5$

$2x \quad = 4$

$$\frac{2x}{2} = \frac{4}{2}$$

$$x = 2$$

The solution is the ordered pair $(2, -1)$.

Example 13

Solve the system of equations:

(1) $2x - y = -1$

(2) $4x - 2y = -2$

◆ **Step 1**   Multiply equation (1) by -2 so that the x variables in equations (1) and (2) are opposites.

(1) $2x(-2) - y(-2) = -1(-2)$

$-4x + 2y = 2$

Let's label this equation (1a).

◆ **Step 2**   Add vertically equations (1a) and (2).

(1a) $-4x + 2y = 2$

(2) $\underline{4x - 2y = -2}$

$0 = 0$

◆ **Step 3**   We can see that both x and y have been eliminated.

We are left with a true equation $0 = 0$.

If we graphed equations (1) and (2) in example 13, we would obtain the same line, because the equations are dependent. We know that there exist an infinite number of solutions, because every point along the line is a solution to the system of equations.

8.4 Word Problems

Now that we have learned methods for solving systems of linear equations, we are ready to apply this knowledge to word problems.

Example 14

> The sum of two numbers is 15 fewer than 45, and the difference between the two numbers is 2. What are the two numbers?

◆ **Step 1** Let x be one number and y be the other number. Remember that *sum* means addition and *difference* means subtraction. The sum of two numbers is 15 less than 45 is expressed algebraically this way:

$x + y = 45 - 15$ or

(1) $x + y = 30$

The difference between the two numbers is 2 can be expressed this way:

(2) $x - y = 2$

◆ **Step 2** Use the elimination method to solve the system of equations.

(1) $x + y = 30$

$$(2) \quad \underline{x - y = 2}$$
$$2x + 0 = 32$$
$$\frac{2x}{2} = \frac{32}{2}$$
$$x = 16$$

◆ **Step 3** Substitute 16 for x in equation (1) and solve for y.

(1) $x + y = 30$

$16 + y = 30$

$$y + 16 - 16 = 30 - 16$$

$$y \qquad = 14$$

The two numbers are 16 and 14.

Do a quick check to see if they satisfy the problem. Is their sum 15 fewer than 45, or 30? Yes. Is the difference between them 2? Yes.

Example 15

John and Mark collect baseball trading cards. The sum of their collection is 73 cards. Find how many cards John has if Mark has 19 fewer than three times the number of John's cards.

◆ **Step 1**   Let $x =$ the number of Mark's cards and $y =$ the number of John's cards. Together they own 73. So equation (1) is as follows:

(1) $x + y = 73$

◆ **Step 2**   Mark has three times as many cards as John less 19, so equation (2) is written like this:

(2) $x = 3y - 19$

◆ **Step 3**   Rewrite equation (2) as follows:

$$x - 3y = -19$$

We'll label this equation (2a).

◆ **Step 4**   The two equations in the system:

(1) $x + y \qquad = 73$

(2) $x \qquad = 3y - 19$

or (2a) $x - 3y = -19$

Solve the system, using the elimination method.

◆ **Step 5** Multiply equation (1) by 3 so that we can eliminate y.

(1) $x + y = 73$

$(3)x + (3)y = 73(3)$

$3x + 3y = 219$

Let's label this equation (1a).

◆ **Step 6** Add equations (1a) and (2a).

(1a) $3x + 3y = 219$

(2a) $\underline{x - 3y = -19}$

$4x + 0 = 200$

$\dfrac{4x}{4} = \dfrac{200}{4}$

$x = 50$

Mark has 50 cards.

◆ **Step 7** To find John's total, substitute 50 for x in equation (1) and solve for y.

(1) $x + y = 73$

$50 + y = 73$

$y + 50 - 50 = 73 - 50$

$y = 23$

Mark has 50 cards and John has 23 cards.

Again, do a quick check. The sum is 73. And Mark does have 19 fewer than $3 \times 23 (= 69)$ cards.

Example 16

Jorge opened his savings box and discovered a number of $1 and $10 bills. After counting them, he found that he had a total of 40 bills whose combined monetary value was $148. How many $1 bills and $10 bills did Jorge have?

◆ **Step 1**　Let x = the number of $1 bills and y = the number of $10 bills. Organize the data in a table (see table 8.1).

◆ **Step 2**　Construct the system of equations.

(1) $x + y = 40$

(2) $x + 10y = 148$

◆ **Step 3**　Multiply equation 2 by -1 so that we can eliminate x.

(2) $x + 10y = 148$

$x(-1) + 10y(-1) = 148(-1)$

$-x - 10y = -148$

Let's label this equation (2a).

◆ **Step 4**　Add and solve for y.

Table 8.1

Denomination of bill	Number of bills	Total value of bills
$1	x	$1 \times x = x$
$10	y	$10 \times y = 10y$
Total	40	$148

(1) $x + y = 40$

(2a) $-x - 10y = -148$

$0 \quad -9y = -108$

$$\frac{-9y}{-9} = \frac{-108}{-9}$$

$y = 12$

◆ **Step 5** Substitute 12 for y in equation (1) and solve for x.

(1) $x + y = 40$

$x + 12 = 40$

$x + 12 - 12 = 40 - 12$

$x = 28$

There were 28 \$1 bills and 12 \$10 bills.

Check: That is 40 bills worth \$28 + \$120 = \$148.

Example 17

Meryl and Miguel leave a highway rest stop at the same time and then travel in opposite directions. Meryl travels 5 miles per hour (mph) faster than Miguel, and after 4 hours, the two cars are 420 miles apart. At what speed are the two cars traveling?

◆ **Step 1** Let x = the rate of speed of Miguel's car and y = the rate of speed of Meryl's car. Remember that distance = rate × time.

◆ **Step 2** Organize the data in a table (see table 8.2).

Table 8.2

Car	Rate	Time	Distance
Miguel	x	4 hours	$4x$ miles
Meryl	y	4 hours	$4y$ miles

◆ **Step 3**   Meryl is traveling an additional 5 mph faster than Miguel, so equation 1 is written like this:

$$y = x + 5$$

$$x + 5 = y$$

$$x + 5 - 5 = y - 5$$

$$x = y - 5$$

$$x - y = y - y - 5$$

$$(1) \quad x - y = -5$$

◆ **Step 4**   The total distance between the two cars is 420 miles. Thus, equation (2) is:

$$(2) \quad 4x + 4y = 420$$

◆ **Step 5**   Multiply equation (1) by 4 so that we can eliminate y.

$$(1) \quad x - y = -5$$

$$x(4) - y(4) = -5(4)$$

$$4x - 4y = -20$$

Let's call this equation (1a).

◆ **Step 6**   Add, solving for x.

$$(1a) \quad 4x - 4y = -20$$

$$(2) \quad \underline{4x + 4y = 420}$$

$$8x + 0 = 400$$

$$8x = 400$$

$$\frac{8x}{8} = \frac{400}{8}$$

$$x = 50$$

◆ **Step 7**   Substitute 50 for x in equation (1) and solve for y.

(1) $x - y \quad = -5$

$\quad 50 - y \quad = -5$

$\quad 50 - 50 - y = -5 - 50$

$\quad -y = -55$

$\quad \dfrac{-y}{-1} = \dfrac{-55}{-1}$

$\quad y = 55$

Miguel is traveling at 50 mph, and Meryl is traveling at 55 mph.

Go back to check the original problem: in 4 hours Miguel traveled 200 miles and Meryl traveled 220 miles. That is correct.

8.5 Systems of Linear Equations in Three Variables

Some standardized mathematics tests require students to select (but not solve) a system of equations in three variables that could be used to solve a given word problem. Usually these are multiple-choice questions. So, we conclude this chapter with two examples for students to read through.

Example 18

After counting his loose change, which is made up of nickels, dimes, and quarters, D'Sean discovered that he had a total of $8.50. His change contains three times as many nickels as quarters, and the number of dimes is five more than the total number of nickels and quarters. Write a system of linear equations in three variables that could determine how many nickels, dimes, and quarters D'Sean had.

◆ **Step 1**   Let n = the number of nickels, d = the number of dimes, and q = the number of quarters. Convert $8.50 to 850 pennies (cents) to standardize the monetary value of the coins. A nickel is worth 5 pennies, or $5n$; a dime is worth 10 pennies, or $10d$; and a quarter is worth 25 pennies, or 25*q*. Together they are worth 850 pennies. The first equation, therefore, is this:

(1) $5n + 10d + 25q = 850$

◆ **Step 2**   There are 3 times as many nickels as quarters. We express that this way:

(2) $n = 3q$

◆ **Step 3**   The number of dimes is equal to 5 more than the total number of nickels and quarters. We write the third equation this way:

(3) $d = n + q + 5$

The complete system is this:

$5n + 10d + 25q = 850$

$n = 3q$

$d = n + q + 5$

Note that if there are three variables, there usually have to be three equations.

Example 19

The sum of three numbers is 46. One number is 6 more than a second and is twice the third number. Write a system of three linear equations to solve this problem.

◆ **Step 1**   Let *x*, *y*, and *z* represent the three numbers. The sum of these numbers is 46. The first equation:

(1) $x + y + z = 46$

◆ **Step 2**   One number is 6 more than a second. The second equation:

(2) $x = y + 6$

◆ **Step 3**   We also know that this number is twice the third number. The third equation:

(3) $x = 2z$

> The complete system of equations is this:
>
> $x + y + z = 46$
>
> $x \qquad\quad = y + 6$
>
> $x \qquad\quad = 2z$

Problems

1. Is the ordered pair $(3, 4)$ a solution of the following system of equations?

   $$4x - 2y = 4$$

   $$3x + 5y = 29$$

2. Is the ordered pair $(-1, -1)$ a solution of the following system of equations?

   $$9x - 5y = -4$$

   $$-5x + y = -4$$

3. If the ordered pair $\left(-\frac{1}{2}, \frac{3}{4}\right)$ satisfies the system of equations, complete the system.

   $$2x + 8y = ?$$

   $$16x - 4y = ?$$

4. Solve the system of equations by graphing.

   $$x + y = -5$$

   $$3x - y = -3$$

5. Solve the system of equations by graphing.

   $$3x - 3y = -18$$

   $$5x + 2y = -2$$

6. Using the substitution method, solve the system of equations.

   $$2a + 2b = 2$$

   $$3a - b = 1$$

7. Using the substitution method, solve the following system of equations.

$$4x - y = -7$$

$$7x + 6y = -51$$

8. Using the elimination method, solve the following system of equations.

$$2x + 3y = 11$$

$$-4x + 2y = 2$$

9. Using the elimination method, solve the following system of equations.

$$-6x - 4y = -8$$

$$4x - 10y = 18$$

10. The sum of two numbers is 7 less than 20, and the difference between the two numbers is 5. What are the two numbers?

11. Matilda and Elena collect fashion dolls. The sum of their collection is 36 dolls. Determine how many dolls both have if Matilda has 6 fewer than twice the number of Elena's dolls.

12. Mrs. Kim took in a number of $5 and $10 bills from her bake sale. After counting her earnings, she found that she had a total of 35 bills whose combined value was $225. How many $5 bills and $10 bills did she have?

13. Rob and Habib leave a highway motel diner at the same time and then travel in opposite directions at a constant rate of speed. Sam travels 10 mph faster than Rob. After 3 hours, their two cars are 420 miles apart. At what speed are the two cars traveling?

14. Arthur found $1 in pennies, nickels, and dimes under the cushions of his couch. There were five times as many pennies as dimes, and the number of nickels was 4 more than the number of dimes. Write three equations to determine how many pennies, nickels, and dimes Arthur found.

15. The sum of three numbers is 6. Twice the first number minus three times the second number is 2 less than the third number. Three times the first number minus twice the second number, minus the third number, is 1. Write a system of equations that could be used to find the three numbers.

Focus on English

Grammar

However

However is a logical connector that suggests conflict or contrast. Frequently, students begin sentences with the word "but." Try improving your writing by using the word *however*. For example, *Susan was certain that she had passed the test. Mary, however, was not as confident.* Write five sentences using the word *however*.

Neither... Nor

Many people say "neither...or." For example, *Neither Bob or Mary can read French.* The formal construction is *neither...nor* as in *Neither Bob <u>nor</u> Mary can read French.* However, *or* is correct in the construction *either...or.*

Fill in the blanks with one of the following: *either*, *or*, *neither*, or *nor*.

1. Neither June _____ Janet can ride horses.

2. It's getting late! Either call Sarah now _____ wait until tomorrow.

3. _____ Rafael nor Ramiro will give the presentation.

4. Neither John _____ Michael passed the test.

5. Either do your chores now _____ do them later.

 ## Improving Mathematical Vocabulary

Pronunciation

Underline the syllable or syllables that are stressed in the following: For example, e<u>lim</u>inate.

1. substitute

2. addition

3. difference

4. subtraction

5. equation

 ## Dictionary Work

Use your dictionary to find the meanings of the following words:

implement

intersect

eliminate

Chapter 9
Radical Expressions

9.0 Understanding Radicals

In chapter 1, we learned about square roots and cube roots and how to simplify square roots. In this chapter, we will continue our work with radical expressions (expressions that contain roots). We are now familiar with the symbol $\sqrt{}$, called a radical. A radicand is the expression located under the radical symbol. Moreover, the small superscript number just to the left of the radical is called the index (see fig. 9.1).

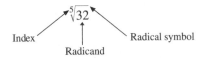

Figure 9.1 Parts of a Radical Expression

As we learned in chapter 1, mathematicians omit the index when writing square roots. Thus, $\sqrt{9}$ (the square root of 9) is not written as $\sqrt[2]{9}$. However, the cube root of 8, which we write as $\sqrt[3]{8}$, includes the number 3 as the index.

Example 1

Evaluate $\sqrt{1}$.

◆ **Step 1**   What number multiplied by itself equals 1?

$1 \times 1 = 1$

The solution is 1.

Example 2

Evaluate $-\sqrt{4}$.

◆ **Step 1**   Find the positive square root of 4. The result is 2.

◆ **Step 2**   We are evaluating a negative square root.

$$-\sqrt{4} = -2$$

Note that this is different from $\sqrt{-4}$, which has no real value, since there is no real number that, when multiplied by itself, will equal a negative.

9.1 Multiplication and the Product Rule

The product rule for radicals states that if $a \geq 0$ and $b \geq 0$, the following is true:

$$\sqrt{a \cdot b} = \sqrt{a} \cdot \sqrt{b}$$

Example 3

Multiply: $\sqrt{2} \cdot \sqrt{7}$

◆ **Step 1**   According to the product rule, $\sqrt{2} \cdot \sqrt{7} = \sqrt{2 \cdot 7} =$

$\sqrt{14}$

Example 4

Multiply and simplify: $\sqrt{8} \cdot \sqrt{2}$

◆ **Step 1** $\sqrt{8} \cdot \sqrt{2} = \sqrt{8 \cdot 2}$

◆ **Step 2** $\sqrt{8 \cdot 2} = \sqrt{16}$

◆ **Step 3**   Find the positive square root of 16.

The solution is 4, since $4 \times 4 = 16$.

Example 5

Simplify: $\sqrt{28}$

◆ **Step 1**   Factor the radicand.

$$\sqrt{28} = \sqrt{4 \cdot 7} =$$
$$\sqrt{4}\sqrt{7}$$

◆ **Step 2**   The positive square root of 4 is 2.

The solution is $2\sqrt{7}$.

Simplifying Square Roots Whose Radicands Contain Variables Raised to Powers

How do we identify the perfect square of a variable? Look at the radicand and check to see if the exponent on the variable is even. If it is, the radicand contains a perfect square. For example, in the radical expression $\sqrt{x^6}$, x^6 is a perfect square, because the exponent is even. We evaluate a radical expression whose radicand contains a perfect square, such as x^6, by using this rule:

> The square root of a variable with an even power = the variable
> raised to one-half of its original power.

This is because $\sqrt{x} = x^{\frac{1}{2}}$. Similarly, $\sqrt[3]{x} = x^{\frac{1}{3}}$. A fractional exponent means a root, with the index being the denominator of the fraction. Thus, $\sqrt{x^3} = x^{\frac{3}{2}}$. This is discussed in more detail at the end of this chapter.

Example 6

Simplify: $\sqrt{x^6}$

◆ **Step 1**   The exponent is even, so the radicand contains a perfect square.
    Multiply the exponent by $\frac{1}{2}$.

$$\sqrt{x^6} =$$
$$(x^6)^{\frac{1}{2}} = x^{\frac{6}{2}} =$$

x^3

Example 7

Simplify: $\sqrt{x^4 y^2}$

◆ **Step 1**   The exponents are even, so the radicand contains perfect squares. Multiply the exponents by $\frac{1}{2}$.

$$\sqrt{x^4 y^2} =$$
$$(x^4 y^2)^{\frac{1}{2}} =$$
$$x^{\frac{4}{2}} y^{\frac{2}{2}} =$$
$$x^2 y^1 =$$

$$x^2 y$$

When we simplify radical expressions containing a variable in the radicand that is not a perfect square—because the exponent is odd—we begin by writing the radicand as the product of two factors, one of which is the perfect square and the other of which is a factor whose exponent = 1. Thus, using the product rule for exponents, we can write $\sqrt{x^7}$ as $\sqrt{x^6 \cdot x^1}$. What we cannot simplify, we leave in radical form.

Example 8

Simplify: $\sqrt{x^7}$

◆ **Step 1**   The exponent is odd, so we must express the radicand as the product of two factors, one of which is a perfect square, and the other a factor whose exponent = 1.

$$\sqrt{x^7} = \sqrt{x^6 \cdot x^1} =$$
$$\sqrt{x^6} \cdot \sqrt{x^1} =$$
$$(x^6)^{\frac{1}{2}} \cdot \sqrt{x^1} =$$
$$x^{\frac{6}{2}} \cdot \sqrt{x^1} =$$
$$x^3 \cdot \sqrt{x} =$$

$$x^3 \sqrt{x}$$

Example 9

Simplify: $\sqrt{x^3 y^9 z^{13}}$

◆ **Step 1** The exponents are odd, so we must express each variable in the radicand as the product of two factors, one of which is a perfect square and the other of which is a factor whose exponent = 1.

$$\sqrt{x^3 y^9 z^{13}} \qquad =$$
$$\sqrt{x^2 y^8 z^{12}} \cdot \sqrt{x^1 y^1 z^1} \quad =$$
$$(x^2 y^8 z^{12})^{\frac{1}{2}} \cdot \sqrt{x^1 y^1 z^1} =$$
$$x^{\frac{2}{2}} y^{\frac{8}{2}} z^{\frac{12}{2}} \cdot \sqrt{x^1 y^1 z^1} \quad =$$
$$x^1 y^4 z^6 \cdot \sqrt{x^1 y^1 z^1} \quad =$$
$$xy^4 z^6 \cdot \sqrt{xyz} \qquad =$$

$$xy^4 z^6 \sqrt{xyz}$$

Example 10

Simplify: $\sqrt{9x^4}$

◆ **Step 1** The radicand contains two perfect squares, 9 and x^4. Simplify.

$$\sqrt{9x^4} \quad =$$
$$\sqrt{3^2 x^4} \quad =$$
$$\sqrt{3^2} \sqrt{x^4} =$$

◆ **Step 2** Multiply the exponent by $\frac{1}{2}$ and remove the radical symbol.

$$3 \cdot (x^4)^{\frac{1}{2}} =$$
$$3 \cdot x^{\frac{4}{2}} \quad =$$
$$3 \cdot x^2 \quad =$$

$$3x^2$$

Example 11

Simplify: $\sqrt{50x^3y^5}$

◆ **Step 1**   Express the radical as the product of two radicals, one of which has a perfect square radicand.

$\sqrt{50x^3y^5} \qquad =$

$\sqrt{25x^2y^4} \cdot \sqrt{2x^1y^1} =$

◆ **Step 2**   Multiply the exponents of the perfect square variables in the radicand by $\frac{1}{2}$, and remove the radical symbol.

$5x^{\frac{2}{2}}y^{\frac{4}{2}} \cdot \sqrt{2x^1y^1} \quad =$

$5xy^2 \cdot \sqrt{2xy} \qquad =$

$5xy^2\sqrt{2xy}$

9.2 Addition and Subtraction of Square Roots

Adding Like Square Roots

Like (similar) square roots are radical expressions that have the same radicand, such as $7\sqrt{5}$ and $4\sqrt{5}$. Using the distributive property, add the coefficients of the radical expressions, and then multiply the sum by the like square root (see fig. 9.2). Essentially, we treat the radical expression like a variable: $7x + 4x = 11x$, and $7\sqrt{5} + 4\sqrt{5} = 11\sqrt{5}$.

Example 12

Add: $3\sqrt{7} + 9\sqrt{7}$

◆ **Step 1**   The radicands are the same, so add the coefficients and multiply by the like square root.

$3\sqrt{7} + 9\sqrt{7} =$

$(3 + 9)\sqrt{7} \quad =$

$(12)\sqrt{7} \qquad =$

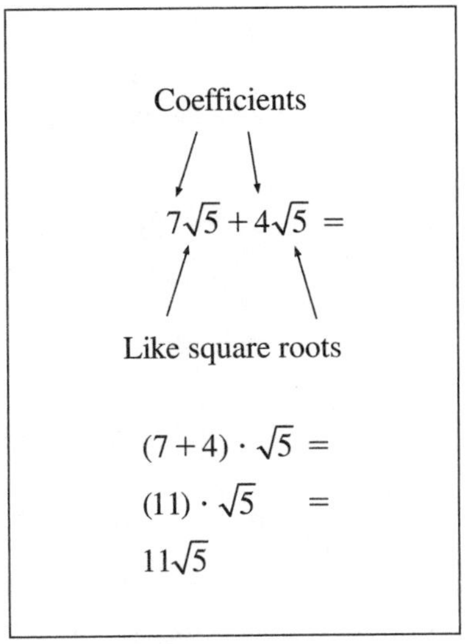

Figure 9.2: Adding Like Square Roots

$$12\sqrt{7}$$

Example 13

Add: $3\sqrt{x} + 5\sqrt{x} + 4x$

◆ **Step 1** Add the like square roots. The $4x$ cannot be combined.

$$3\sqrt{x} + 5\sqrt{x} + 4x =$$
$$(3+5)\sqrt{x} + 4x =$$
$$(8)\sqrt{x} + 4x =$$

$$8\sqrt{x} + 4x$$

Subtracting Like Square Roots

Subtracting like square roots is similar to adding them. Again, using the distributive property, subtract the coefficients of the radical expressions, and then multiply the difference by the like square root (see fig. 9.3).

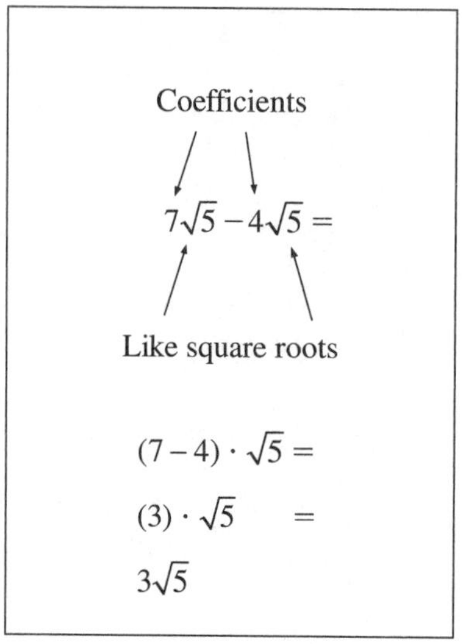

Figure 9.3: Subtracting Like Square Roots

Example 14

Subtract: $5\sqrt{6} - 7\sqrt{6}$

◆ **Step 1**   Subtract the coefficients, and then multiply the difference by the like square root.

$5\sqrt{6} - 7\sqrt{6} =$
$(5-7)\sqrt{6}\ =$
$(-2)\sqrt{6}\ \ =$

$-2\sqrt{6}$

Adding Unlike Square Roots

Unlike square roots are those that have different radicands. We cannot add two or more unlike square roots unless we can change them from unlike to like. This is not always possible, however.

Example 15

Add: $\sqrt{18} + \sqrt{2}$

◆ **Step 1**   The radicands are different, so the square roots are unlike. If we simplify $\sqrt{18}$, we might obtain a like square root, which we can add to $\sqrt{2}$.

$$\sqrt{18} + \sqrt{2} \ =$$
$$\sqrt{9 \cdot 2} + \sqrt{2} \ =$$
$$\sqrt{9}\sqrt{2} + \sqrt{2} \ =$$

◆ **Step 2**   Evaluate the perfect square, and remember that the coefficient of $\sqrt{2}$ is 1.

$$(3)\sqrt{2} + 1\sqrt{2} \ =$$
$$(3 + 1)\sqrt{2} \ \ =$$

$$4\sqrt{2}$$

Example 16

Add: $5\sqrt{12} + 3\sqrt{27} + 27$

◆ **Step 1**   Simplify the unlike square roots to find, if possible, like square roots.

$$5\sqrt{12} \ + 3\sqrt{27} \ + 27 =$$
$$5\sqrt{4 \cdot 3} \ + 3\sqrt{9 \cdot 3} \ + 27 =$$
$$5\sqrt{4}\sqrt{3} \ + 3\sqrt{9}\sqrt{3} \ + 27 =$$

◆ **Step 2**   Simplify the perfect squares.

$$5(2)\sqrt{3} + 3(3)\sqrt{3} + 27 \ =$$
$$10\sqrt{3} \ + 9\sqrt{3} \ \ + 27 \ =$$

◆ **Step 3**   Add the like square root terms.

$$(10 + 9)\sqrt{3} + 27 =$$

$$19\sqrt{3} + 27$$

Example 17

Add: $3\sqrt{2} + 7\sqrt{27}$

◆ **Step 1**   Simplify the unlike square roots to find, if possible, like square roots.

$3\sqrt{2} + 7\sqrt{27}$ =

$3\sqrt{2} + 7\sqrt{9 \cdot 3}$ =

$3\sqrt{2} + 7\sqrt{9}\sqrt{3}$ =

$3\sqrt{2} + 7(3)\sqrt{3}$ =

$3\sqrt{2} + 21\sqrt{3}$

◆ **Step 2**   We can proceed no further, because the radical expressions are unlike.

Subtracting Unlike Square Roots

To subtract unlike square roots, we first need to change them from unlike to like roots, if possible, as we did for adding them.

Example 18

Subtract: $3\sqrt{125} - 5\sqrt{20}$

◆ **Step 1**   Simplify to search for like square roots.

$3\sqrt{125} - 5\sqrt{20}$ =

$3\sqrt{25 \cdot 5} - 5\sqrt{4 \cdot 5}$ =

$3\sqrt{25}\sqrt{5} - 5\sqrt{4}\sqrt{5}$ =

$3(5)\sqrt{5} - 5(2)\sqrt{5}$ =

$15\sqrt{5} - 10\sqrt{5}$ =

$(15 - 10)\sqrt{5}$ =

$5\sqrt{5}$

9.3 The Quotient Rule for Radicals

We can also simplify square roots by using the quotient rule for radicals, which states that if $a \geq 0$ and $b \geq 0$, then $\sqrt{\dfrac{a}{b}} = \dfrac{\sqrt{a}}{\sqrt{b}}$.

Example 19

Simplify: $\sqrt{\dfrac{32}{2}}$

◆ **Step 1**   Reduce the radicand to its lowest terms.

$$\sqrt{\frac{32}{2}} = \sqrt{\frac{16}{1}} =$$
$$\sqrt{16} \qquad =$$
$$\sqrt{4^2}$$

4

Example 20

Simplify: $\sqrt{\dfrac{16}{9}}$

◆ **Step 1**   Use the quotient rule for radicals.

$$\sqrt{\frac{16}{9}} = \frac{\sqrt{16}}{\sqrt{9}}$$

◆ **Step 2**   Simplify the perfect squares.

$$\frac{\sqrt{4^2}}{\sqrt{3^2}} =$$

$$\frac{4}{3}$$

Example 21

Simplify: $\sqrt{\dfrac{27x^6}{3y^2}}$

- ◆ **Step 1**   Reduce the radicand to its lowest terms by dividing the numerator and the denominator by the common factor, 3.

$$\sqrt{\frac{27x^6}{3y^2}} = \sqrt{\frac{9x^6}{1y^2}} =$$

- ◆ **Step 2**   Use the quotient rule.

$$\frac{\sqrt{9x^6}}{\sqrt{y^2}} =$$

- ◆ **Step 3**   Simplify the perfect squares.

$$\frac{\sqrt{3^2 x^6}}{\sqrt{y^2}} =$$

$$\frac{(3)\cdot(x^6)^{\frac{1}{2}}}{(y^2)^{\frac{1}{2}}} =$$

$$\frac{3x^3}{y^1} =$$

$$\frac{3x^3}{y}$$

9.4 Rationalizing the Denominator

Sometimes, we see fractions whose denominators are radicals, such as $\dfrac{2}{\sqrt{3}}$. We can simplify them by rationalizing the denominator, which involves removing the radical from the denominator. We proceed this way:

1. Multiply both the numerator and the denominator by the radical contained in the denominator.

2. Simplify the numerator and denominator, if possible. For example, we make sure that there are no fractions or perfect squares left in the radicands.

Example 22

Simplify: $\dfrac{3}{\sqrt{2}}$

◆ **Step 1**   Multiply the numerator and the denominator by $\sqrt{2}$.

$$\frac{3}{\sqrt{2}} \cdot \frac{\sqrt{2}}{\sqrt{2}} =$$

$$\frac{3 \cdot \sqrt{2}}{\sqrt{2} \cdot \sqrt{2}} =$$

$$\frac{3\sqrt{2}}{\sqrt{4}} =$$

◆ **Step 2**   Simplfiy the perfect square.

$$\frac{3\sqrt{2}}{\sqrt{2^2}} =$$

$$\frac{3\sqrt{2}}{(2)} =$$

$$\frac{3\sqrt{2}}{2}$$

Example 23

Simplify: $\dfrac{4}{\sqrt{8}}$

◆ **Step 1**   Multiply the numerator and the denominator by $\sqrt{8}$.

$$\frac{4}{\sqrt{8}} \cdot \frac{\sqrt{8}}{\sqrt{8}} =$$

$$\frac{4\sqrt{8}}{\sqrt{64}} =$$

◆ **Step 2**   Factor the radicand in the numerator.

$$\frac{4\sqrt{4 \cdot 2}}{\sqrt{64}} =$$

◆ **Step 3**   Simplify the perfect squares.

$$\frac{4(2)\sqrt{2}}{(8)} =$$

$$\frac{8\sqrt{2}}{8} =$$

◆ **Step 4**   Reduce to simplest form by canceling out the eights.

$$\sqrt{2}$$

Example 24

Simplify: $\dfrac{\sqrt{7}}{\sqrt{12}}$

◆ **Step 1**   Multiply by $\dfrac{\sqrt{12}}{\sqrt{12}}$.

$$\frac{\sqrt{7}}{\sqrt{12}} \cdot \frac{\sqrt{12}}{\sqrt{12}} =$$

$$\frac{\sqrt{7}\sqrt{12}}{\sqrt{12}\sqrt{12}} =$$

$$\frac{\sqrt{84}}{\sqrt{144}} =$$

◆ **Step 2**   Factor the radicand in the numerator.

$$\frac{\sqrt{4 \cdot 21}}{\sqrt{144}} =$$

◆ **Step 3**   Simplify the perfect squares.

$$\frac{\sqrt{4}\sqrt{21}}{\sqrt{144}} =$$

$$\frac{(2)\sqrt{21}}{(12)} =$$

◆ **Step 4**   Simplify the fraction.

$$\frac{^1(\cancel{2})\sqrt{21}}{^6(\cancel{12})} =$$

$$\frac{1\sqrt{21}}{6} =$$

$$\boxed{\frac{\sqrt{21}}{6}}$$

9.5 Rationalizing the Numerator

A fractional expression that contains a radical in the numerator looks like this example:

$$\frac{8+4\sqrt{3}}{4}$$

We simplify rational expressions that contain radicals in the numerator in this way:

- Before proceeding, simplify the radical expression (if possible) by factoring out the greatest common factor (GCF) from each term in the numerator.

- If possible, cancel out a common factor from the already factored numerator and denominator.

Example 25

Simplify: $\dfrac{2+8\sqrt{7}}{2}$

◆ **Step 1**   Factor the numerator. The GCF is 2.

$$\frac{2+8\sqrt{7}}{2} =$$

$$\frac{2(1+4\sqrt{7})}{2} =$$

◆ **Step 2**   Cancel out the common factor 2 from the numerator and the denominator.

$$\frac{\cancel{2}(1+4\sqrt{7})}{\cancel{2}} =$$

$$1+4\sqrt{7}$$

Example 26

Simplify: $\dfrac{5+2\sqrt{50}}{5}$

◆ **Step 1**   Factor the radicand.

$$\frac{5+2\sqrt{50}}{5} =$$

$$\frac{5+2\sqrt{25\cdot 2}}{5} =$$

$$\frac{5+2\sqrt{25}\sqrt{2}}{5} =$$

$$\frac{5+2(5)\sqrt{2}}{5} =$$

◆ **Step 2**   Continue to simplify the numerator.

$$\frac{5+10\sqrt{2}}{5} =$$

◆ **Step 3**   Factor the numerator.

$$\frac{5(1+2\sqrt{2})}{5} =$$

◆ **Step 4**   Cancel out the common factor.

$$\frac{\cancel{5}(1+2\sqrt{2})}{\cancel{5}} =$$

$$1+2\sqrt{2}$$

9.6 Equations with Radicals

In this section, we will learn how to solve radical equations that contain one or two square root terms. A radical equation is one that includes a variable located in the radicand. For example, $\sqrt{x} = 9$ and $\sqrt{x+3} = 3$ are radical equations. We follow these general steps to solve a radical equation:

1. Isolate the radical expression on one side of the equation.

2. Square both sides of the equation to remove the square root.

3. Solve for the variable.

4. Check the result.

Solving Radical Equations that Contain One Square Root Term

Example 27

Solve for x: $\sqrt{x} = 9$

◆ **Step 1**   Square both sides of the equation to remove the square root.

$$\left(\sqrt{x}\right)^2 = 9^2$$
$$x = (9)(9)$$

$$x = 81$$

Is 9 the square root of 81? Yes, since $9 \times 9 = 81$.

Example 28

Solve for x: $\sqrt{x-4} = 6$

◆ **Step 1**   Square both sides of the equation to remove the square root.

$$\left(\sqrt{x-4}\right)^2 = 6^2$$
$$x - 4 = (6)(6)$$
$$x - 4 = 36$$

◆ **Step 2**   Solve for *x*.

$$x - 4 + 4 = 36 + 4$$

$$x = 40$$

◆ **Step 3**   Check the answer.

Does $\sqrt{40 - 4} = 6$?

Does $\sqrt{36} \quad = 6$?

$$6 \quad = 6$$

The solution is correct.

Solving Radical Equations That Contain Two Square Root Terms

Here are two examples of radical equations that contain two square root terms:

$$\sqrt{x + 5} = \sqrt{13 - x}$$
$$\sqrt{3x} - \sqrt{2x + 12} = 0$$

To solve equations of this form, follow these steps:

1. Make sure that there is one square root term on each side of the equation.

2. Square both sides of the equation.

3. Solve for the variable.

4. Check the result.

Example 29

Solve for *x*: $\sqrt{x + 5} = \sqrt{13 - x}$

◆ **Step 1**   Square each term.

$$\left(\sqrt{x + 5}\right)^2 = \left(\sqrt{13 - x}\right)^2$$

◆ **Step 2**   Solve for x

$$
\begin{array}{rcl}
x + 5 & = & 13 - x \\
x + 5 - 5 & = & 13 - x - 5 \\
x & = & 13 - x - 5 \\
x + x & = & 13 - x + x - 5 \\
2x & = & 13 - 5 \\
2x & = & 8 \\
\dfrac{2x}{x} & = & \dfrac{8}{2}
\end{array}
$$

$$x = 4$$

◆ **Step 3**   Check the result.

$$\sqrt{x + 5} = \sqrt{13 - x}$$

Does $\sqrt{4 + 5} = \sqrt{13 - 4}$?

Does $\sqrt{9} = \sqrt{9}$?

$$
\begin{array}{rcl}
3 & = & 3
\end{array}
$$

True

9.7 Rational Exponents

In this section we will convert radical expressions to exponential form and vice versa. As we saw earlier in this chapter, the rule for rational exponents is displayed below. The variable a is positive, m and n are integers, and $n > 0$. Notice that the index of the radical expression is the same as the denominator of the fractional exponent.

$$a^{\frac{m}{n}} = \sqrt[n]{a^m} \text{ or}$$

$$a^{\frac{m}{n}} = \left(\sqrt[n]{a}\right)^m$$

Example 30

Change $\sqrt[3]{9^5}$ to exponential form.

◆ **Step 1**   Use the rule $\left(\sqrt[n]{a}\right)^m = a^{\frac{m}{n}}$ or $\sqrt[n]{a^m} = a^{\frac{m}{n}}$ where $a = 9$, $m = 5$, and $n = 3$.

$$\sqrt[3]{9^5} =$$

$$9^{\frac{5}{3}}$$

Example 31

Change $8^{\frac{2}{3}}$ to a radical expression.

◆ **Step 1**   Let $a^{\frac{m}{n}} = \sqrt[n]{a^m}$ or $a^{\frac{m}{n}} = \left(\sqrt[n]{a}\right)^m$, where $a = 8$, $m = 2$, and $n = 3$.

The radical expressions are as follows:

$$8^{\frac{2}{3}} = \sqrt[3]{8^2} \text{ or}$$

$$8^{\frac{2}{3}} = \left(\sqrt[3]{8}\right)^2$$

Using Rational Exponents to Simplify Radical Expressions

Sometimes it is easier to simplify a radical expression by first converting it to its exponential form and then, if possible, expressing the result as a radical.

Example 32

Use rational exponents to simplify: $\sqrt[6]{x^3}$

◆ **Step 1**   Use the rule $\sqrt[n]{a^m} = a^{\frac{m}{n}}$ where $a = x$, $m = 3$, and $n = 6$. Thus, we get the following:

$$\sqrt[6]{x^3} = x^{\frac{3}{6}} = x^{\frac{1}{2}}$$

◆ **Step 2**   Since $a^{\frac{1}{n}} = \sqrt[n]{a}$, then the following is true:

$$x^{\frac{1}{2}} = \sqrt[2]{x^1} = \sqrt{x}$$

Example 33

Use rational exponents to simplify: $\sqrt[4]{(x+4)^2}$

◆ **Step 1**   Use the rule $\sqrt[n]{a^m} = a^{\frac{m}{n}}$ where $a = (x+4)$, $m = 2$, and $n = 4$. Thus,

$$\sqrt[4]{(x+4)^2} = (x+4)^{\frac{2}{4}} = (x+4)^{\frac{1}{2}}$$

◆ **Step 2**   Since $a^{\frac{1}{n}} = \sqrt[n]{a}$, then

$$(x+4)^{\frac{1}{2}} = \sqrt[2]{(x+4)^1} =$$

$$\sqrt{x+4}$$

Problems

1. Evaluate: $\sqrt{16}$

2. Simplify: $\sqrt{x^8}$

3. Simplify: $\sqrt{x^4 y^2}$

4. Simplify: $\sqrt{x^7}$

5. Simplify: $\sqrt{x^9 y^{12}}$

6. Add: $5\sqrt{5x} + 3\sqrt{5x} + 5x$

7. Subtract: $5\sqrt{6} - 7\sqrt{6} - 3$

8. Add: $2\sqrt{8} + 5\sqrt{32}$

9. Add: $\sqrt{12} + 2\sqrt{27} + 4$

10. Simplify: $\dfrac{\sqrt{1}}{\sqrt{49}}$

11. Simplify: $\dfrac{2}{\sqrt{3}}$

12. Simplify: $\sqrt{\dfrac{x^8}{5}}$

13. Simplify: $\dfrac{8 - \sqrt{20}}{2}$

14. Convert $\sqrt[5]{32x}$ to exponential form.

15. Simplify: $\sqrt[6]{x^4}$

Focus on English

Grammar

The present perfect tense is used to ask about a general experience in the past. For example, *Have you seen Jackie Chan's new movie?* We use the past simple, however, to discuss a specific moment in the past, such as *I went to the store yesterday*. Here are some regular and irregular verbs in the present perfect.

Infinitive	Present perfect
Regular Verbs	
to kiss	have kissed
to cry	have cried
to learn	have learned
Irregular Verbs	
to leave	have left
to speak	have spoken
to buy	have bought
to see	have seen
to write	have written
to meet	have met

Complete the sentences with the present perfect tense, using the verb in the parentheses.

1. Have you _____ the newspaper? (see)

2. Have you _____ his wife? (meet)

3. I have _____ many poems. (write)

4. Have you _____ any milk? (buy)

5. Have you _____ to Margaret? (speak)

Improving Mathematical Vocabulary

Discuss with your classmates the following words:

radical

radicand

index

rational equation

 Dictionary Work

Look up the meanings of the following words:

radical

rational

Chapter 10

Quadratic Equations and Functions

10.0 Understanding Quadratic Equations

A quadratic equation is one that contains a squared term. The standard form of a quadratic equation in one variable is as follows, where a, b, and c are real numbers and $a \neq 0$:

$$ax^2 + bx + c = 0$$

Examples of quadratic equations in standard form are the following:

$$x^2 + 3x + 2 = 0 \qquad\qquad y^2 + 8y + 7 = 0$$

The equation $x^2 - 10x = -9$ is also a quadratic equation, but it is not in standard form. In order to rewrite this equation in standard form, perform the following operations:

$$x^2 - 10x = -9$$

$$x^2 - 10x + 9 = -9 + 9$$

$$x^2 - 10x + 9 = 0$$

We solve a quadratic equation by finding a value or values for the variable that make the equation true. Again, we can check the results by inserting our values back into the original equation to see if they are true solutions to the equation.

10.1 Solving by Factoring

We will discover in this chapter that there is more than one way to solve quadratic equations. In this section we will use the factoring method. At the heart of this method is the zero-factor property, which states that if a and b are real numbers, and $a \cdot b = 0$, then either $a = 0$, $b = 0$, or both $a = 0$ and $b = 0$. For example, if $8 \cdot x = 0$, then x must be zero. Similarly, if $(x - 1)(x - 9) = 0$, then at least one of these two factors $(x - 1)$ or $(x - 9)$ must be zero. Here are the steps we take to solve a quadratic equation by factoring:

1. Make sure the equation is in standard form. Rewrite it if necessary.

2. Factor the polynomial on the left side of the equation by one of the methods shown in chapter 4.

3. Using the zero-factor property, set each factor equal to zero.

4. Solve for the variable in the resulting equations.

5. Check each result by inserting the values obtained back into the original equation.

Example 1

Solve: $x^2 + 11x + 24 = 0$

◆ **Step 1**   Note that the equation is in standard form, so we can now factor it.

$$x^2 + 11x + 24 = 0$$

$$(x + 3)(x + 8) = 0$$

◆ **Step 2**   Using the zero-factor property, set each binomial factor to 0 and solve for x in both equations.

$(x + 3) = 0$ or $(x + 8) = 0$

$x + 3 = 0$ or $x + 8 = 0$

$x + 3 - 3 = 0 - 3$ or $x + 8 - 8 = 0 - 8$

$x = 0 - 3$ or $x = 0 - 8$

$x = -3$ or $x = -8$

◆ **Step 3**   Check the results by inserting them into the original equation.

(1) Let $x = -3$

$$x^2 + 11x + 24 \qquad = 0$$

Does $(-3)^2 + 11(-3) + 24 = 0$?

Does $(9) + 11(-3) + 24 \quad = 0$?

Does $9 - 33 + 24 \qquad = 0$?

Does $-24 + 24 \qquad = 0$?

$$0 \qquad\qquad = 0$$

True

(2) Let $x = -8$

$$x^2 + 11x + 24 \qquad = 0$$

Does $(-8)^2 + 11(-8) + 24 = 0$?

Does $(64) + 11(-8) + 24 \quad = 0$?

Does $64 - 88 + 24 \qquad = 0$?

Does $-24 + 24 \qquad = 0$?

$$0 \qquad\qquad = 0$$

True

The solution set is $\{-8, -3\}$

Example 2

Solve: $a^2 + 9 = 10a$

◆ **Step 1**   Write the equation in standard form.

$a^2 + 9 \quad\quad = 10a$

$a^2 + 9 - 10a = 10a - 10a$

$a^2 + 9 - 10a = 0$

$a^2 - 10a + 9 = 0$

◆ **Step 2**   Factor the trinomial $a^2 - 10a + 9$.

$(a - 1)(a - 9) = 0$

◆ **Step 3**   Using the zero-factor property, set each factor to 0, and solve for a in both equations.

$(a - 1) = 0 \quad\quad$ or $(a - 9) = 0$

$a - 1 + 1 = 0 + 1$ or $a - 9 + 9 = 0 + 9$

$a = 0 + 1 \quad\quad$ or $a = 0 + 9$

$a = 1$ or $a = 9$

◆ **Step 4**   Check the results by inserting them into the original equation.

(1) Let $a = 1$.

$a^2 + 9 \quad\quad = 10a$

Does $(1)^2 + 9 = 10(1)$?

Does $1 + 9 = 10$?

$10 \qquad = 10$

Yes

(2) Let $a = 9$.

$a^2 + 9 \qquad = 10a$

Does $(9)^2 + 9 = 10(9)$?

Does $81 + 9 \ = 90$?

$90 \qquad\qquad = 90$

Yes

Example 3

Solve: $x^2 - 16 = 0$

◆ **Step 1:** Note that $x^2 - 16$ is the difference of squares, so we can quickly factor this as

$(x - 4)(x + 4) = 0$

◆ **Step 2:** Using the zero-factor property, set each factor to 0 and solve for x in both equations.

$(x - 4) = 0 \qquad$ or $(x + 4) = 0$

$x - 4 + 4 = 0 + 4$ or $x + 4 - 4 = 0 - 4$

$x = 4$ or $x = -4$

The solution set is $\{-4, 4\}$.

◆ **Step 3**	Does $(-4)^2 - 16 = 0$?	Does $(+4)^2 - 16 = 0$?
	Does $16 - 16 = 0$?	Does $16 - 16 = 0$?
	$0 = 0$	$0 = 0$
	Yes	Yes

10.2 Solving by the Square Root Property

The square root property states that for any positive number a, if $x^2 = a$, then $x = \sqrt{a}$ or $x = -\sqrt{a}$. Be sure the minus sign is in front of the radical, not within it.

Example 4

Solve: $x^2 = 9$

◆ **Step 1**   Use the square root property.

$x = \sqrt{9}$ or $x = -\sqrt{9}$

$x = 3$ or $x = -3$

The solution set is $\{-3, 3\}$.

We can also write "$x = \sqrt{9}$ or $x = -\sqrt{9}$" as $x = \pm\sqrt{9}$, which we read as "x is equal to plus or minus the square root of nine."

Example 5

Solve: $x^2 = 48$

◆ **Step 1**   Use the square root property.

$x = \sqrt{48}$ or $x = -\sqrt{48}$

◆ **Step 2**   Simplify the square roots.

$x = \sqrt{16 \cdot 3}$ or $x = -\sqrt{16 \cdot 3}$

$x = \sqrt{16}\sqrt{3}$ or $x = -\sqrt{16}\sqrt{3}$

$x = (4)\sqrt{3}$ or $x = -(4)\sqrt{3}$

$$x = 4\sqrt{3} \quad \text{or} \quad x = -4\sqrt{3}$$

The solution set is $\left\{-4\sqrt{3}, 4\sqrt{3}\right\}$

Example 6

Solve: $4x^2 - 8 = 64$

◆ **Step 1**   Rewrite the equation to isolate the squared term.

$$4x^2 - 8 + 8 = 64 + 8$$
$$4x^2 = 64 + 8$$
$$4x^2 = 72$$
$$\frac{4x^2}{4} = \frac{72}{4}$$
$$x^2 = 18$$

◆ **Step 2**   Use the square root property.

$$x = \sqrt{18} \quad \text{or} \quad x = -\sqrt{18}$$

◆ **Step 3**   Simplify the square roots.

$$x = \sqrt{9 \cdot 2} \quad \text{or} \quad x = -\sqrt{9 \cdot 2}$$
$$x = \sqrt{9}\sqrt{2} \quad \text{or} \quad x = -\sqrt{9}\sqrt{2}$$
$$x = 3\sqrt{2} \quad \text{or} \quad x = -3\sqrt{2}$$

The solution set is $\left\{-3\sqrt{2}, 3\sqrt{2}\right\}$.

10.3   Solving by Using the Quadratic Formula

In this section, we will learn how to use the quadratic formula, which enables us to find the solutions for any quadratic equation. This formula works all the time. This important formula is as follows:

$$\text{For any quadratic equation } ax^2 + bx + c = 0,$$

$$x = \frac{-b \pm \sqrt{b^2 - 4ac}}{2a}, \text{ where } a \neq 0$$

Before we use the quadratic formula, we must make sure to do two things:

1. Write the quadratic equation in the standard form of $ax^2 + bx + c = 0$.

2. Write down the values of a, b, and c before proceeding.

Note that if $b^2 < 4ac$, the radicand is negative and there can be no real solution for x. It is a good idea before starting to use the quadratic formula to make sure that $b^2 - 4ac$ is a positive number.

Example 7

Solve $x^2 + 6x + 5 = 0$ by using the quadratic formula.

◆ **Step 1**   Find out whether the equation is written in standard form.

◆ **Step 2**   If so, assign values for a, b, and c.

$$ax^2 + bx + c = 0$$

$$a = 1, b = 6, \text{ and } c = 5$$

◆ **Step 3**   Use the quadratic formula where $a = 1$, $b = 6$, and $c = 5$.

$$x = \frac{-(6) \pm \sqrt{(6)^2 - 4(1)(5)}}{2(1)}$$

$$x = \frac{-6 \pm \sqrt{(36) - 4(1)(5)}}{2(1)}$$

$$x = \frac{-6 \pm \sqrt{(36) - (4)(5)}}{(2)}$$

$$x = \frac{-6 \pm \sqrt{(36) - (20)}}{(2)}$$

$$x = \frac{-6 \pm \sqrt{(16)}}{(2)}$$

$$x = \frac{-6 \pm 4}{(2)}$$

$$x = \frac{-6 + 4}{2} \quad \text{or} \quad x = \frac{-6 - 4}{2}$$

$$x = \frac{-2}{2} \quad \text{or} \quad x = \frac{-10}{2}$$

$$x = -1 \quad \text{or} \quad x = -5$$

The solution set for x is $\{-5, -1\}$.

◆ **Step 4**   Check the results by inserting the values for x into the original equation in this example.

(1) Let $x = -1$.

$$x^2 + 6x + 5 = 0$$

Does $(-1)^2 + 6(-1) + 5 = 0$?

Does $1 - 6 + 5 \qquad = 0$?

Does $-5 + 5 \qquad = 0$?

$$0 \qquad = 0$$

Yes

(2) Let $x = -5$.

$$x^2 + 6x + 5 = 0$$

Does $(-5)^2 + 6(-5) + 5 = 0$?

Does $25 - 30 + 5 \qquad = 0$?

Does $-5 + 5 \qquad = 0$?

$$0 \qquad = 0$$

Yes

Example 8

Solve $2x^2 - 4x - 3 = -6x + 9$ by using the quadratic formula.

◆ **Step 1**   Rewrite the equation in standard form.

$$2x^2 - 4x - 3 + 6x \quad = -6x + 9 + 6x$$

$$2x^2 - 4x - 3 + 6x - 9 = 9 - 9$$

$$2x^2 - 4x - 3 + 6x - 9 = 0$$

◆ **Step 2**   Combine like terms.

$$2x^2 - 4x + 6x - 3 - 9 = 0$$

$$2x^2 + 2x - 12 \quad\quad = 0$$

◆ **Step 3**   Assign values for a, b, and c.

Let $a = 2$, $b = 2$, and $c = -12$

◆ **Step 4**   Use the quadratic formula.

$$x = \frac{-(2) \pm \sqrt{(2)^2 - 4(2)(-12)}}{2(2)}$$

$$x = \frac{-(2) \pm \sqrt{(4) - 4(2)(-12)}}{2(2)}$$

$$x = \frac{-(2) \pm \sqrt{(4) - (8)(-12)}}{(4)}$$

$$x = \frac{-(2) \pm \sqrt{(4) - (-96)}}{(4)}$$

$$x = \frac{-(2) \pm \sqrt{(4) + 96}}{(4)}$$

$$x = \frac{-(2) \pm \sqrt{100}}{(4)}$$

$$x = \frac{-2 \pm 10}{4}$$

$$x = \frac{-2 + 10}{4} \quad \text{or} \quad x = \frac{-2 - 10}{4}$$

$$x = \frac{8}{4} \quad \text{or} \quad x = \frac{-12}{4}$$

$$x = 2 \quad \text{or} \quad x = -3$$

The solution set for x is $\{-3, 2\}$.

Example 9

Use the quadratic formula to solve $x^2 + 4 = 4x$.

◆ **Step 1** Rewrite the equation in standard form.

$$x^2 + 4 - 4x = 4x - 4x$$

$$x^2 + 4 - 4x = 0$$

$$x^2 - 4x + 4 = 0$$

◆ **Step 2** Use the quadratic formula where $a = 1$, $b = -4$, and $c = 4$.

$$x = \frac{-(-4) \pm \sqrt{(-4)^2 - 4(1)(4)}}{2(1)}$$

$$x = \frac{-(-4) \pm \sqrt{(16) - 4(1)(4)}}{2(1)}$$

$$x = \frac{-(-4) \pm \sqrt{(16) - (4)(4)}}{2(1)}$$

$$x = \frac{-(-4) \pm \sqrt{(16) - (16)}}{2}$$

$$x = \frac{-(-4) \pm \sqrt{0}}{2}$$

$$x = \frac{4 \pm 0}{2}$$

$$x = \frac{4+0}{2} \quad \text{or} \quad x = \frac{4-0}{2}$$

$$x = \frac{4}{2} \quad \text{and} \quad x = \frac{4}{2}$$

Since these are identical, there is just one solution.

$x = 2$

The solution set is $\{2\}$.

10.4 Graphing Quadratic Equations and Inequalities

In this section, we will learn how to graph quadratic equations in two variables of the following type:

$$y = ax^2 + bx + c$$

As an example of graphing quadratic equations in two variables, we begin by graphing the equation $y = x^2 + 0x + 0$, simplified as $y = x^2$. Proceed by choosing several values for x, and then calculate the corresponding values for y (see example 10).

Example 10

Graph: $y = x^2$

♦ **Step 1**   Draw up a table of ordered pairs. For example, if $y = x^2$ and $x = 1$, then $y = 1^2 = 1$.

x	-2	-1	0	1	2
y	4	1	0	1	4

♦ **Step 2**   Plot the points on a rectangular coordinate system and connect the points by drawing a curve through them (see fig. 10.1).

Notice the distinctive shape of the graph; this is called a parabola. If $a \neq 0$, the graph of every equation of the type $y = ax^2 + bx + c$ is a parabola.

Figure 10.2 illustrates that the parabola opens upward. This is because the coefficient of the x^2 term in the equation $y = x^2$ is positive. When a parabola opens upward, the vertex is the lowest point of the graph, which is $(0, 0)$ in figure 10.2.

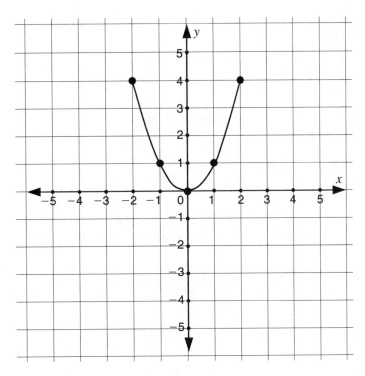

Figure 10.1: Graphing the Equation $y = x^2$

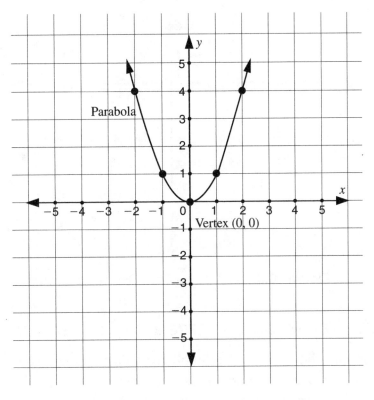

Figure 10.2: A Parabola That Opens Upward

Example 11

Graph the equation: $y = -x^2 + 2$

◆ **Step 1**   Draw up a table of ordered pairs.

x	-2	-1	0	1	2
y	-2	1	2	1	-2

◆ **Step 2**   Plot the points on a rectangular coordinate system and connect the points by drawing a curve through them (see fig. 10.3).

Figure 10.3 illustrates that the vertex (0, 2) is the highest point of the parabola, because it opens downward, an indication that the coefficient of the x^2 term is negative.

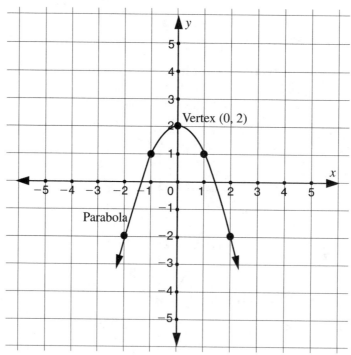

Figure 10.3: A Parabola That Opens Downward

Finding the Vertex and Intercepts of a Parabola

We can find the vertex of a graph by using the vertex formula for the x value, where a and b correspond to the variables in the graph of the quadratic equation of the type $y = ax^2 + bx + c$ (and $a \neq 0$).

$$x = \frac{-b}{2a}$$

The y value of the vertex is found by substituting this x value into the original equation.

Example 12

Find the vertex of the graph of the equation: $y = x^2 + 8x + 7$

◆ **Step 1**   Solve for x, using the vertex formula where $a = 1$ (the coefficient of the squared term), and $b = 8$ (the coefficient of the x term).

$$x = \frac{-8}{2(1)}$$

$$x = \frac{-8}{2}$$

$$x = -4$$

◆ **Step 2**   To find the y value of the vertex, let $x = -4$ in the equation of the graph and solve for y.

$$y = x^2 + 8x + 7$$

$$y = (-4)^2 + 8(-4) + 7$$

$$y = (16) + 8(-4) + 7$$

$$y = (16) - (32) + 7$$

$$y = 16 - 32 + 7$$

$$y = -16 + 7$$

$$y = -9$$

Because $x = -4$ and $y = -9$, the coordinates of the vertex are $(-4, -9)$.

Example 13

Given the equation $y = x^2 + 8x + 7$, find the x-intercepts and the y-intercept. In other words, find the points where the parabola crosses the x-axis and the y-axis.

◆ **Step 1**   To find the x-intercepts, let $y = 0$, and solve for x.

$y = x^2 + 8x + 7$

$0 = x^2 + 8x + 7$

◆ **Step 2**   Factor the trinomial.

$0 = (x + 1)(x + 7)$

◆ **Step 3**   Using the zero-factor property, set each factor to 0 and solve for x in both equations.

$(x + 1) = 0$ or $(x + 7) = 0$

$x + 1 = 0$ or $x + 7 = 0$

$x = -1$ or $x = -7$

The x-intercepts are $(-1, 0)$ and $(-7, 0)$.

◆ **Step 4**   To find the y-intercept, let $x = 0$ in the equation and solve for y.

$y = x^2 + 8x + 7$

$y = (0)^2 + 8(0) + 7$

$y = 0 + 0 + 7$

$y = 7$

The y-intercept is $(0, 7)$.

Graphing Quadratic Inequalities

Graphing quadratic inequalities is similar to graphing quadratic equations, except we must shade either the region of the graph outside the parabola or the region inside the parabola. Similarly, we use a test point to determine which side of the graph to shade.

Furthermore, to graph a quadratic inequality with either the $>$ symbol or the $<$ symbol, we draw the parabola as a dashed curve. If the inequality contains either the $\leq$ symbol or the $\geq$ symbol, however, the parabola is drawn as a solid curve. The solid line indicates that the solution also includes all of the points on the line.

Example 14

Graph the quadratic inequality: $y \leq x^2 - 2x - 3$

◆ **Step 1** Rewrite the inequality as a quadratic equation.

$y = x^2 - 2x - 3$

◆ **Step 2** Compile a table of ordered pairs.

x	-2	-1	0	1	2	3
y	5	0	-3	-4	-3	0

◆ **Step 3** Plot the points on a rectangular coordinate system (see fig. 10.4).

◆ **Step 4** Connect the points by drawing a solid curve through them, because the inequality contains a $\leq$ symbol.

◆ **Step 5** Choose a test point either inside or outside the parabola. Let's select the inside point (1, 2), which we mark here with a larger dot.

◆ **Step 6** Let $x = 1$ and $y = 2$, and insert these values into the original inequality to discover whether the result is true or false.

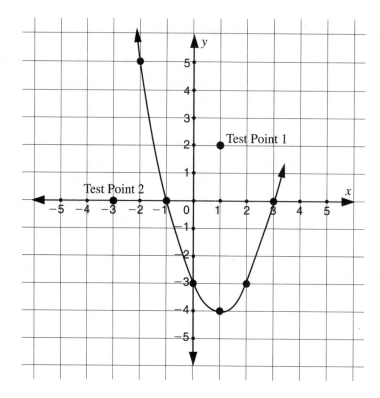

Figure 10.4: Graphing a Quadratic Inequality

$y \qquad \leq x^2 - 2x - 3$

Is $2 \leq (1)^2 - 2(1) - 3$?

Is $2 \leq 1 - 2 - 3$?

Is $2 \leq 1 - 5$?

Is $2 \leq -4$?

No

◆ **Step 7**   Because the test point is false, we shade the other side of the parabola. Thus, we shade the region outside the parabola (see fig. 10.5).

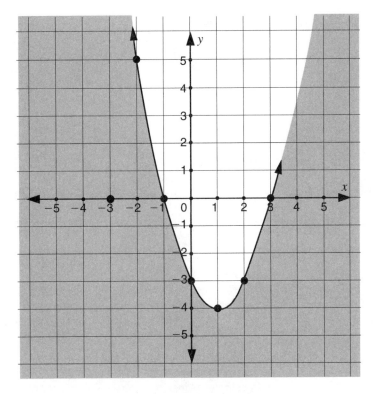

Figure 10.5: Graphing $y \leq x^2 - 2x - 3$

Example 15

Does the graph shown in figure 10.6 illustrate the inequality $y < -x^2 + 3$?

◆ **Step 1**   Look at the coefficient of the squared term. If it is negative, then the parabola must open downward. It does.

◆ **Step 2**   Calculate the vertex of the parabola by using the formula $x = \frac{-b}{2a}$.

$y < -x^2 + 3$

$y < -x^2 + 0x + 3$

Thus, $a = -1$ and $b = 0$.

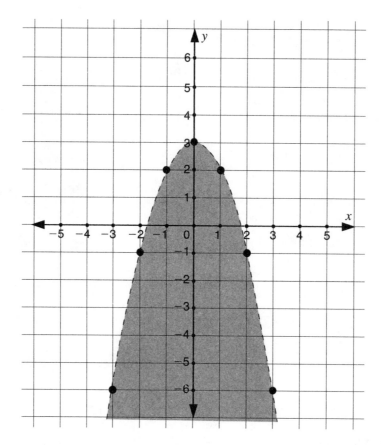

Figure 10.6: Does this graph illustrate the inequality $y < -x^2 + 3$?

$$x = \frac{-(0)}{2(-1)}$$

$$x = \frac{-0}{-2}$$

$$x = 0$$

◆ **Step 4**   To find the y value of the vertex, let $x = 0$ and solve for y in the equation $y = -x^2 + 3$.

$$y = -x^2 + 3$$

$$y = -(0)^2 + 3$$

$$y = -0 + 3$$

$$y = 3$$

The coordinates of the vertex are (0, 3), which is true for the parabola in figure 10.6.

◆ **Step 5**   Plot a few points and compare them with the points on the graph. If they correspond, we have more evidence that the parabola shown in figure 10.6 illustrates the inequality $y < -x^2 + 3$.

◆ **Step 6**   Determine whether the correct region is shaded. Select a test point, such as (0, 1), located inside the parabola, and insert the values of the ordered pair into the inequality to discover whether the result is true or false.

$y < -x^2 + 3$

Is $1 < -0^2 + 3$?

Is $1 < -0 + 3$?

Is $1 < 3$?

Yes

Because the ordered pair (0, 1) whose point is located inside the parabola is part of the solution set, the correct area is shaded.

◆ **Step 7**   Find out whether the parabola is a dashed curve (required if the inequality contains either the symbol $<$ or the symbol $>$). It is not.

The parabola in figure 10.6 is *not* the graph of the inequality $y < -x^2 + 3$.

10.5 Functions

A function can be described as a set of ordered pairs in which each x value has only one corresponding y value. For example, imagine that Jane buys one towel on sale for $2. The amount of money she spends ($2) is related to the number of towels she purchases (one). Similarly, if Mary decides to buy five towels in the same sale, the amount of money she spends ($10) is still related to the number of towels she buys (five). We can express this relationship as follows, where x represents the number of towels purchased, and y represents the total cost of the towels:

$$y = 2x$$

Each value for x corresponds to only one value for y.

Functional Notation

Mathematicians used a special symbol, $f(x)$ (pronounced "f of x"), to indicate a function, although they may also use other letters, such as $g(x)$ or $h(x)$. We can write $y = 3x + 2$ as a function $f(x) = 3x + 2$, because every value for x has exactly one corresponding value for y. If the function is written as $f(4) = 3x + 2$, this means that we have to replace x with the number 4 and then find the corresponding y value.

Example 16

For the function $f(x) = 3x + 2$, find $f(4)$.

◆ **Step 1**   This means that we are looking for the value of y when $x = 4$. Replace x with 4 in the equation and solve.

$f(x) = 3x + 2$

$f(4) = 3x + 2$

$f(4) = 3(4) + 2$

$f(4) = 12 + 2$

$f(4) = 14$

Because $f(x) = 3x + 2$ is the equivalent of $y = 3x + 2$, $y = 14$.

Example 17

Evaluate $g(x) = x^2 + 6x - 4$ for $g(3)$.

◆ **Step 1**   Replace x with 3 and solve the equation.

$g(3) = 3^2 + 6(3) - 4$

$g(3) = 9 + 6(3) - 4$

$g(3) = 9 + 18 - 4$

$g(3) = 27 - 4$

$g(3) = 23$

Example 18

Find: $h(5) - h(-3)$ if $h(x) = |x + 2| - 1$

◆ **Step 1**   Find $h(5)$ and then $h(-3)$ by replacing x with 5 and then with -3.

$h(5)\ = |x + 2| - 1$

$h(5)\ = |5 + 2| - 1$

$h(5)\ = |7| - 1$

$h(5)\ = (7) - 1$

$h(5)\ = 6$

$h(-3) = |x + 2| - 1$

$h(-3) = |-3 + 2| - 1$

$h(-3) = |-1| - 1$

$$h(-3) = (1) - 1$$

$$h(-3) = 1 - 1$$

$$h(-3) = 0$$

◆ **Step 2**   Perform the operation $h(5) - h(-3)$, where $h(5) = 6$ and $h(-3) = 0$.

$$h(5) - h(-3)$$

$$6 - 0 = 6$$

Graphing Absolute Value Functions

Finally, many standardized tests require students to have knowledge of the graphs of absolute value functions.

Example 19

Graph the function: $f(x) = |x|$

◆ **Step 1**   Compile a table of values by assigning positive and negative values for x and $f(x) = y$.

$$f(x) = |x|$$

$$f(-3) = |-3| = 3$$

$$f(-2) = |-2| = 2$$

$$f(-1) = |-1| = 1$$

$$f(0) = |0| = 0$$

$f(1) = |1| = 1$

$f(2) = |2| = 2$

$f(3) = |3| = 3$

x	$f(x) = y$
−3	3
−2	2
−1	1
0	0
1	1
2	2
3	3

◆ **Step 2**   Plot the points (see fig. 10.7).

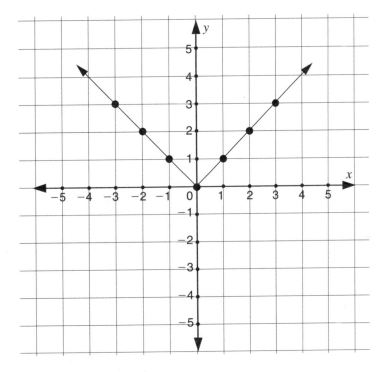

Figure 10.7: Graphing $f(x) = |x|$

Example 20

Graph the function: $f(x) = -|x|$

◆ **Step 1**   Compile a table of values by assigning positive and negative values for x and $f(x) = y$.

$f(x) \quad = -|x|$

$f(-3) = -|-3| = -3$

$f(-2) = -|-2| = -2$

$f(-1) = -|-1| = -1$

$f(0) \quad = -|0| = 0$

$f(1) \quad = -|1| = -1$

$f(2) \quad = -|2| = -2$

$f(3) \quad = -|3| = -3$

x	y
−3	−3
−2	−2
−1	−1
0	0
1	−1
2	−2
3	−3

◆ **Step 2**   Plot the points (see fig. 10.8).

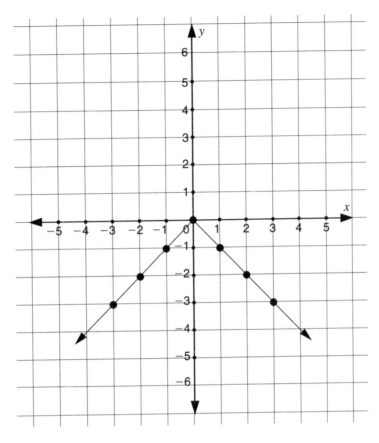

Figure 10.8: Graphing $f(x) = -|x|$

Notice that the graph shown in figure 10.7 is the inverted form of the graph in figure 10.8. This is because there is a negative sign in front of the absolute value. Notice also that the graphs are symmetric around the y-axis. This means that if you folded the graph on the y-axis, the points would match exactly.

Problems

1. Solve $x^2 - 10x + 24 = 0$ by factoring.

2. Solve $x^2 = 16$ by using the square root property.

3. Solve $x^2 = 54$ by using the square root property.

4. Solve $2x^2 + 7 = 61$ by using the square root property.

5. Solve $(x - 3)^2 = 18$ by using the square root property.

6. Solve $(2x - 3)^2 = 48$ by using the square root property.

7. Solve $x^2 + 12x - 13 = 0$ by using the quadratic formula.

8. Solve $3z^2 - 2z + 5 = 10z + 1$ by using the quadratic formula.

9. Solve $2x^2 + 3x + 8 = 0$ by using the quadratic formula, if possible.

10. Graph the equation: $y = -x^2 + 2$

11. Does the parabola of the equation $y = -x^2 + 2x - 8$ open upward or downward? Explain your choice.

12. Find the vertex of the graph of the equation: $y = 3x^2 + 6x + 4$

13. Find the x-intercepts and the y-intercept of the graph of the equation: $y = x^2 + 8x + 7$

14. Evaluate: $f(x) = x^2 + 6x - 2$ for $f(2)$

15. Evaluate: $g(x) = x^2 + 6x - 4$ for $g(5)$

Focus on English

Grammar

Will (Future)

Use *will* and the infinitive of the verb for decisions, offers, and promises. For example:

Decisions: I will call my friend.

Offers: I will help you.

Promises: I will visit you tomorrow.

Will is often contracted to *'ll,* such as *I'll call you tomorrow.* The negative *will* is contracted to *won't.*

Note the following examples:

I'll come.	I won't come.
You'll come.	You won't come.
He'll come.	He won't come.
She'll come.	She won't come.
It'll come.	It won't come.
We'll come.	We won't come.
They'll come.	They won't come.

Don't use the contraction *'ll* when responding to positive questions. For example, *Will you write? Yes, I will.* However, for negative responses, you can use the contraction *won't,* such as *Will he write? No, he won't.*

Fill in the blanks with either *will* or *won't.*

1. Will you write? Yes, I _____.

2. Will you call me? No, I _____.

3. Will she come tomorrow? Yes, she _____.

4. Will you help me? Yes, we _____.

5. Will they visit them? No, they _____.

Future (Be) Going To

We use *be going to* with the infinitive to talk about future plans and predictions. For example, *Are you going to the concert next week? Is it going to snow?*

Positive sentences

I'm going to buy a car tomorrow.
You're going to buy a car tomorrow.
He's going to buy a car tomorrow.
She's going to buy a car tomorrow.
We're going to buy a car tomorrow.
They're going to buy a car tomorrow.

Negative sentences

I'm not going to buy a car tomorrow.
You're not going to buy a car tomorrow.
He's not going to buy a car tomorrow.
She's not going to buy a car tomorrow.
We're not going to buy a car tomorrow.
They're not going to buy a car tomorrow.

Positive and Negative Questions

Am I going to buy a car tomorrow? Yes, I am. No, I'm not.

Fill in the blanks:

1. _____ you going to the concert with me tomorrow?

2. Are you going to New York tomorrow? Yes, _____ _____.

3. Will it snow next week? Yes, _____ _____.

4. Will John pass his driver's test? No, _____ _____.

5. Will your aunt visit next week? Yes, _____ _____.

Dictionary Work

Define the following terms:

parabola

function

Answer Key

Chapter 1

Problems

1. **Solution: -14**

   $-10 + 20 \div (-5) =$

   $-10 + (-4) \quad =$

   $-10 - 4 \quad =$

   -14

2. **Solution: -24**

   $6 - 3[2 - 4(2 - 4)] =$

   $6 - 3[2 - 4(-2)] \quad =$

   $6 - 3[2 + 8] \quad =$

   $6 - 3(10) \quad =$

   $6 - 30 \quad =$

   -24

3. **Solution: 32**

   $(2 + 1)^3 + 5 =$

   $(3)^3 + 5 \quad =$

$$(3)(3)(3) + 5 =$$

$$(9)(3) + 5 \quad =$$

$$(27) + 5 \quad =$$

$$27 + 5 \quad =$$

$$32$$

4.   **Solution: −625**

$$-(-5)^4 \qquad =$$

$$-(-5)(-5)(-5)(-5) =$$

$$-(25)(-5)(-5) \quad =$$

$$-(-125)(-5) \quad =$$

$$-625$$

5.   **Solution: $\dfrac{1}{49}$**

$$7^{-2} \quad =$$

$$\frac{1}{7^2} \quad =$$

$$\frac{1}{(7)(7)} =$$

$$\frac{1}{49}$$

6.   **Solution: 16**

$$\frac{4^4}{4^2} \quad =$$

$$4^{4-2} \quad =$$

$$4^2 \quad =$$

$$(4)(4) =$$

$$16$$

7. **Solution: 1,728**

    $4^3 \cdot 3^3$ $=$

    $(12)^3$ $=$

    $(12)(12)(12) =$

    $(144)(12)$ $=$

    $1,728$

8. **Solution: 5**

    $\sqrt[3]{125}$ $=$

    $\sqrt[3]{(25)(5)} = \sqrt[3]{(5)(5)(5)}$

    5

9. **Solution: 75**

    $3\sqrt{49} + 6\sqrt{81} =$

    $3(7) + 6(9)$ $=$

    $21 + 54$ $=$

    75

10. **Solution: Thousands**

    Reading from right to left, enter each digit in a place value box.

Thousands	Hundreds	Tens	Units
1	3	8	4

11. **Solution: 6.74219×10^{-3}**

    0.00674219

    Move the decimal point three places to the right. Because the standard form number is less than 1, the second factor, 10, is raised to a negative integer power equal to the number of places that the decimal point is moved.

12. **Solution: 81,833,325,000,000 km**

8.1833325×10^{13} km

Move the decimal point 13 places to the right, adding zeros where necessary.

13. **Solution: 0.0480305**

4.80305×10^{-2}

Move the decimal point two places to the left, adding zeros where necessary.

14. **Solution: 3.3×10^{-10}**

$(1.1 \times 10^{-7})(3 \times 10^{-3}) =$

$(1.1 \times 3)(10^{-7} \times 10^{-3}) =$

$(3.3) \times (10^{-7 + (-3)}) \qquad =$

$(3.3) \times (10^{-10})$

15. **Solution: $\dfrac{3}{16}, \dfrac{2}{8}, \dfrac{3}{8}, \dfrac{3}{4}, \dfrac{7}{8}$**

Express each fraction as a decimal, and order them from smallest to largest.

$\dfrac{3}{8}$:

```
   .375
8)3.000
  24
  ──
   60
   56
   ──
   40
   40
   ──
```

$\dfrac{7}{8}$:

```
   .875
8)7.000
  64
  ──
   60
   56
   ──
   40
   40
   ──
```

$\dfrac{2}{8}$:

```
   .25
8)2.00
  16
  ──
   40
   40
   ──
```

$\dfrac{3}{16}$:

```
     .1875
16)3.0000
   16
   ──
   140
   128
   ───
   120
   112
   ───
    80
    80
    ──
```

$\dfrac{3}{4}$:

```
   .75
4)3.00
  28
  ──
   20
   20
   ──
```

.1875, .25, .375, .75, .875 or $\dfrac{3}{16}, \dfrac{2}{8}, \dfrac{3}{8}, \dfrac{3}{4}, \dfrac{7}{8}$

Focus on English

1. thicker

2. safer

3. hottest

4. higher

5. kindest

1. The denominator is 4, and the numerator is 3.

2. The symbol for positive is $+$, and the symbol for negative is $-$.

3. "greater than," "less than," "equal to"

4. *Cross multiplication* means "multiplying the numerator of one of a pair of fractions by the denominator of the other."

5. A *square root* is a number that, when multiplied by itself, results in a given number. The square root of 4 is 2. A *cube root* is a number that, when multiplied by itself twice, results in a given number. The cube root of 9 is 3; that is, $3 \times 3 \times 3 = 9$.

6. *Absolute value* is the numerical value of a real number without regard to its sign. For example, the absolute value of -4 (written $|-4|$) is 4.

7. *Scientific notation* is a method of writing or displaying numbers in terms of a decimal number between 1 and 10 multiplied by a power of 10. The scientific notation of 33,099, for example, is 3.3099×10^4.

8. It is important to learn the order of operations because often we have to use more than one operation when solving problems. If we used the wrong order, we would arrive at the wrong answer.

Chapter 2

Problems

1.   **Solution: $9b - 26$**

$$6(2b - 3) - 2(4b + 4) + 5b \quad =$$

$$6(2b) + 6(-3) - 2(4b) - 2(4) + 5b =$$

$$12b - 18 - 8b - 8 + 5b \quad =$$

$$12b - 8b + 5b - 18 - 8 \quad =$$

$$4b + 5b - 18 - 8 \quad =$$

$$9b - 26$$

2.   **Solution: -15**

Let $x = 4$ and $y = 6$.

$$(-6)^0 - |3x - 6y| - 4^2 + xy \quad =$$

$$(-6)^0 - |3(4) - 6(6)| - 4^2 + (4)(6) =$$

$$(-6)^0 - |(12) - (36)| - 4^2 + (4)(6) =$$

$$(-6)^0 - |-24| - 4^2 + (4)(6) \quad =$$

$$(-6)^0 - (24) - 4^2 + (4)(6) \quad =$$

$$(1) - (24) - (16) + (4)(6) \quad =$$

$$1 - 24 - 16 + (24) \quad =$$

$$1 - 24 - 16 + 24 \quad =$$

$$-23 - 16 + 24 \quad =$$

$$-39 + 24 \quad =$$

$$-15$$

3. **Solution: 1**

$$
\begin{aligned}
7(x+3) &= 3x+25 \\
7(x)+7(3) &= 3x+25 \\
7x+21-3x &= 3x+25-3x \\
4x+21 &= 25 \\
4x+21-21 &= 25-21 \\
4x &= 4 \\
\frac{4x}{4} &= \frac{4}{4} \\
x &= 1
\end{aligned}
$$

4. **Solution: 16**

$$\frac{x}{8}+1=3$$

Multiply by 8 to clear the fractions.

$$
\begin{aligned}
8\left(\frac{x}{8}+1\right) &= 8(3) \\
8\left(\frac{x}{8}\right)+8(1) &= 8(3) \\
x+8 &= 24 \\
x+8-8 &= 24-8 \\
x &= 16
\end{aligned}
$$

5. **Solution: −5**

$$
\begin{aligned}
-4(3x-1) &= 5(x-5)+114 \\
-4(3x)-4(-1) &= 5(x)+5(-5)+114 \\
-12x+4 &= 5x-25+114 \\
-12x+4 &= 5x+89 \\
-12x+4-4 &= 5x+89-4 \\
-12x &= 5x+85 \\
-12x-5x &= 5x+85-5x \\
-17x &= 85 \\
\frac{-17x}{-17} &= \frac{85}{-17} \\
x &= -5
\end{aligned}
$$

6.   **Solution:** $-\dfrac{1}{13}$

$$\frac{x+1}{6} + \frac{x-1}{7} = 0$$

Multiply throughout the equation by 42, the LCD of the three denominators 1, 6, and 7.

$$42\left(\frac{x+1}{6}\right) + 42\left(\frac{x-1}{7}\right) = 42(0)$$
$$7(x+1) + 6(x-1) = 42(0)$$
$$7x + 7 + 6x - 6 = 0$$
$$13x + 1 = 0$$
$$13x + 1 - 1 = 0 - 1$$
$$13x = -1$$
$$\frac{13x}{13} = -\frac{1}{13}$$
$$x = -\frac{1}{13}$$

7.   **Solution: 9,000 calories from saturated fat, and 36,000 calories from enriched flour.**

Mike gets half of ("division") his monthly calorie total of 90,000 from refined sugar alone. So, the number of calories he gets from sugar is $\frac{90,000}{2} = 45,000$. Let the number of calories from saturated fat be represented by the variable t. Thus, the number of calories he gets from sugar (five times what he takes in from saturated fat) can be expressed as $5t$. We know that the number of calories Mike takes in from sugar is 45,000, so $5t = 45,000$. What is the value of t?

$$\frac{5t}{5} = \frac{45,000}{5}$$
$$t = 9,000$$

Now we know that he consumes 45,000 calories in sugar and 9,000 calories in saturated fat (t). But how many calories does he get from enriched flour? Let the number of calories from flour be represented by the variable *f*. When added to the calories from refined sugar and saturated fat, the monthly total is 90,000. So write the equation as

$$f + 45{,}000 + 9{,}000 \quad = 90{,}000$$

$$f + 54{,}000 \qquad\qquad = 90{,}000$$

$$f + 54{,}000 - 54{,}000 = 90{,}000 - 54{,}000$$

$$f \qquad\qquad\qquad = 36{,}000$$

Thus, Mike consumes 9,000 calories from saturated fat (*t*), and 36,000 calories from enriched flour (*f*).

8. **Solution:** $W = \dfrac{Z + V}{T}$

$$
\begin{aligned}
WT - V &= Z \\
WT - V + V &= Z + V \\
WT &= Z + V \\
\frac{WT}{T} &= \frac{Z + V}{T} \\
W &= \frac{Z + V}{T}
\end{aligned}
$$

9. **Solution:** $T = SXZ + SY$

$$
\begin{aligned}
\frac{T}{S} &= XZ + Y \\
S\left(\frac{T}{S}\right) &= S(XZ + Y) \\
T &= SXZ + SY
\end{aligned}
$$

10. **Solution: 9 in.**

Use the formula for calculating the area of a rectangle, $A = lw$, and insert the known values.

$$
\begin{aligned}
36 &= 4(w) \\
4(w) &= 36 \\
\frac{4(w)}{4} &= \frac{36}{4} \\
w &= 9 \text{ in.}
\end{aligned}
$$

11.   **Solution: 8 ft**

The formula for calculating the perimeter of a rectangle is $P = 2(w) + 2(l)$. Let sides A and $C = 2(w)$, and $B = l$. We know that the sum of sides A and $C = \frac{1}{3}(P)$ and $P = 24$. So,

$$2(w) = \frac{1}{3}(P)$$
$$2(w) = \frac{1}{3}(24)$$
$$2(w) = 8$$

Insert $2(w) = 8$ into the formula $P = 2(w) + 2(l)$ and solve for l.

$$
\begin{aligned}
2(w) + 2(l) &= P \\
8 + 2(l) &= 24 \\
8 - 8 + 2(l) &= 24 - 8 \\
2(l) &= 16 \\
\frac{2(l)}{2} &= \frac{16}{2} \\
l &= 8
\end{aligned}
$$

$l = B$, so side $B = 8$ ft.

12.   **Solution: 12**

Cross multiply: $\dfrac{25}{2x+1} = \dfrac{26}{2x+2}$

$$
\begin{aligned}
25(2x + 2) &= 26(2x + 1) \\
25(2x) + 25(2) &= 26(2x) + 26(1) \\
50x + 50 &= 52x + 26 \\
50x + 50 - 50 &= 52x + 26 - 50 \\
50x &= 52x - 24 \\
50x - 52x &= 52x - 52x - 24 \\
-2x &= -24 \\
\frac{-2x}{-2} &= \frac{-24}{-2} \\
x &= 12
\end{aligned}
$$

13.   **Solution: 20%**

Use the formula $\dfrac{\text{change}}{\text{starting point}}$ = percent change.

The change in price of the overcoat is $450 − $360 = $90.

The starting point is $450. Let x = percent change (decrease).

Use the formula, inserting the known values.

$$\frac{90}{450} = x$$
$$\frac{1}{5} = x$$

Express the fraction as a decimal by dividing 1 by 5. The result is 0.20. To change the decimal to a percentage, move the decimal point two places to the right and add a percentage sign: 20%.

14.   **Solution: $\dfrac{8}{1}$**

There are eight pieces of red glass for every piece of yellow glass.

Eliminate unnecessary information. The question asks us about the red and yellow glass only, not the pieces of white glass. Write a fraction to show the ratio of the number of pieces of red glass to the number of pieces of yellow glass used in the mosaic.

$$\frac{440}{55} = \frac{8}{1}$$

15.   **Solution: $\dfrac{5}{8} = \dfrac{t}{640}$**

The dealer sells five trucks for every three compact cars. This means that, for every 8 (5 + 3) vehicles sold, five are trucks. The first ratio is $\frac{5}{8}$. The next ratio shows the unknown number of trucks (t) to the total number of vehicles sold: $\frac{t}{640}$.

The proportion is $\dfrac{5}{8} = \dfrac{t}{640}$.

Focus on English

1. Laura speaks Spanish as a first language and is learning to speak English.

2. She is a receptionist at a hotel.

3. She is from Cuba.

4. She wants to learn English to do her job better and to watch English-language television.

1. Variable: A quantity, such as x, that can assume any one of a set of values.

2. Numerical coefficient: A factor that is a number; for example, in $3ab$, 3 is the numerical coefficient of ab.

3. Like terms: Terms whose variable factors and coefficients are the same, such as $2x^2$ and $3x^2$.

4. Unlike terms: Terms whose variable factors and coefficients are not the same, such as $3ab$ and $3a^2$.

5. Constant: A value that cannot change.

6. Lowest common denominator: The smallest number that can be divided evenly into two larger numbers.

7. Least common multiple: The smallest number that two or more numbers will divide into evenly.

Chapter 3

Problems

1. Solution: $\dfrac{1}{2}n - 9 \geq 30$

2. Solution: $Z < (x + y)^2 \left(\dfrac{x}{4y} \right)$

3. Solution: See below.

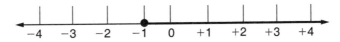

Graphing $x \geq -1$ on a Number Line

4. Solution: See below.

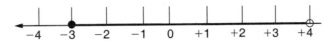

Graphing $-3 \leq y < 4$ on a Number Line

5. Solution: $z \geq -4$

6. Solution: $\{x \mid -3 < x \leq 1\}$

7. Solution: $x \geq 2$

   Multiply by 100 to clear the decimals.

   $-0.03x \leq -0.06$

   $-3x \quad \leq -6$

   Divide by -3 and reverse the inequality symbol.

   $\dfrac{-3x}{-3} \geq \dfrac{-6}{-3}$

   $x \quad \geq 2$

8. Solution: $x \geq -5$

   $5x + 1 \geq 3x - 9$

$$5x + 1 - 1 \geq 3x - 9 - 1$$

$$5x \qquad \geq 3x - 10$$

$$5x - 3x \quad \geq 3x - 10 - 3x$$

$$2x \qquad \geq -10$$

$$\frac{2x}{2} \qquad \geq \frac{-10}{2}$$

$$x \qquad \geq -5$$

9.   **Solution: $a < 1$**

$$\frac{2}{3}(a + 3) < -\frac{2}{3}(a - 5)$$

Multiply by 3 to clear the fractions.

$$(3) \cdot \frac{2}{3}(a + 3) < (3) \cdot -\frac{2}{3}(a - 5)$$

$$2(a + 3) \quad < -2(a - 5)$$

$$2(a) + 2(3) < -2(a) - 2(-5)$$

$$2a + 6 \quad < -2a + 10$$

$$2a + 6 - 6 < -2a + 10 - 6$$

$$2a \qquad < -2a + 4$$

$$2a + 2a \quad < -2a + 4 + 2a$$

$$4a \qquad < 4$$

$$\frac{4a}{4} \qquad < \frac{4}{4}$$

$$a \qquad < 1$$

10. **Solution:** $\{x \mid x \geq 13\}$

$$\frac{x+1}{6} + \frac{x-5}{12} \geq 3$$

Multiply by 12 throughout to clear the fractions.

$$12\left(\frac{x+1}{6}\right) + 12\left(\frac{x-5}{12}\right) \geq 12(3)$$

$2(x+1) + (x-5)$	≥ 36
$2(x) + 2(1) + (x-5)$	≥ 36
$2x + 2 + x - 5$	≥ 36
$3x - 3$	≥ 36
$3x - 3 + 3$	$\geq 36 + 3$
$3x$	≥ 39
$\dfrac{3x}{3}$	$\geq \dfrac{39}{3}$
x	≥ 13

11. **Solution:** $\{z \mid z > -2\}$

$$2z - (4z + 3) < 6z + 3(z + 4) + 7$$

$$2z - (4z + 3) < 6z + 3(z) + 3(4) + 7$$

$$2z - 4z - 3 < 6z + 3z + 12 + 7$$

$$-2z - 3 < 9z + 19$$

$$-2z - 3 + 3 < 9z + 19 + 3$$

$$-2z \quad < 9z + 22$$

$$-2z - 9z < 9z + 22 - 9z$$

$$-11z \quad < 22$$

Divide by -11 and reverse the inequality symbol.

$$\frac{-11z}{-11} > \frac{22}{-11}$$

$$z \quad > -2$$

12.   **Solution:** $-1 \le x \le 4$

$$-5 \quad \le 2x - 3 \le 5$$

$$-5 + 3 \le 2x - 3 + 3 \le 5 + 3$$

$$-2 \quad \le 2x \le 8$$

$$\frac{-2}{2} \le \frac{2x}{2} \le \frac{8}{2}$$

$$-1 \le x \le 4$$

13.   **Solution:** $-4 \le a \le 0$

$$|a + 2| + 1 \quad \le 3$$

$$|a + 2| + 1 - 1 \quad \le 3 - 1$$

$$|a + 2| \quad \le 2$$

$$-2 \quad \le a + 2 \quad \le 2$$

$$-2 - 2 \le a + 2 - 2 \le 2 - 2$$

$$-4 \quad \le a \quad \le 0$$

14.   **Solution: 33**

Let x represent the first and smallest odd integer. The second and middle odd integer is therefore $(x + 2)$, and the third and largest is $(x + 4)$. We know that twice the middle integer is at least 9 more than the largest integer. Translate this into an inequality and solve for x.

$$2(x + 2) \geq 9 + (x + 4)$$

$$2x + 4 \geq 9 + x + 4$$

$$2x + 4 \geq 13 + x$$

$$2x + 4 - 4 \geq 13 + x - 4$$

$$2x \geq 13 + x - 4$$

$$2x \geq 9 + x$$

$$2x - x \geq 9 + x - x$$

$$x \geq 9$$

If x is equal to or greater than 9, then the minimum value for x must be 9. Then the three odd integers are 9, 11, and 13, and the minimum sum is $9 + 11 + 13 = 33$.

15.   **Solution: 60**

If x represents the number of nickels, then $3x$ represents the number of dimes. Notice that the money is not expressed in the same denomination, so we must determine the common monetary value of the coins before solving the problem.

What is the value of a nickel? 5 pennies.

What is the value of a dime? 10 pennies.

So the value of the nickels in Sarah's jar is 5x, and the value of the dimes is 10(3x).

Together they total no more than $21, or 2,100 pennies. Write the inequality and solve for x.

$5(x) + 10(3x) \leq 2,100$

$5x + 30x \quad \leq 2,100$

$35x \quad\quad \leq 2,100$

$\dfrac{35x}{35} \quad \leq \dfrac{2,100}{35}$

$x \quad\quad \leq 60$

So the maximum number of nickels in Sarah's jar is 60.

Focus on English

1. on

2. with

3. of

4. on

5. to

1. at

2. on

3. In

4. on

5. at

6. on

7. in

1. but

2. because

3. or

4. or

5. but

6. and

Chapter 4

Problems

1.   **Solution: 31**

Let $x = 3$.

$x^3 + x^2 - 5$ =

$(3)(3)(3) + (3)(3) - 5$ =

$(9)(3) + 9 - 5$ =

$27 + 9 - 5$ =

$36 - 5$ = 31

2.   **Solution:** $-b^2 - 7b + 5$

Change the sign in front of each term of the polynomial that is being subtracted and then add the two polynomials.

$(-6b + 2) - (b^2 + b - 3)$ =

$(-6b + 2) + (-b^2 - b + 3)$ =

$-6b + 2 - b^2 - b + 3$ =

$-b^2 - 6b - b + 2 + 3$ =

$-b^2 - 7b + 5$

3.   **Solution:** $-3a^2b - 3ab^2 - 15ab$

$(5a^2b - 2ab + 9ab^2) - (8a^2b + 13ab + 12ab^2) \quad =$

$(5a^2b - 2ab + 9ab^2) + (-8a^2b - 13ab - 12ab^2) =$

$5a^2b - 2ab + 9ab^2 - 8a^2b - 13ab - 12ab^2 \quad =$

$5a^2b - 8a^2b + 9ab^2 - 12ab^2 - 2ab - 13ab \quad =$

$-3a^2b - 3ab^2 - 15ab$

4.   **Solution:** $45x^{11}$

Multiply the constants and add the exponents.

$(-5x^4)(-9x^7) =$

$45x^{4+7} \qquad =$

$45x^{11}$

5.   **Solution:** $15x^6y^3z^3$

$(5x^3y^2z^2)(3x^3yz) \qquad\qquad =$

$(5 \cdot 3)(x^3 \cdot x^3)(y^2 \cdot y^1)(z^2 \cdot z^1) =$

$15x^6y^3z^3$

6.   **Solution:** $36z^4 - 18z^2 + 24z$

$3z(8 - 6z + 12z^3) \qquad\qquad =$

$3z(8) + 3z(-6z) + 3z(12z^3) =$

$24z - 18z^2 + 36z^4$ or, in descending order, $36z^4 - 18z^2 + 24z$

7.   **Solution:** $-4y^4 + 6y^3 - 2y^2 - 13y + 10$

$$2y^2 + y - 2$$

$$-2y^2 + 4y - 5$$

$$-10y^2 - 5y + 10 \text{ (multiplying by } -5)$$

$$8y^3 + 4y^2 - 8y \qquad \text{(multiplying by } +4y)$$

$$-4y^4 - 2y^3 + 4y^2 \qquad \text{(multiplying by } -2y^2)$$

$$-4y^4 + 6y^3 - 2y^2 - 13y + 10$$

8.   **Solution:** $\dfrac{x^2}{2y} - \dfrac{5x}{2y^2} + \dfrac{1}{xy^3}$

$$\frac{3x^4y^2 - 15x^3y + 6x}{6x^2y^3} \quad =$$

$$\frac{3x^4y^2}{6x^2y^3} - \frac{15x^3y}{6x^2y^3} + \frac{6x}{6x^2y^3} =$$

$$\frac{x^4y^2}{2x^2y^3} - \frac{5x^3y}{2x^2y^3} + \frac{x}{x^2y^3} \quad =$$

$$\frac{x^2}{2y} - \frac{5x}{2y^2} + \frac{1}{xy^3}$$

9.   **Solution:** $13x^2(x^4 - 2x^3 + 3)$

The GCF of the constants 13, 26, and 39 is 13, and the GCF of the variables is x^2.

$$13x^6 - 26x^5 + 39x^2 =$$

$$13x^2(x^4 - 2x^3 + 3)$$

10.   **Solution: $(x + 3)(x + 7)$**

We know that the first term of each binomial factor is x. The trinomial's middle term is $10x$, so select the factors of 21 as 3 and 7. Insert them into the two binomial factors:

$x^2 + 10x + 21 \qquad =$

$x^2 + 7x + 3x + 21 \quad =$

$x(x + 7) + 3(x + 7) =$

$(x + 3)(x + 7)$

11.   **Solution: $\dfrac{2x - 5}{6}$**

The denominators are the same, so add the numerators.

$\dfrac{x - 5}{6} + \dfrac{x}{6} \quad =$

$\dfrac{x - 5 + x}{6} \quad =$

$\dfrac{2x - 5}{6}$

12.   **Solution: $\dfrac{-8}{x}$**

$\dfrac{x - 4}{x} - \dfrac{x + 4}{x} \quad =$

$\dfrac{x - 4 - (x + 4)}{x} \quad =$

$\dfrac{x - 4 - x - 4}{x} \quad =$

$\dfrac{-8}{x}$

13.   **Solution: $(7b - a)(b + 2)$**

Arrange the terms in the polynomial into two groups:

$7b^2 + 14b$ and $-ab - 2a$

Find the GCF in both groups:

$7b(b + 2) - a(b + 2)$

$(7b - a)(b + 2)$

14.   **Solution:** $\dfrac{z+4}{z-1}$

$\dfrac{z^2 + 5z + 4}{z^2 - 1}$

Factor the trinomials.

$\dfrac{\cancel{(z+1)}(z+4)}{\cancel{(z+1)}(z-1)} =$

Cancel where possible.

$\dfrac{z+4}{z-1}$

15.   **Solution:** $\dfrac{x-8}{x+2}$

$\dfrac{x^2 - 12x + 32}{x^2 - 6x - 16} \div \dfrac{x^2 - x - 12}{x^2 - 5x - 24} =$

$\dfrac{x^2 - 12x + 32}{x^2 - 6x - 16} \cdot \dfrac{x^2 - 5x - 24}{x^2 - x - 12} =$

Factor the trinomials.

$\dfrac{(x-4)(x-8)}{(x+2)(x-8)} \cdot \dfrac{(x+3)(x-8)}{(x+3)(x-4)} =$

Cancel out where possible.

$\dfrac{\cancel{(x-4)}\,\cancel{(x-8)}}{(x+2)\cancel{(x-8)}} \cdot \dfrac{\cancel{(x+3)}(x-8)}{\cancel{(x+3)}\,\cancel{(x-4)}} =$

$\dfrac{x-8}{x+2}$

Focus on English

1. Whose

2. Who's

3. Whose

4. Who's

5. Whose

1. I can't come tomorrow evening.

2. John's a mathematician.

3. You're in class 3.

4. It's not working.

5. They're going to France this summer.

1. tri<u>no</u>mial

2. poly<u>no</u>mial

3. square of a bi<u>no</u>mial

4. <u>di</u>fference of squares

5. di<u>vi</u>sor

6. <u>di</u>vidend

7. re<u>ma</u>inder

8. <u>grea</u>test <u>com</u>mon <u>fac</u>tor

9. <u>ra</u>tional ex<u>pres</u>sion

10. de<u>gree</u>

Chapter 5

Problems

1. **Solution: Yes**

   Let $x = 5$ and $y = 3$. Insert these values into the equation.

   $3x + 4y \quad = 27$

   Does $3(5) + 4(3) = 27$?

   Does $15 + 12 \quad = 27$?

   $27 \qquad = 27$

   Yes

2. **Solution: (1, 3)**

   Let $y = 3$ and solve for x.

   $4y \quad = 8x + 2(5 - 3)$

   $4(3) \quad = 8x + 2(2)$

   $12 \quad = 8x + 4$

   $12 - 4 = 8x + 4 - 4$

   $8 \qquad = 8x$

   $\dfrac{8}{8} \quad = \dfrac{8x}{8}$

   $1 \qquad = x$

   $x = 1$, $y = 3$ so the ordered pair is $(1, 3)$.

3.   **Solution: See the values below.**

x	1	−1	0
y	5	1	3

Substitute $x = 1$ into the equation $3y = 6x + 9$;

$3y = 6(1) + 9$

$3y = 6 + 9$

$3y = 15$

$\dfrac{3y}{3} = \dfrac{15}{3}$

$y = 5$

then substitute $y = 1$,

$3(1) = 6x + 9$

$3 = 6x + 9$

$3 - 9 = 6x + 9 - 9$

$-6 = 6x$

$\dfrac{-6}{6} = \dfrac{6x}{6}$

$-1 = x$

and finally $x = 0$

$3y = 6(0) + 9$

$3y = 0 + 9$

$3y = 9$

$\dfrac{3y}{3} = \dfrac{9}{3}$

$y = 3$

to compile a table of values.

4.   **Solution: Plotting the ordered pair (−3, 2) (see fig. 5a)**

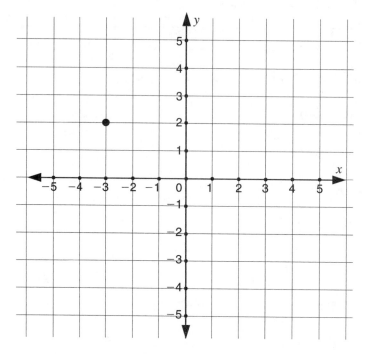

Figure 5a: Plotting (−3, 2)

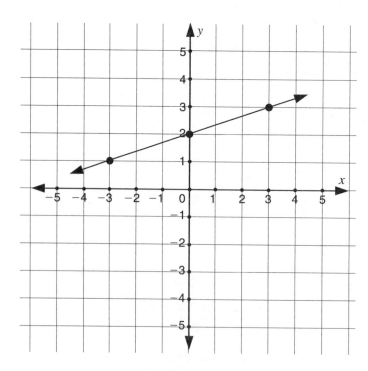

Figure 5b

5. **Solution: Find the three ordered pairs by substituting the known values into $3y - x = 6$. See figure 5b on page 386.**

$(0, y): 3y - 0 = 6 \quad y = 2 \,(0, 2)$

$(x, 1): 3(1) - x = 6 \quad x = 3 - 6 = -3 \,(-3, 1)$

$(3, y): 3y - 3 = 6 \quad 3y = 9 \; y = 3 \,(3, 3)$

6. **Solution:**

Pick any three x (or y) values and find three ordered pairs that satisfy $2y = x - 4$. For example,

for $x = 0: 2y = 0 - 4$

$2y = -4$

$y = -2 \,(0, -2)$

for $x = 2: 2y = 2 - 4$

$2y = -2$

$y = -1 \,(2, -1)$

for $y = 0: 2(0) = x - 4$

$4 = x \,(4, 0)$

See figure 5c.

7. **Solution: slope $m = \dfrac{4}{3}$**

The slope m is the coefficient of x when the equation is written in the form $y = mx + b$.

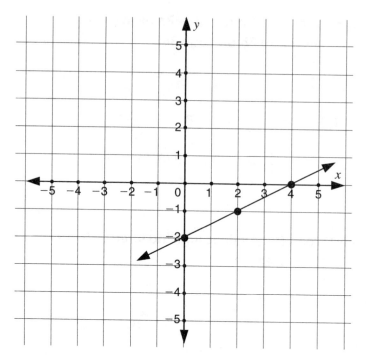

Figure 5c

$$3y = 4x - 7$$

$$\frac{3y}{3} = \frac{4x}{3} - \frac{7}{3}$$

$$y = \frac{4x}{3} - \frac{7}{3}$$

$$m = \frac{4}{3}$$

8.   **Solution: The *x*-intercept = (2, 0) and the *y*-intercept = (0, −8)**

To find the *x*-intercept, let $y = 0$ and solve for *x*.

$$4x - y = 8$$

$$4x + 0 = 8$$

$$4x = 8$$

$$\frac{4x}{4} = \frac{8}{4}$$

$$x = 2$$

To find the *y*-intercept, let $x = 0$, and solve for *y*.

$$4x - y = 8$$

$$4(0) - y = 8$$

$$0 - y = 8$$

$$-y = 8$$

$$y = -8$$

9. **Solution: slope *m* = −2 and the *y*-intercept = (0, 4)**

Rewrite the equation in slope-intercept form $y = mx + b$.

$$4x + 2y = 8$$
$$4x - 4x + 2y = -4x + 8$$
$$2y = -4x + 8$$
$$\frac{2y}{2} = \frac{-4x}{2} + \frac{8}{2}$$
$$y = -2x + 4$$

The slope m = the coefficient of x. Thus $m = -2$, and the *y*-intercept $(0, b) = (0, 4)$.

10. **Solution: Find three ordered pairs: See figure 5d.**

$$y = -3x$$

x	0	−1	1
y	0	3	−3

11. **Solution: *y* = 5**

The slope-intercept equation is $y = mx + b$.

$$y = 0x + 5$$

$$y = 5$$

12. **Solution: See figure 5e. Plot the *y*-intercept (0, 5) and then find a second point by going down 3 units and to the right 4 units, since the slope is $m = \dfrac{-3}{4} = \dfrac{\text{rise}}{\text{run}}$.**

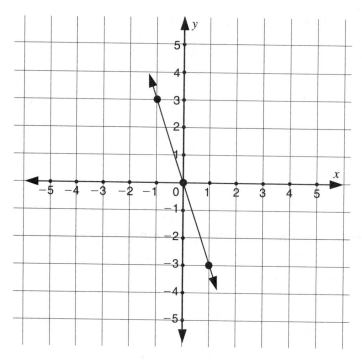

Figure 5d

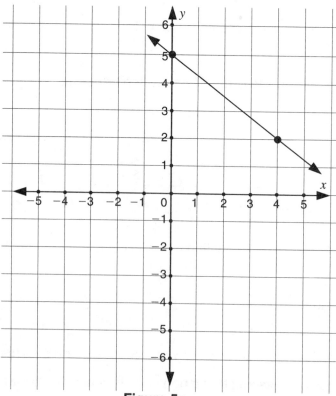

Figure 5e

13. **Solution: $y - (-10) = -2(x - 3)$**

Let $x_1 = 3; y_1 = -10; m = -2$.

Insert the known values into the point-slope equation.

$$y - y_1 \quad = m(x - x_1)$$

$$y - (-10) = -2(x - 3)$$

14. **Solution: $d = 6\sqrt{2}$**

Use the distance formula: $d = \sqrt{(x_2 - x_1)^2 + (y_2 - y_1)^2}$ where $x_1 = -3$, $x_2 = 3$, $y_1 = -2$, $y_2 = 4$

$$d = \sqrt{(3 - (-3))^2 + (4 - (-2))^2}$$

$$d = \sqrt{(3 + 3)^2 + (4 + 2)^2}$$

$$d = \sqrt{(6)^2 + (6)^2}$$

$$d = \sqrt{36 + 36}$$

$$d = \sqrt{72}$$

$$d = \sqrt{36}\sqrt{2}$$

$$d = 6\sqrt{2}$$

15. **Solution: See figure 5f.**

Since $x \geq 3$, the graph is a vertical solid line. Which part of the plane do we shade? Select any point, such as (4, 4), that is not on the line. Insert the ordered pair into the inequality and determine whether the point is a possible solution. $x \geq 3$ can be expressed as follows:

$x + 0y \geq 3$, where $x = 4$ and $y = 4$

$4 + 0(4) \geq 3$?

$4 + 0 \quad \geq 3$?

$4 \qquad \geq 3$

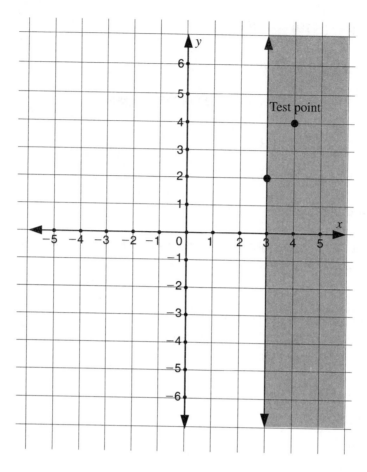

Figure 5f

This is a true statement, so shade the part of the plane that contains the test point (4, 4).

Focus on English

1. can't

2. Can

3. can

4. Can

5. can't

6. can't

1. The food was very good.

2. Drive carefully!

3. My mother dresses very well.

4. The boss likes her because she works hard.

5. Everything happened very quickly.

6. The table can be presented vertically.

Correct spelling of the misspelled words in the e-mail: *studying, graphing, There are, hypotenuse, distance, formula, equations, intercept, equations*

Chapter 6

Problems

1. **Solution: 45°**

Let x = the angle we are looking for. The supplement of the angle can be written as $180 - x$, and the complement of the angle can be expressed as $90 - x$. So:

$$
\begin{aligned}
180 - x &= 3(90 - x) \\
180 - x &= 270 - 3x \\
180 - x + 3x &= 270 - 3x + 3x \\
180 + 2x &= 270 \\
180 - 180 + 2x &= 270 - 180 \\
2x &= 270 - 180 \\
2x &= 90 \\
\frac{2x}{2} &= \frac{90}{2} \\
x &= 45
\end{aligned}
$$

2. **Solution: 110°**

$\angle AGF$ and $\angle BGE$ are vertical (opposite) angles, so if $m\angle AGF = 110°$, then $m\angle BGE = 110°$.

3. **Solution: $m\angle 6 = 80°$, $m\angle 2 = 80°$, and $m\angle 5 = 100°$**

$\angle 6$ and $\angle 4$ are supplementary angles. Since $m\angle 4 = 100°$, then $m\angle 6 = 180° - 100° = 80°$. $\angle 6$ and $\angle 2$ are corresponding angles, so they have the same measure. Thus, if $m\angle 6 = 80°$, then $m\angle 2$ also $= 80°$. Since $\angle 4$ and $\angle 5$ are alternate interior angles, they have the same measure. Thus, if $m\angle 4 = 100°$, then $m\angle 5 = 100°$.

4. **Solution: 15 cm**

The perimeter formula for a triangle is $P = a + b + c$, where a, b, and c are the three sides of the figure. Thus, to find the length of each side, divide the perimeter total by 3.

$$\frac{45}{3} = 15 \text{ cm}$$

5. **Solution: $\angle CDB = 105°$, $\angle BCD = 16°$, and $\angle ACB = 66°$**

Notice that $\angle ADC$ and $\angle CDB$ together form the straight angle ADB. Since $\angle ADB$ is a straight angle whose measure is 180°, and we know that $m\angle ADC = 75°$, we can calculate $m\angle CDB$ by subtracting 75° from 180°. Thus, $\angle CDB = 105°$. $\angle BCD$ is also an unmarked angle in $\triangle DCB$, but we now know that $m\angle CDB = 105°$, and $m\angle DBC = 59°$. Since the sum of the angles of a triangle = 180°, we can find $m\angle BCD$ by adding the known measures and subtracting this sum from 180°.

$m\angle BCD = 180° - (105° + 59°)$

$m\angle BCD = 180° - 164°$

$m\angle BCD = 16°$

To find $m\angle ACB$, add $m\angle ACD = 50°$ and $m\angle BCD = 16°$:

$m\angle ACB = 50° + 16° = 66°$

6. **Solution: $m\angle 1 = 45°$**

Since the figure is a rectangle, $\angle CDA = 90°$. Thus, if $m\angle BDA = 45°$, then $m\angle 1 = \angle CDA - \angle BDA$.

$m\angle 1 = 90° - 45°$

$m\angle 1 = 45°$

7. **Solution: $AC = 5$ cm**

Since $AB = 3$ cm, then $CD = 3$ cm. To find the length of AC, use the Pythagorean theorem: $a^2 + b^2 = c^2$. Let $a = CD = 3$ cm, $b = AD = 4$ cm, and $c = AC$. Insert the known values and solve for c.

$$a^2 + b^2 = c^2$$
$$3^2 + 4^2 = c^2$$
$$9 + 16 = c^2$$
$$25 = c^2$$
$$c^2 = 25$$
$$\sqrt{c^2} = \sqrt{25}$$
$$c = 5$$

If $c = 5$ cm, then $AC = 5$ cm.

8.   **Solution: $m\angle 1 = 55°$ and $m\angle 2 = 35°$**

Diagonal DB bisects $\angle ADC$ into two equal angles: $\angle ADE$ and $\angle 1$. Since $m\angle ADE = 55°$, $m\angle 1 = 55°$. Since the diagonals of a rhombus are perpendicular, $m\angle DEC = 90°$. We know that $m\angle 1 = 55°$, so

$$m\angle 2 = 180° - (90° + 55°)$$

$$m\angle 2 = 180° - 145°$$

$$m\angle 2 = 35°$$

9.   **Solution: $CD = 10$ in.**

Let $DE =$ side a and $EC =$ side b of $\triangle DEC$. Since $m\angle DEC = 90°$, $\triangle DEC$ is a right triangle. So, let $CD =$ side c, the triangle's hypotenuse. If $a = 6$ in. and side $b = 8$ in., we can find the length of side c by using the Pythagorean theorem, $a^2 + b^2 = c^2$.

$$c^2 = 6^2 + 8^2$$
$$c^2 = 36 + 64$$
$$c^2 = 100$$
$$\sqrt{c^2} = \sqrt{100}$$
$$c = 10$$

Since $c = 10$, side $CD = 10$ in.

10. **Solution: Arc $\overset{\frown}{CD}$ = 55°, and arc $\overset{\frown}{DB}$ = 90°**

Since $m\angle COD = 55°$, the measure of arc $\overset{\frown}{CD}$, which the central angle intersects, is the same. Thus, arc $\overset{\frown}{CD}$ = 55°. We know that arc $\overset{\frown}{BAC}$ = 215°, and arc $\overset{\frown}{CD}$ = 55°. Arcs $\overset{\frown}{BAC}$, $\overset{\frown}{CD}$, and $\overset{\frown}{DB}$ make up a complete circle whose measure = 360°. Since we know that arc $\overset{\frown}{BAC}$ = 215° and arc $\overset{\frown}{CD}$ = 55°, we can find the measure of arc $\overset{\frown}{DB}$ by adding the measures of arcs $\overset{\frown}{BAC}$ and $\overset{\frown}{CD}$, and then subtracting the sum from 360°.

$\overset{\frown}{DB}$ = 360° − (215° + 55°)

$\overset{\frown}{DB}$ = 360° − 270°

$\overset{\frown}{DB}$ = 90°

11. **Solution: $m\angle BAC = 60°$**

Since the central angle $\angle BOC = 120°$, the measure of arc $\overset{\frown}{BC}$ is also 120°. $\angle BAC$ is an inscribed angle whose measure is half the measure of the arc it intercepts (arc $\overset{\frown}{BC}$). Thus,

$$m\angle BAC = \frac{1}{2}(120°)$$

$m\angle BAC = 60°$

12. **Solution: $\angle GHD$**

When two parallel lines are cut by a transversal, corresponding angles will be formed on the same side as the transversal, and in corresponding locations with respect to the lines. One corresponding angle will be positioned outside the parallel lines, and the other will be located inside the lines. Since $\angle EGB$ is outside the parallel lines, its corresponding angle $\angle GHD$ will be located on the same side of the transversal inside the lines.

13. **Solution: $m\angle 1 = 55°$ and $m\angle 2 = 45°$**

Since $ABCD$ is a parallelogram, its opposite angles have the same measure. If $m\angle 1 = m\angle BCD$, then $m\angle 1 = 55°$. Notice that, as BD is a transversal intersecting the two parallel lines *BC* and *DA*, ∠2 and ∠*BDA* are alternate interior angles with equal measure. Since *m*∠*BDA* = 45°, *m*∠2 = 45°.

14.   **Solution: *CD* = 8 cm**

The opposite sides of a parallelogram are equal. Therefore, if *AB* = 8 cm, then *CD* = 8 cm.

15.   **Solution: 24 sq yd**

Use the formula $S = 6s^2$, where $s = 6$ feet

$S = (6)(6)^2$

$S = 36^2$

$S = 216$ sq ft

Since Fred plans to buy wood by the square yard, convert 216 square feet to square yards by dividing by 9. (There are 9 square feet in a square yard.)

$$\frac{216}{9} = 24$$

Fred needs 24 square yards of wood.

Focus on English

1. two

2. too

3. to

4. too

5. two

1. con<u>gru</u>ent

2. trans<u>ver</u>sal

3. perpen<u>dic</u>ular

4. <u>bi</u>sect

5. <u>tan</u>gent

6. ad<u>ja</u>cent

Chapter 7

Problems

1.   **Solution: Company A**

Examine the figure and find the company whose production is represented by the shortest bar.

2.   **Solution: Company E**

Examine the figure and find the company whose production is represented by the tallest bar.

3.   **Solution: 25%**

First, find the total production of the six companies:

$(150 + 300 + 400 + 700 + 1{,}000 + 250)$ million $= 2{,}800$ million

Company D produced 700 million, so express this as a percentage of the total of the six companies (here we use the fact that $\frac{700 \text{ million}}{2{,}800 \text{ million}} = \frac{700}{2{,}800}$):

$$\frac{700}{2{,}800} \cdot 100 =$$

$$\frac{70{,}000}{2{,}800} = 25\%$$

4.   **Solution: Company D**

Company B produced 300 million pencils and company C produced 400 million. The sum is 300 million + 400 million = 700 million, which is the same as the production of company D.

5.   **Solution: $150**

The amount spent on gasoline = $100 and the cost of parking = $50. The sum of the two is $150.

6. **Solution: 28%**

The total expenses:

$50 + $100 + $350 + $150 + $600 = $1,250

The amount spent on food = $350. Thus, the percentage of the total budget spent on food is as follows:

$$\frac{350}{1,250} \cdot 100 =$$

$$\frac{35,000}{1,250} = 28\%$$

7. **Solution: $1,340**

If the rent of $600 is raised by 15%, the new rent is:

$$\frac{15}{100} \cdot 600 =$$

$$\frac{9,000}{100} = \$90$$

The new rent is $600 + $90 = $690. Thus, the new total budget is:

$690 + $150 + $350 + $100 + $50 = $1,340

8. **Solution: 1994**

Examine the line graphs and look for the year where the two lines representing the companies merge.

9. **Solution: 1996**

Examine the graph and look for the year when the distance between the two symbols is the greatest vertically.

Item	Unit price	Quantity	Total price
Math textbook	$60.00	3	$180.00
Graphing calculator	$90.10	4	$360.40
Ballpoint pens	$0.75	11	$8.25
File folders	$1.23	5	$6.15
Package of paper	$0.99	4	$3.96

10. **Solution: See the completed table (above).**

11. **Solution: 39**

Add 6 to each number to find the next number in the sequence.

12. **Solution: 0, −7**

Subtract 7 from each number to find the next number in the sequence.

13. **Solution: 32, 30**

The pattern is an alternating one in which 6 is added and then 2 is subtracted.

$18 + 6 = 24$

$24 - 2 = 22$

$22 + 6 = 28$

$28 - 2 = 26$

$26 + 6 = 32$

$32 - 2 = 30$

14. **Solution: 15.71**

Add up the numbers and divide by the total number of numbers in the sequence.

$$10 + 13 + 12 + 16 + 19 + 18 + 22 = 110$$

$$\frac{110}{7} = 15.71$$

15.   **Solution: Candace sits between Mark and Arthur.**

Let A = Arthur, C = Candace, F = Frank, J = Jane, K = Katy, M = Mark, R = Robert, and S = Susan. Draw a diagram to illustrate the problem: Frank sits opposite Mark. They cannot sit at either end of the table because at least one female has to sit at one of the ends. Place Frank on one side of the table and Mark opposite him. Jane sits between Frank and Robert, so she sits on the same side as these two men. Robert sits to the left of Katy, so Katy must occupy one of the ends of the table. Arthur sits to her right, so he must sit opposite Robert. Susan refuses to sit next to Arthur, so she must sit opposite Katy on the other end of the table. Now there is only one place for Candace to sit—between Mark and Arthur.

Focus on English

I	Spain
I'm	Paris
Mexico	I'm
United States	August
France	Tuesday

1. Open

2. Turn on

3. Don't fill in

4. Answer

5. Don't look

1. A *pie chart* is a graph shaped like a circle divided into pieces, each piece displaying the size of some related piece of information. A *bar graph* consists of an axis and a series of labeled horizontal or vertical bars showing different values for each bar.

2. An *empty set* (or null set) is a set that contains no elements.

3. The *mean* is the arithmetic average, which we get by adding up the numbers and dividing by how many there are. The *median* is the number in the middle, which we find by ordering the numbers from smallest to largest. The *mode* is the value that occurs most often.

Chapter 8

Problems

1.   **Solution: Yes**

Substitute 3 for x and 4 for y in both equations.

$4x - 2y$	$= 4$		$3x + 5y$	$= 29$
Does $4(3) - 2(4) = 4$?			Does $3(3) + 5(4) = 29$?	
Does $12 - 8$	$= 4$?		Does $9 + 20$	$= 29$?
4	$= 4$		29	$= 29$
	Yes			Yes

Since both equations are true, the ordered pair is a solution of the system.

2.   **Solution: No**

Substitute -1 for x and -1 for y in both equations in the system.

$9x - 5y$	$= -4$	$-5x + y$	$= -4$
Does $9(-1) - 5(-1) = -4$?		Does $-5(-1) + (-1) = -4$?	
Does $-9 + 5$	$= -4$?	Does $5 - 1$	$= -4$?
-4	$= -4$	4	$\neq -4$
	Yes		No

3.   **Solution: $2x + 8y = 5$**

$16x - 4y = -11$

Substitute $-\dfrac{1}{2}$ for x and $\dfrac{3}{4}$ for y in the system.

$2x + 8y$	$=$	$16x - 4y$	$=$
$2\left(-\dfrac{1}{2}\right) + 8\left(\dfrac{3}{4}\right)$	$=$	$16\left(-\dfrac{1}{2}\right) - 4\left(\dfrac{3}{4}\right)$	$=$
$-1 + 6$	$= 5$	$-8 - 3$	$= -11$

4.   **Solution:** $(-2, -3)$

Graph both equations by letting $x = 0$, $y = 0$, and $x = 1$.

(1) $x + y = -5$

x	0	−5	1
y	−5	0	−6

(2) $3x - y = -3$

x	0	−1	1
y	3	0	6

Plot the points for both equations and draw a line through them. See figure 4a.

We find the solution to the problem by reading the coordinates of the point where the two graphs intersect.

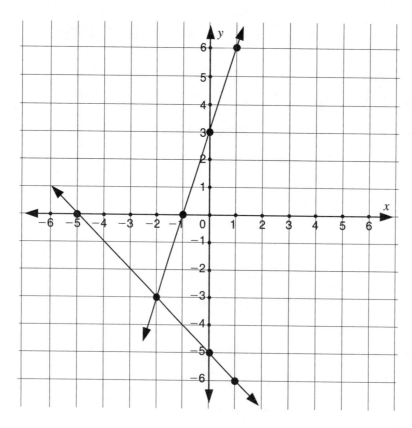

Figure 4a

5.   **Solution: (−2, 4)**

Graph both equations by letting $x = 0$, $y = 0$, and $x = 1$.

(1) $3x - 3y = -18$

x	0	−6	1
y	6	0	7

(2) $5x + 2y = -2$

x	0	$-\dfrac{2}{5}$	1
y	−1	0	$-3\dfrac{1}{2}$

Plot the points for both equations, and draw a line through them. See figure 5a.

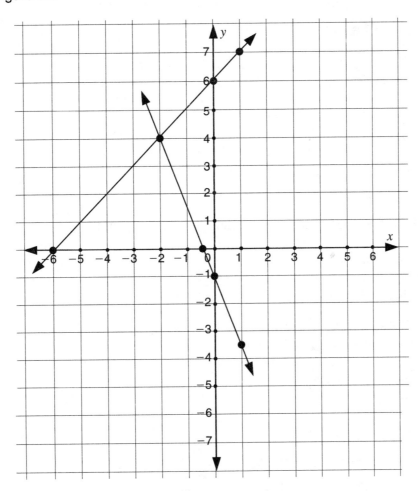

Figure 5a

The solution to the problem is found by reading the coordinates of the point where the two graphs intersect.

6. **Solution:** $\left(\dfrac{1}{2}, \dfrac{1}{2}\right)$

Isolate b in equation (2) by writing the equation as

$$3a - b = 1$$
$$3a - 3a - b = 1 - 3a$$
$$-b = 1 - 3a$$
$$b = -1 + 3a$$

Substitute $b = -1 + 3a$ for b in equation (1) and solve for a.

$$2a + 2b = 2$$
$$2a + 2(-1 + 3a) = 2$$
$$2a - 2 + 6a = 2$$
$$8a - 2 = 2$$
$$8a - 2 + 2 = 2 + 2$$
$$8a = 4$$
$$\frac{8a}{8} = \frac{4}{8}$$
$$a = \frac{1}{2}$$

Find the value of b by substituting $\dfrac{1}{2}$ for a into equation (1).

$$2a + 2b = 2$$
$$2\left(\frac{1}{2}\right) + 2b = 2$$
$$1 + 2b = 2$$
$$1 - 1 + 2b = 2 - 1$$
$$2b = 1$$
$$\frac{2b}{2} = \frac{1}{2}$$
$$b = \frac{1}{2}$$

The solution is the ordered pair $\left(\dfrac{1}{2}, \dfrac{1}{2}\right)$.

7. **Solution: $(-3, -5)$**

Isolate y in equation (1) by writing the equation as follows:

$4x - y = -7$

$4x - 4x - y = -7 - 4x$

$-y = -7 - 4x$

$y = 7 + 4x$

Substitute $7 + 4x$ for y in equation (2) and solve for x.

$7x + 6y = -51$

$7x + 6(7 + 4x) = -51$

$7x + 42 + 24x = -51$

$31x + 42 = -51$

$31x + 42 - 42 = -51 - 42$

$31x = -93$

$\dfrac{31x}{31} = \dfrac{-93}{31}$

$x = -3$

Find the value of y by substituting -3 for x into equation (1).

$4x - y = -7$

$4(-3) - y = -7$

$-12 - y = -7$

$-12 + 12 - y = -7 + 12$

$-y = 5$

$y = -5$

The solution is the ordered pair $(-3, -5)$.

8.   **Solution: (1, 3)**

Multiply equation (1) by 2 so we can later eliminate x.

$2x + 3y \qquad = 11$

$2x(2) + 3y(2) = 11(2)$

$4x + 6y \qquad = 22$

Add vertically $4x + 6y = 22$ and equation (2).

$$\begin{aligned} 4x + 6y &= 22 \\ -4x + 2y &= 2 \\ \hline 0x + 8y &= 24 \\ 8y &= 24 \\ \frac{8y}{8} &= \frac{24}{8} \\ y &= 3 \end{aligned}$$

Let $y = 3$ in equation (1) and solve for x.

$$\begin{aligned} 2x + 3y &= 11 \\ 2x + 3(3) &= 11 \\ 2x + 9 &= 11 \\ 2x + 9 - 9 &= 11 - 9 \\ 2x &= 2 \\ \frac{2x}{2} &= \frac{2}{2} \\ x &= 1 \end{aligned}$$

9.   **Solution: (2, −1)**

Multiply equation (1) by 4 and multiply equation (2) by 6 so we can later eliminate x.

(1) $-6x(4) - 4y(4) = -8(4)$

$\qquad -24x - 16y \quad = -32$

(2) $4x(6) - 10y(6) = 18(6)$

$\qquad 24x - 60y \qquad = 108$

Add vertically:

$$\begin{array}{rcl} -24x - 16y & = & -32 \\ 24x - 60y & = & 108 \\ \hline 0x - 76y & = & 76 \\ \dfrac{-76y}{-76} & = & \dfrac{76}{-76} \\ y & = & -1 \end{array}$$

Let $y = -1$ in equation (2) and solve for x.

$$\begin{array}{rcl} 4x - 10y & = & 18 \\ 4x - 10(-1) & = & 18 \\ 4x + 10 & = & 18 \\ 4x + 10 - 10 & = & 18 - 10 \\ 4x & = & 8 \\ \dfrac{4x}{4} & = & \dfrac{8}{4} \\ x & = & 2 \end{array}$$

10. **Solution: 9 and 4**

Let x = one number and y = the other number. The sum of the two numbers is 7 less than 20: $x + y = 20 - 7$, which we can simplify as follows:

(1) $x + y = 13$

The difference between the two numbers is 5.

(2) $x - y = 5$

Solve the system of equations.

11. **Solution: Matilda has 22 dolls and Elena has 14 dolls.**

Let x = the number of Matilda's dolls and y = the number of Elena's dolls.

The sum of their collection is 36 dolls.

(1) $x + y = 36$

Matilda has 6 fewer than twice the number of dolls that Elena has.

(2) $x = 2y - 6$

Solve the system of equations.

12. **Solution: Mrs. Kim has 25 $5 bills and 10 $10 bills.**

Organize the data in a table.

Denomination of bill	Number of bills	Total value of bills
$5	x	$5 \times x = 5x$
$10	y	$10 \times y = 10y$
Total	35	$225

Build the system of equations.

(1) $x + y = 35$

(2) $5x + 10y = 225$

Solve the system of equations.

13. **Solution: Rob travels at 65 mph, and Habib travels at 75 mph.**

Organize the data in a table.

Car	Rate	Time	Distance
Rob	x	3 hours	$3x$ miles
Habib	y	3 hours	$3y$ miles

Habib is traveling an additional 10 mph faster than Rob, so the following is true:

(1) $y = x + 10$

The total distance between both cars is 420 miles. Thus, the following is true:

(2) $3x + 3y = 420$

Solve the system of equations.

14. **Solution: $p + 5n + 10d = 100$**

$p = 5d$

$n = d + 4$

Let p = the number of pennies, n = the number of nickels, and d = the number of dimes. A penny is worth one cent or p; a nickel is worth 5 cents, or $5n$; and a dime contains 10 cents, or $10d$. Together they are worth one dollar, or 100 cents.

Thus, the first equation is as follows:

(1) $p + 5n + 10d = 100$

There are five times as many pennies as dimes, so we write the second equation thus:

(2) $p = 5d$

The number of nickels is 4 more than the number of dimes. The third equation is this:

$n = d + 4$

15.   **Solution:** $x + y + z = 6$

$$2x - 3y \quad = z - 2$$

$$3x - 2y - z = 1$$

Let x, y, and z represent the three numbers. The sum of these numbers is 6, so the first equation is as follows:

(1) $x + y + z = 6$

"Twice the first number minus three times the second number is two less than the third number" can be expressed thus:

(2) $2x - 3y = z - 2$

The third equation is derived from this statement: "Three times the first number minus twice the second number less the third number is 1."

(3) $3x - 2y - z = 1$

Focus on English

1. nor

2. or

3. Neither

4. nor

5. or

1. <u>sub</u>stitute

2. ad<u>di</u>tion

3. <u>di</u>fference

4. sub<u>trac</u>tion

5. e<u>qua</u>tion

Chapter 9

Problems

1. **Solution: 4**

What number multiplied by itself equals 16? It is 4.

2. **Solution: x^4**

$$\sqrt{x^8} = (x^8)^{\frac{1}{2}}$$
$$x^{\frac{8}{2}} = x^4$$

3. **Solution: x^2y**

$$\sqrt{x^4y^2} \quad =$$
$$(x^4y^2)^{\frac{1}{2}} \quad =$$
$$x^{\frac{4}{2}}y^{\frac{2}{2}} \quad =$$
$$x^2y^1 \quad =$$
$$x^2y$$

4. **Solution: $x^3\sqrt{x}$**

The exponent in the radicand is odd, so we must express the radicand as the product of two factors, one of which is a perfect square, and the other whose exponent = 1.

$$\sqrt{x^7} = \sqrt{x^6 \cdot x^1} =$$
$$\sqrt{x^6} \cdot \sqrt{x^1} \quad =$$
$$(x^6)^{\frac{1}{2}} \cdot \sqrt{x^1} \quad =$$
$$x^{\frac{6}{2}} \cdot \sqrt{x^1} \quad =$$
$$x^3 \cdot \sqrt{x^1} \quad =$$
$$x^3\sqrt{x}$$

5.   Solution: $x^4 y^6 \sqrt{x}$

$$\sqrt{x^9 y^{12}} \quad =$$
$$\sqrt{x^8 y^{12}} \cdot \sqrt{x^1} \quad =$$
$$(x^8 y^{12})^{\frac{1}{2}} \cdot \sqrt{x^1} \quad =$$
$$x^{\frac{8}{2}} y^{\frac{12}{2}} \cdot \sqrt{x^1} \quad =$$
$$x^4 y^6 \sqrt{x}$$

6.   Solution: $8\sqrt{5x} + 5x$

$$5\sqrt{5x} + 3\sqrt{5x} + 5x =$$
$$(5+3)\sqrt{5x} + 5x \quad =$$
$$(8)\sqrt{5x} + 5x \quad =$$
$$8\sqrt{5x} + 5x$$

7.   Solution: $-2\sqrt{6} - 3$

$$5\sqrt{6} - 7\sqrt{6} - 3 \quad =$$
$$(5-7)\sqrt{6} - 3 \quad =$$
$$-2\sqrt{6} - 3$$

8.   Solution: $24\sqrt{2}$

Simplify the square roots to search for like roots to add.

$$2\sqrt{8} + 5\sqrt{32} \quad =$$
$$2\sqrt{4 \cdot 2} + 5\sqrt{16 \cdot 2} \quad =$$
$$2\sqrt{4}\sqrt{2} + 5\sqrt{16}\sqrt{2} \quad =$$
$$2(2)\sqrt{2} + 5(4)\sqrt{2} \quad =$$
$$4\sqrt{2} + 20\sqrt{2} \quad =$$
$$(4+20)\sqrt{2} \quad =$$
$$(24)\sqrt{2} \quad =$$
$$24\sqrt{2}$$

9. **Solution:** $8\sqrt{3} + 4$

$$
\begin{aligned}
\sqrt{12} + 2\sqrt{27} + 4 \quad &= \\
\sqrt{4 \cdot 3} + 2\sqrt{9 \cdot 3} + 4 \quad &= \\
\sqrt{4}\sqrt{3} + 2\sqrt{9}\sqrt{3} + 4 \quad &= \\
(2)\sqrt{3} + 2(3)\sqrt{3} + 4 \quad &= \\
2\sqrt{3} + 6\sqrt{3} + 4 \quad &= \\
(2 + 6)\sqrt{3} + 4 \quad &= \\
(8)\sqrt{3} + 4 \quad &= \\
8\sqrt{3} + 4
\end{aligned}
$$

10. **Solution:** $\dfrac{1}{7}$

$$
\frac{\sqrt{1}}{\sqrt{49}} =
$$

$$
\frac{1}{7}
$$

11. **Solution:** $\dfrac{2\sqrt{3}}{3}$

$$
\begin{aligned}
\frac{2}{\sqrt{3}} \cdot \frac{\sqrt{3}}{\sqrt{3}} \quad &= \\
\frac{2\sqrt{3}}{\sqrt{9}} \quad &= \\
\frac{2\sqrt{3}}{(3)} \quad &= \\
\frac{2\sqrt{3}}{3}
\end{aligned}
$$

12. **Solution:** $\dfrac{x^4\sqrt{5}}{5}$

$$
\sqrt{\frac{x^8}{5}} \cdot \frac{\sqrt{5}}{\sqrt{5}} =
$$

$$\frac{\sqrt{x^8}\sqrt{5}}{\sqrt{25}} =$$

$$\frac{(x^{\frac{8}{2}})\sqrt{5}}{\sqrt{25}} =$$

$$\frac{(x^4)\sqrt{5}}{(5)} =$$

$$\frac{x^4\sqrt{5}}{5}$$

Evaluate the perfect squares.

13. **Solution: $4 - \sqrt{5}$**

$$\frac{8 - \sqrt{20}}{2} =$$

$$\frac{8 - \sqrt{4 \cdot 5}}{2} =$$

$$\frac{8 - \sqrt{4}\sqrt{5}}{2} =$$

$$\frac{2(4) - (2)\sqrt{5}}{2} =$$

Factor the numerator.

$$\frac{2(4 - 1\sqrt{5})}{2} =$$

$$(4 - 1\sqrt{5}) =$$

$$4 - \sqrt{5}$$

14. **Solution: $(32x)^{\frac{1}{5}}$**

Use the rule $\sqrt[n]{a} = a^{\frac{1}{n}}$, where the index $n = 5$, and the radicand $a = 32x$.

$$\sqrt[5]{32x} = (32x)^{\frac{1}{5}}$$

15. **Solution: $\sqrt[3]{x^2}$**

$$\sqrt[6]{x^4}$$

Use the rule $\sqrt[n]{a^m} = a^{\frac{m}{n}}$, where $a = x$, $m = 4$, and $n = 6$.

$$a^{\frac{4}{6}} = a^{\frac{2}{3}}$$

$$\sqrt[3]{x^2}$$

Focus on English

1. seen

2. met

3. written

4. bought

5. spoken

Chapter 10

Problems

1. **Solution: {4, 6}**

    $$x^2 - 10x + 24 = 0$$

    $$(x - 4)(x - 6) = 0$$

    $$(x - 4) = 0 \quad \text{or} \quad (x - 6) = 0$$

    $$x - 4 + 4 = 0 + 4 \quad \text{or} \quad x - 6 + 6 = 0 + 6$$

    $$x = 4 \qquad\qquad \text{or} \quad x = 6$$

2. **Solution: {−4, 4}**

    $$x^2 = 16$$

    $$\sqrt{x^2} = \sqrt{16}$$

    $$x = 4 \quad \text{or} \quad x = -4$$

3. **Solution: $\left\{-3\sqrt{6}, 3\sqrt{6}\right\}$**

    $$x^2 = 54$$

    $$\sqrt{x^2} = \sqrt{54}$$

    $$x = \sqrt{54} \quad \text{or} \quad x = -\sqrt{54}$$

    Simplify the square roots.

    $$x = \sqrt{9 \cdot 6} \quad \text{or} \quad x = -\sqrt{9 \cdot 6}$$

    $$x = \sqrt{9}\sqrt{6} \quad \text{or} \quad x = -\sqrt{9}\sqrt{6}$$

    $$x = 3\sqrt{6} \quad \text{or} \quad x = -3\sqrt{6}$$

4. **Solution:** $\left\{-3\sqrt{3},\ 3\sqrt{3}\right\}$

$$2x^2 + 7 = 61$$
$$2x^2 + 7 - 7 = 61 - 7$$
$$2x^2 = 61 - 7$$
$$2x^2 = 54$$
$$\frac{2x^2}{2} = \frac{54}{2}$$

$$x^2 = \sqrt{27} \quad \text{or} \quad x = -\sqrt{27}$$

Simplify the square roots.

$$x = \sqrt{9 \cdot 3} \quad \text{or} \quad x = -\sqrt{9 \cdot 3}$$

$$x = \sqrt{9}\sqrt{3} \quad \text{or} \quad x = -\sqrt{9}\sqrt{3}$$

$$x = 3\sqrt{3} \quad \text{or} \quad x = -3\sqrt{3}$$

5. **Solution:** $\left\{3 - 3\sqrt{2},\ 3 + 3\sqrt{2}\right\}$

$$(x - 3)^2 = 18$$

$$x - 3 = \sqrt{18} \quad \text{or} \quad x - 3 = -\sqrt{18}$$

Simplify the square roots.

$$x - 3 = \sqrt{9 \cdot 2} \quad \text{or} \quad x - 3 = -\sqrt{9 \cdot 2}$$

$$x - 3 = \sqrt{9}\sqrt{2} \quad \text{or} \quad x - 3 = -\sqrt{9}\sqrt{2}$$

$$x - 3 = 3\sqrt{2} \quad \text{or} \quad x - 3 = -3\sqrt{2}$$

$$x - 3 + 3 = 3 + 3\sqrt{2} \quad \text{or} \quad x - 3 + 3 = 3 - 3\sqrt{2}$$

$$x = 3 + 3\sqrt{2} \quad \text{or} \quad x = 3 - 3\sqrt{2}$$

6. **Solution:** $\left\{ \dfrac{3-4\sqrt{3}}{2}, \dfrac{3+4\sqrt{3}}{2} \right\}$

$(2x - 3)^2 = 48$

$2x - 3 = \sqrt{48}$ or $2x - 3 = -\sqrt{48}$

Simplify the square roots.

$2x - 3 = \sqrt{16 \cdot 3}$ or $2x - 3 = -\sqrt{16 \cdot 3}$

$2x - 3 = \sqrt{16}\sqrt{3}$ or $2x - 3 = -\sqrt{16}\sqrt{3}$

$2x - 3 = 4\sqrt{3}$ or $2x - 3 = -4\sqrt{3}$

$2x - 3 + 3 = 3 + 4\sqrt{3}$ or $2x - 3 + 3 = 3 - 4\sqrt{3}$

$2x = 3 + 4\sqrt{3}$ or $2x = 3 - 4\sqrt{3}$

$\dfrac{2x}{2} = \dfrac{3 + 4\sqrt{3}}{2}$ or $\dfrac{2x}{2} = \dfrac{3 - 4\sqrt{3}}{2}$

$x = \dfrac{3 + 4\sqrt{3}}{2}$ or $x = \dfrac{3 - 4\sqrt{3}}{2}$

7. **Solution:** $\{-13, 1\}$

$x^2 + 12x - 13 = 0$

Let $a = 1$, $b = 12$, and $c = -13$. Use these values in the quadratic formula.

$$x = \frac{-12 \pm \sqrt{12^2 - 4(1)(-13)}}{2(1)}$$

$$x = \frac{-12 \pm \sqrt{144 - 4(-13)}}{2(1)}$$

$$x = \frac{-12 \pm \sqrt{144 - (-52)}}{2}$$

$$x = \frac{-12 \pm \sqrt{144 + 52}}{2}$$

$$x = \frac{-12 \pm \sqrt{196}}{2}$$

$$x = \frac{-12 \pm 14}{2}$$

$$x = \frac{-12 + 14}{2} \quad \text{or} \quad x = \frac{-12 - 14}{2}$$

$$x = \frac{2}{2} \quad \text{or} \quad x = \frac{-26}{2}$$

$$x = 1 \quad \text{or} \quad x = -13$$

8. **Solution:** $\left\{ \dfrac{6 - 2\sqrt{6}}{3}, \dfrac{6 + 2\sqrt{6}}{3} \right\}$

$$3z^2 - 2z + 5 = 10z + 1$$

Write the equation in standard form.

$$3z^2 - 2z + 5 - 1 = 10z + 1 - 1$$

$$3z^2 - 2z + 5 - 1 = 10z$$

$$3z^2 - 2z + 5 - 1 - 10z = 10z - 10z$$

$$3z^2 - 2z + 5 - 1 - 10z = 0$$

$$3z^2 - 12z + 4 = 0$$

Use the quadratic formula where $a = 3$, $b = -12$, and $c = 4$.

$$z = \frac{-(-12) \pm \sqrt{(-12)^2 - 4(3)(4)}}{2(3)}$$

$$z = \frac{-(-12) \pm \sqrt{(-12)^2 - 4(12)}}{2(3)}$$

$$z = \frac{-(-12) \pm \sqrt{(144) - 4(12)}}{2(3)}$$

$$z = \frac{-(-12) \pm \sqrt{(144) - 48}}{2(3)}$$

$$z = \frac{-(-12) \pm \sqrt{96}}{6}$$

$$z = \frac{-(-12) \pm \sqrt{16 \cdot 6}}{6}$$

$$z = \frac{-(-12) \pm \sqrt{16}\sqrt{6}}{6}$$

$$z = \frac{-(-12) \pm 4\sqrt{6}}{6}$$

$$z = \frac{(12) \pm 4\sqrt{6}}{6}$$

$$z = \frac{12 + 4\sqrt{6}}{6} \quad \text{or} \quad z = \frac{12 - 4\sqrt{6}}{6}$$

Divide by a common factor of 2.

$$z = \frac{6 + 2\sqrt{6}}{3} \quad \text{or} \quad z = \frac{6 - 2\sqrt{6}}{3}$$

9.   **Solution: There are no real solutions.**

Use the quadratic formula where $a = 2$, $b = 3$, and $c = 8$.

$$x = \frac{-(3) \pm \sqrt{(3)^2 - 4(2)(8)}}{2(2)}$$

$$x = \frac{-(3) \pm \sqrt{(3)^2 - (8)(8)}}{2(2)}$$

$$x = \frac{-(3) \pm \sqrt{(3)^2 - (64)}}{2(2)}$$

$$x = \frac{-(3) \pm \sqrt{9 - 64}}{2(2)}$$

$$x = \frac{-(3) \pm \sqrt{-55}}{4}$$

Since the radical $\sqrt{-55}$ has a negative radicand, it is not a real number. Therefore, there are no real-number solutions to the equation.

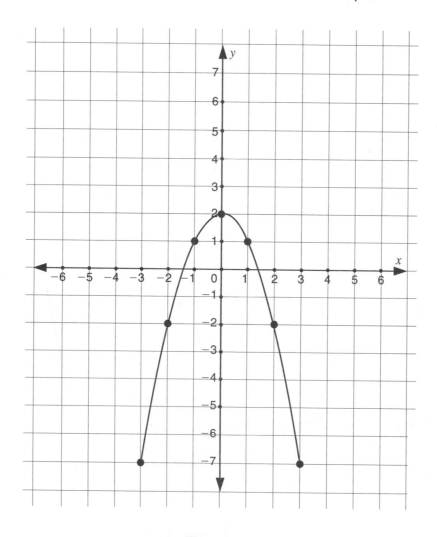

Figure 10a

10. **Solution: See figure 10a.**

Draw up a table of values for $y = -x^2 + 2$.

x	-3	-2	-1	0	1	2	3
y	-7	-2	1	2	1	-2	-7

Plot the points on a rectangular coordinate system, and connect the points by drawing a curve through them.

11. **Solution: The parabola opens downward, because the coefficient of the squared term is negative.**

12. **Solution: $(-1, 1)$**

$y = 3x^2 + 6x + 4$

Solve for x, using the vertex formula: $x = \dfrac{-b}{2a}$

Let $a = 3$ and $b = 6$. Use these values in the vertex formula.

$x = \dfrac{-6}{2(3)}$

$x = \dfrac{-6}{6}$

$x = -1$

To find the y value of the vertex, let $x = -1$, and solve for y.

$y = 3x^2 + 6x + 4$

$y = 3(-1)^2 + 6(-1) + 4$

$y = 3(1) + 6(-1) + 4$

$y = 3 - 6 + 4$

$y = -3 + 4$

$y = 1$

Since $x = -1$ and $y = 1$, the coordinates of the vertex are $(-1, 1)$.

13.   **Solution: $(-1, 0)$, $(-7, 0)$, and $(0, 7)$**

To find the x-intercepts, let $y = 0$ and solve for x.

$y = x^2 + 8x + 7$

$0 = x^2 + 8x + 7$ Rearrange.

$x^2 + 8x + 7 = 0$ Factor the trinomial.

$(x + 1)(x + 7) = 0$

$x + 1 = 0$ or $x + 7 = 0$

$x = -1$ or $x = -7$

The x-intercepts are $(-1, 0)$ and $(-7, 0)$.

To find the y-intecept, let $x = 0$ and solve for y.

$y = x^2 + 8x + 7$

$y = 0^2 + 8(0) + 7$

$y = 7$

The y-intercept is $(0, 7)$.

14.   **Solution: $f(2) = 14$**

$f(x) = x^2 + 6x - 2$

Replace x with 2 and solve.

$f(x) = x^2 + 6x - 2$

$f(2) = 2^2 + 6(2) - 2$

$$f(2) = 4 + 12 - 2$$

$$f(2) = 16 - 2$$

$$f(2) = 14$$

15. **Solution: $g(5) = 51$**

$$g(x) = x^2 + 6x - 4$$

Replace x with 5 and solve.

$$g(x) = x^2 + 6x - 4$$

$$g(5) = 5^2 + 6(5) - 4$$

$$g(5) = 25 + 30 - 4$$

$$g(5) = 55 - 4$$

$$g(5) = 51$$

Focus on English

1. will

2. won't

3. will

4. will

5. won't

1. Are

2. I am

3. it will

4. he won't

5. she will

NOTES

NOTES

NOTES

NOTES

NOTES

NOTES